# Teacher Education Yearbook XIII

## EDITORS

Julie Rainer Dangel, Georgia State University
Edith M. Guyton, Georgia State University

## EDITORIAL ADVISORY BOARD

Violet Allain, James Madison University
Wendy Burke, Eastern Michigan University
Angela Case, University of Delaware
Teresa Harris, James Madison University
Jeanette Haynes Writer, New Mexico State University
Scott Hopkins, University of South Alabama
Lijun Jin, Towson University
Catherine A. Kelly, The University of Colorado at Colorado Springs
Rudy Mattai, SUNY–College at Buffalo
Loren Miller, Cooper Elementary School
Binyao Zheng, Kennesaw State University
David M. Byrd, University of Rhode Island
John McIntyre, Southern Illinois University at Carbondale
Sandra J. Odell, University of Nevada at Las Vegas
Mary John O'Hair, University of Oklahoma

## EXECUTIVE DIRECTOR

David Ritchey, Association of Teacher Educators, Reston, Virginia

# Research on Alternative and Non-Traditional Education

## Teacher Education Yearbook XIII

EDITED BY JULIE RAINER DANGEL AND
EDITH M. GUYTON

Published by
The Association of Teacher Educators
with
SCARECROWEDUCATION
*Lanham, Maryland • Toronto • Oxford*
*2005*

Published in the United States of America
by the Association of Teacher Educators with ScarecrowEducation
An imprint of The Rowman & Littlefield Publishing Group, Inc.
4501 Forbes Boulevard, Suite 200, Lanham, Maryland 20706
www.scarecroweducation.com

PO Box 317
Oxford
OX2 9RU, UK

1-57886-237-X (pbk.: alk.paper)
Library of Congress Control Number: 2004117613

∞ ™ The paper used in this publication meets the minimum requirements of
American National Standard for Information Sciences—Permanence of
Paper for Printed Library Materials, ANSI/NISO Z39.48-1992.
Manufactured in the United States of America.

# Contents

# List of Tables and Figures

## List of Tables

# List of Figures

# Foreword

*Ed Pultorak*
Southern Illinois University—Carbondale

Ed Pultorak is a faculty member in the Department of Curriculum and Instruction at Southern Illinois University (Carbondale) and is the 2004-2005 President of the Association of Teacher Educators (ATE). Ed, an ATE member for 19 continuous years, has served the organization and teacher education in a number of leadership roles including membership in numerous ATE committees, commissions, and task forces and has served on the Delegate Assembly and ATE Board of Directors. As a member of conference planning committees, he initiated the inclusion of a featured preservice teacher strand. Ed is the author of more than 45 professional articles on teacher education.

*What office is there which involves more responsibility, which requires more qualifications, and which ought, therefore, to be more honorable, than that of teaching?*

—Harriet Martineau (1837)

Teacher educators face many challenges such as preparing high-quality teachers, maintaining up-to-date and research-based information for programs, recruiting high-quality individuals that will withstand the rigorous standards that face preservice students and teachers, and preparing enough teachers to meet the significant shortages that currently exist in certain areas. For example, in Texas in 2002, more than 63,000 new teachers were needed while only approximately 22,000 certified teachers were available.

In an attempt to meet the challenge of preparing a sufficient number of teaching candidates, many alternative routes to teacher certification have appeared across the country. In fact, more than 45 states currently offer alternative route programs with approximately 80% provided by institutions of higher education, often in partnership with local education agencies (AACTE, 2004; NCEI, 2003). Without considering past research investigating the quality of such programs, several states went so far as to require that alternative route programs be developed and implemented. To many, this implied that teachers do not need to be fully prepared and that anyone can teach. To further this issue, in July of 2002, the U.S. Secretary of Education cited the Abell Foundation paper in his Annual Report on Teacher Quality as the only source for concluding that teacher education does not contribute to teacher effectiveness. He went on to recommend that requirements for education coursework not be required for certification and that field experiences, including student teaching, be made optional.

In September of 2002, an article written by Linda Darling-Hammond highlighted the inadequacies of the Abell Foundation paper (Darling-Hammond, 2002). Among other items, she clarified how the paper dismissed or misreported much of the existing evidence in order to argue that teacher education made no difference to teacher performance or student learning. She also reported research studies indicating that the Abell Foundation report, if followed, could bring harm to many children, especially those living in more challenging areas.

Whether a traditional or non-traditional program, our focus must remain on the preparation of high-quality teachers. We must continue to consider the appropriate preparation for all grade levels, content areas, demographic regions, socioeconomic conditions, ethnic backgrounds, and personal situations just to mention a few. The complexity is enormous.

*Teacher Education Yearbook XIII* provides a collection of well-researched chapters on Alternative and Non-traditional approaches to teacher preparation. The editors provide three divisions to frame the dialogue: successes and challenges, effects of models, and non-traditional models of professional development.

Division I includes four chapters on successes and challenges for alternative routes to certification. In this section, one will learn of a program designed to prepare recent immigrants and refugees, of whom many were certified teachers in their home nations, to be certified teachers in this country. In the next chapter the writers raise a very interesting point about retention. As part of the New York City Teaching Fellows program, researchers followed cohort Fellows for three years and discovered the reasons why many were strongly considering leaving the urban schools for which they were recruited. The following chapter provides a cross-case description and analysis of a five-site program ranging from small town to highly urban. The final chapter in this section provides a description of four distinctly different routes to certification that were developed to recruit diverse and non-traditional individuals into teaching.

Division 2 provides four chapters regarding the effects of models of alternative routes to certification. Chapter 5 summarizes the findings of an alternative certification program that compares a group of recent college graduates with a group of career changers. They found that career changers either performed well below or exceeded expectations. Further, the study raises questions about the ability of alternative programs to address sociocultural issues prior to entering inner-city classrooms. Chapter 6 describes a program that has been in operation for four years. Assessment results show that dispositions, rather than teaching skills or knowledge, are the most frequent cause of less than satisfactory ratings. Chapter 7 provides a comparison study of regularly certified first-year teachers with Teach for America first-year teachers (TFA1) and Teach for America second-year teachers (TFA2). Researchers concluded that student achievement was lower with both TFA1 and TFA2 teachers than with regularly certified teachers. The final chapter in this division, chapter 8, provides information about a longitudinal study of 1,702 novice teachers. Findings indicate that 34% left by the end of the fifth year and that those entering the teaching field without being fully prepared to teach (e.g., no student teaching) were more likely to leave.

Finally, Division III includes three chapters addressing non-traditional models of professional development. Chapter 9 provides a summary of a unique approach to offering professional development opportunities to meet the academic and personal needs of teachers of English language learners. Chapter 10 identifies several barriers to coaching practice, including lack of time, teacher resistance to change, lack of trust, and inconsistencies in definition of the coaching role. The final chapter, chapter 11, provides information on how online events can be useful and usable by a broad population of teachers.

In addition to research provided in this yearbook, additional studies of teacher education will continue on an even larger scale. As part of the fiscal 2004 appropriations bill, Congress has mandated a wholesale cataloging of the work done by teacher-preparation programs to better understand the academic content and field experiences provided to prospective teachers. Congress intends for existing data to be synthesized on the consistency of required course work, how reading and math are taught, and the degree to which programs are aligned with scientific evidence on the subjects.

Conversations with other educational leaders regarding their thoughts on this landmark project—including individuals from National Council for Accreditation of Teacher Education (NCATE), American Association of Colleges for Teacher Education (AACTE), and American Educational Research Association (AERA)—have occurred. Most seemed to agree that the initial idea of this mandated study was neither positive nor in the best interest of student learning. Currently, however, more are agreeing that this could be helpful if conducted appropriately. For example, in a 2004 publication of *Education Week* (Blair, 2004) Arthur E. Wise, president of NCATE, was quoted as saying, "We do have a lot of small-scale studies, but the big policy questions have not been well studied. This is very, very ambitious." (p. 13). In addition, David G. Imig, president and chief executive officer of AACTE, was quoted as saying, "The value-added of teacher education is going to be demonstrated if the study is set up in a way that looks at outcomes and . . . the impact on student learning." (p. 13).

Teaching is a very complex and noble profession. To answer the question quoted at the beginning of this foreword, there is no other office that involves more responsibility, requires more qualifications, and deserves more honor than that of a teacher. In preparing teachers, we must recruit the best, provide rigorous and beneficial standards, research best approaches, and provide each student with an opportunity for a quality education. To quote Jean-Jacques Rousseau (1762), "We are born weak, we need strength; helpless, we need aid; foolish, we need reason. All that we lack at birth, all that we need when we come to man's estate, is the gift of education." The responsibility of teacher preparation is to help ensure that the bearers of the gift of education are up to the challenge.

# References

American Association of Colleges for Teacher Education. (2004). *Teacher Education Primer 2004. Information for Members of Congress for the Reauthorization of the Higher Education Act*. Washington, DC: AACTE.

Blair, J. (2004, March 3). Congress Orders Thorough Study of Teacher Education Programs. *Education Week*, 23, p. 13.

Darling-Hammond, L. (2002). Research and Rhetoric on Teacher Certification: A Response to Teacher Certification Reconsidered. *Education Policy Analysis Archives*, *10*(36), 1–42.

Harriet Martineau (1837). *Society in America*. London: Saunders & Otley.

Jean-Jacques Rousseau (1762). *Emile*. Barbara Foxley, trans. London: Dent.

National Center for Education Information (2003). *Alternative teacher certification: A state-by-state analysis*. Retrieved from http://www.ncei.com/2003/executive_summary.htm.

# Introduction

*Julie Rainer Dangel*
Georgia State University

*Edith M. Guyton*
Georgia State University

Julie Rainer Dangel is Associate Professor in Early Childhood Education at Georgia State University and currently coordinates the Educational Specialist Program. Her research interests include teacher development and constructivist theory. She has published articles in a variety of journals and edited the recent publication by ATE: *Reframing Teacher Education: Dimensions of a Constructivist Approach.*

Edi Guyton is Professor and Chair of the Early Childhood Department at Georgia State University. Her most recent articles, published in various teacher education journals, have focused on constructivist teacher education. University-based teacher induction programs also have been an area of development and research.

*Teacher Education Yearbook XIII: Research on Alternative and Non-Traditional Teacher Education* provides teachers and teacher educators with current research and practical guidelines as they examine critically the research, practice and policies related to alternative and non-traditional teacher education. In recent years, a perceived teacher shortage, a high demand for qualified teachers in classrooms, and legislative actions have pressed teacher educators to increase the number of teacher candidates they prepare for the classroom. Alternative routes to certification are developing rapidly with approved program routes varying enormously among and within states. Academic arguments are taking place regarding the efficacy of these programs (Darling-Hammond, Chung & Fredlow, 2002; Walsh, 2001), and these arguments for and against alternative preparation are multi-faceted.

Many types of teacher education have become more prevalent, including teacher education by school systems or other local education agencies, distance teacher education, private-for-profit teacher education; and varied post-graduate programs at colleges and universities. All programs claim to produce high-quality teachers, but the research basis for such claims is not well developed nor is what constitutes a highly qualified teacher as well defined. There are limitations in existing studies of alternative certification and there are many questions for further inquiry.

In this *Yearbook*, you will see research in three areas: (1) the successes and challenges of alternative teacher preparation; (2) the effects of alternative preparation programs on teacher performance; and (3) innovative approaches to professional development. You will find evidence of successful models, including those that target diverse and non-traditional populations, alternatively trained teachers' perceptions of themselves and their teaching practice, and innovations in program design. There are cross-case analyses and comparison studies, suggestions for improving recruitment and selection of new teachers, longitudinal perspectives on teacher attrition, and recommendations for further development of teacher assessment technology. In addition, you will find the effects of innovative professional development practices such as coaching and online environments.

# Organization of the Yearbook

The purpose of the yearbook is to inform and guide teachers and teacher educators on complex issues and provide researchers interested in teacher education with current research in the area addressed by the yearbook. A conceptual framework, based on a triadic definition of scholarship—the production of knowledge, the interpretation and synthesis of knowledge, and the application of knowledge—is used to support this purpose. This framework also provides the organization for the yearbook. Each year, research reports based on a significant topic are solicited for publication in the yearbook.

All research reports are blind reviewed and two to four reports in multiple divisions are published. Within the divisions, authors address a variety of issues illustrating the complex nature of the topic. A responder, a recognized scholar in the field, synthesizes, interprets, and applies results drawn from the selected research papers in each division. By providing interpretations and possible application of research, as well as the research report, the *Yearbook* offers recommendations, raises questions and generates rich conversation around issues of importance. In this spirit of scholarship, the editors of *Teacher Education Yearbook XIII* find this issue to be both enlightening and provocative. We welcome conversation, questions, recommendations, and continued research to further the dialogue about alternative and non-traditional teacher education. We also encourage you to look for the *Yearbook XIV: Research on Teacher Induction*.

# References

Darling-Hammond, L., Chung, R., & Fredlow, F. (2002). Variations in teacher preparation: How well do different pathways prepare teachers to teach? *Journal of Teacher Education* 53 (4), 286–302.

Walsh, K. (2001). *Teacher certification reconsidered: Stumbling for quality*. Baltimore, MD: The Abell Foundation

# Acknowledgement

As editors, we would like to acknowledge that this work was made manageable and enjoyable by the participation of Sujatha Bhagvati. Her initiative and organizational skills are a valuable contribution to this edition.

Division 1

# SUCCESSES AND CHALLENGES FOR ALTERNATIVE ROUTES TO CERTIFICATION

# Overview and Framework

## SUCCESSES AND CHALLENGES FOR ALTERNATIVE ROUTES TO CERTIFICATION

*Melba Spooner*
University of North Carolina at Charlotte

> Melba Spooner is Associate Professor in the Department of Reading and Elementary Education at the University of North Carolina at Charlotte where she is also the faculty coordinator for Professional Development Schools. She has also served as Assistant Dean and Coordinator of Field Experiences and Student Teaching in the College of Education. Her research interests include effective teaching and impact on student learning and university-school partnerships with a focus on Professional Development Schools.

> *It was the best of times; it was the worst of times,*
> *It was the age of wisdom; it was the age of foolishness,*
> *It was the epoch of belief; it was the epoch of incredulity,*
> *It was the season of Light; it was the season of Darkness,*
> *It was the spring of hope; it was the winter of despair,*
> *We had everything before us; we had nothing before us,*
> *We were all going direct to Heaven, we were all going direct the other*
> *way—in short, the period was so far like the present period, that some of*
> *its noisiest authorities insisted on its being received, for good or for evil,*
> *in the superlative degree of comparison only.*
>
> —Charles Dickens, 1894

In many ways this quotation describes the dichotomy of alternative routes to teacher certification in our society today. Alternative routes to teacher certification began to surface in the early 1980s. In 1983, only eight states reported alternative routes (other than through a regular teacher education program). Feistritzer and Chester (2003) report that now, all but a handful of states offer some type of alternative certification program for teachers. The National Center for Education Information (NCEI), of which Feistritzer is president, has been polling state departments of education on an annual basis since 1983.

Most of the literature related to the development of alternative certification points to the threat of teacher shortages, as well as to the academic quality of the current traditional teacher education practices. Another issue is the decline in the number of minorities entering teaching fields (Stoddart and Floden, 1995). Whatever the impetus, routes to alternative teacher certification have gained momentum, and do not show evidence of slowing down, even in the light of the most recent report of the National Commission on Teaching and America's Future, *No Dream Denied: A Pledge to America's Children* (2003). This report calls for the abandonment of the futile debate over "traditional" vs. "alternative" preparation for teachers. According to Roach and Cohen (2002) alternative certification programs are generally defined as pathways to a teaching certificate that fall outside of a full-time, four- or five-year teacher preparation program. The majority of the programs are designed for individuals who already have a bachelor's degree and who are employed as teachers while they earn their initial teaching license as a result of the alternative certification program. Typically the teaching license is earned in an abbreviated time frame, but finding two programs that are alike is as challenging as finding two individuals who are alike.

## The Best of Times (Successes)

The diversity of alternative certification programs provides many success stories for individuals who decide to become teachers, whether it is a mid-career changer, a paraprofessional, or a college graduate who decides post graduation that they would like to become a teacher. An argument can be made that these programs, while typically abbreviated in the time students spend in college and university coursework, offer employers a workforce that has more diversity and more content/subject-matter expertise. These programs, while diverse in nature, also typically offer mentoring support along with field work and internship experiences.

Alternative certification programs are regarded as an opportunity for creating multiple pathways for entering the field of teaching. These programs also bring individuals such as the mid-career changers to the profession who bring much strength with them. They are more mature, have a diverse range of life experiences, and typically have a sound work ethic. They give real-world answers to the age-old student question, Why do we have to learn this? (Resta, Huling, and Rainwater, 2001).

# The Worst of Times (Challenges)

Projected teacher shortages and the decline in the number of minorities entering teaching fields are just two of a myriad of reasons that alternative certification programs have gained momentum since the early 1980s. Another contention that is particularly troublesome for traditional teacher certification programs is the argument that traditional teacher certification programs fail in their preparation of teachers for urban school settings. Haberman (1994) argues this point, citing that urban schools and students in those schools have unique needs and characteristics that are not being met in the traditional preparation programs.

The federal No Child Left Behind Act of 2001 has created yet another source of challenge for educators and all education stakeholders. No Child Left Behind requires that by the end of the 2005–2006 school year, all public school teachers of core academic subjects must meet a set of standards that require demonstrated competency in the subject in which they teach. The stressors are then compounded in terms of meeting standards and competencies through high-quality traditional teacher preparation programs and making sure that alternative certification programs have the same, competency-based, rigorous education requirements. Many times the concern is that traditional preparation programs are under much more scrutiny than the alternative programs, yet with this Act, all teachers, no matter the preparation route, will have to be "highly qualified."

# The Many Faces of Alternative Certification

Alternative certification was originally conceived as a way of confronting the teacher shortage problems in areas such as mathematics, science, and special education. Today alternative certification is a rather generic term, or blanket term for assisting individuals to become licensed to teacher other than through a traditional teacher preparation program. Feistritzer, 2000, posits that alternative certification runs the gamut from emergency certification to well-designed professional preparation programs for individuals who have at least a baccalaureate degree and considerable life experience and want to become teachers.

Alternative certification programs range from national to state to local programs. Troops to Teachers and Teach for America are two well-known national programs. Troops to Teachers has placed more than 3,000 military veterans in classrooms since 1994 and Teach for America has more than 4,000 applicants for 1,000 slots each year (Finn and Madigan, 2001). In many states school districts have begun to develop programs for particular shortage areas and more states and districts are working with private companies, such as Sylvan Learning Systems and the New Teacher Project (a Teach for America spin-off), to create alternative routes to certification (Finn and Madigan, 2001).

Feistritzer, 1998, however shares that the biggest increase in interest is from higher education officials in schools, colleges, or departments of education. This leads to an interesting and important concept—utilizing the best practice in traditional teacher education preparation to inform alternative certification program development and refinement, and vice versa. The number of stakeholders is immense, and the political agendas and turf issues sometimes undermine the ultimate goal of strengthening teacher preparation, period! With more institutions of higher education developing unique alternatives for qualified individuals while continuing the traditional paths to teacher preparation, a focus can and should be on developing standards that correlate with and complement the two tracks—traditional and alternative.

Another important facet to consider is the challenge of keeping teachers in the profession once they are recruited. Ingersoll (2001) acknowledges a looming teacher shortage, but attributes it more to the fact that the profession is a "revolving door" in which teachers are constantly leaving for reasons largely related to job dissatisfaction rather than to pending retirements. He further indicates that 39 percent of new teachers leave the classroom within five years. Ingersoll advocates for alternative certification that is embedded within a comprehensive system of teacher development, recruitment, and retention. Taking this advice, the odds of preparing teachers in the traditional manner and in the alternative method(s) will yield programs that produce high-quality teachers.

# What to Look for in Quality Teacher Preparation

As more pathways become possible for entering the teaching profession it is important to stay focused on high standards that support all teacher preparation programs, including alternative routes. The National Council for the Accreditation of Teacher Education (NCATE), Interstate New Teacher Assessment and Support Consortium (INTASC), National Board for Professional Teaching Standards (NBPTS), and various specialized professional associations are current examples of the influences that create the foundation for traditional teacher preparation programs that prepare highly qualified teachers. As alternative routes become more mainstreamed into the Colleges of Education, the issue will not be how teachers are prepared, but how well they are prepared. The alternative path may very well be the most appropriate path for more experienced, mature individuals, but undergirding those paths with standards and systems of quality assurance is critical. The National Commission on Teaching and America's Future most recent report, *No Dream Denied: A Pledge to America's Children* (2003), provides six dimensions of quality teacher preparation that will build the foundation for successful pathways to teacher preparation. The dimensions include:

1. Careful recruitment and selection of teacher candidates;
2. Strong academic preparation for teaching, including deep knowledge of the subjects to be taught, and a firm understanding of how children learn;
3. Extensive clinical practice to develop effective teaching skills, including an ability to teach specific content effectively, at specific grade levels, to diverse students;
4. Entry-level teaching support through residencies and mentored induction;
5. Modern learning technologies that are embedded in academic preparation, clinical practice, induction, and ongoing professional development; and
6. Assessment of teacher preparation program effectiveness.

# The Four Chapters

Currently a wide range of alternative certification programs have been established. The chapters in this division of the *Teacher Education Yearbook XIII* describe four alternative certification programs; while different in concept, evolution, and implementation, they have a major goal to encourage individuals with diverse backgrounds and experiences to participate.

The first two chapters examine programs that are adaptations of nationally recognized programs such as the Teach for America Program. Chapter 1 presents a program that targets the immigrant and refugee population who wish to become certified teachers. The Newcomer Extended Teacher Education Program (ETEP) is an adaptation of the existing Extended Teacher Education Program, a fifth-year program built on the core principles of professional development schools. The Newcomer ETEP stresses the socio-transformative constructivism theory and uses a cohort model to promote the socialization process through intentional reflection, open dialogue, and substantial time in schools with mentor teachers.

Chapter 2 focuses on an alternative certification program that is based on the Teach for America model and is considered a "traditional" alternative certification program. The researcher's main focus is to follow a cohort of Fellows for three years to determine how the teachers understand themselves as teachers and how their thinking changed during their first years of teaching in poor urban schools. A main concern is to determine why the teachers make decisions to remain teaching in poor urban areas, leave for more attractive teaching positions in the suburbs, or leave teaching all together. Autobiographical experiences provide insights into the thinking of the Fellows as they face discrepancies in their ideals of teaching and the realities of high-stakes testing, scripted curricula, and a lack of autonomy.

The last two chapters present multi-program models or routes to teacher certification and use case study methodology to research the successes and challenges of their extended programs. Chapter 3, "Project TEAM Expansions at Indiana University: A Cross-Campus Analysis," is an example of a university-based program originally designed to recruit students of color into teacher education, as well as students planning to teach in urban and/or ethnically diverse schools. This program began on a large, residential campus and has now expanded to four regional institutions. This program is grounded in theories of campus climate and integrated pluralism, ethnic identity development, and teaching for social justice.

Chapter 4, "Innovation in Teacher Preparation: Creating Alternative Routes to Teacher Quality," is an example of an alternative certification program that has been developed to target non-traditional and diverse teacher candidates. Challenges and successes of four distinct programs are addressed using the common elements of peer cohorts, intensive and directed field experiences, creative partnership, the use of mentor teachers who are considered master practitioners, and the use and modeling of educational instructional technologies. The four programs include a community college learning community, a "district-grown" on-site teacher preparation program, an elementary education accelerated certification program, and a grant-supported university–community college emergency certification program.

# References

Dickens, C. (1894). *A Tale of Two Cities*. Boston: Houghton-Mifflin.

Finn, Jr., C. E. and Madigan, K. (2001). Removing the barriers for teacher candidates. *Educational Leadership, 58*(3), 29–31.

Feistritzer, C. E. (1998). *Alternative teacher certification: An overview* (The Center for Education Information). Retrieved May 11, 2004, from http://www.ncei.com/Alt-Teacher-Cert.htm.

Feistritzer, C. E. and Chester, D. T. (2000). *A state-by-state analysis*. Washington, DC: National Center for Education Information.

Feistritzer, C. E. and Chester, D. T. (2003). *Alternative teacher certification*. Washington, DC: National Center for Education Information.

Haberman, M. (1994). Preparing teachers for the real world of urban schools. *Educational Forum, 58*(2), 162–68.

Ingersoll, R. (2001, January). *Teacher turnover, teacher shortages, and the organization of schools.* University of Washington: Center for the Study of Teaching and Policy. Document R-01-1.

National Commission on Teaching and America's Future. (2003). *No dream denied: A pledge to America's children.* Washington, DC: National Commission on Teaching and America's Future.

Resta, V., Huling, L. and Rainwater, N. (2001). Preparing second-career teachers. *Educational Leadership, 58*(8), 60–63.

Roach V. and Cohen, B. A. (2002) *Moving past the politics: How alternative certification can promote comprehensive teacher development reforms.* Alexandria, VA: National Association of State Boards of Education.

Stoddart, T. and Floden, R. E. (1995). *Traditional and alternative routes to teacher certification: Issues, assumptions, and misconceptions. Issue paper 95-2.* National Center for Research on Teacher Learning, Michigan State University. (ERIC Document Reproduction Service No. ED 383697.)

CHAPTER 1

# Looking Through a New Lens: Learning About the American Educational System through the Perspectives of Foreign-Born Teaching Candidates

*Flynn Ross*
University of Southern Maine

Dr. Ross is an Assistant Professor of Teacher Education at the University of Southern Maine. She is the university-based coordinator of Extended Teacher Education Program (ETEP) in Portland and also the faculty coordinator of the Newcomer-ETEP program. Her areas of research include professional development school programs and multicultural education.

ABSTRACT

This chapter documents the successes and challenges of a teacher preparation program designed to prepare recent immigrants and refugees to be certified teachers for mainstream classrooms. Many of the program participants were teachers in their home nations. The program is an adaptation of a nationally recognized fifth-year, graduate-level teacher preparation program. Building on the model of programs that capture the dedication and experience of paraprofessionals, the program has been modified to allow extended time for the participants to reach the same high standards as native-born students. The successes include benefits to the K–12 classroom and the graduate school classes. These include connections with individual students, enrichment of curriculum, and education of veteran teachers about cross-cultural communication and student needs. The challenges include standardized tests, cultural differences in educational philosophy, preparation of mentor teachers for working with non-traditional teaching candidates, employment, interviewing, and education of hiring boards.

*If we are to achieve a richer culture, rich in contrasting values, we must recognize the whole gamut of human potentialities, and so weave a less arbitrary social fabric, one in which each diverse human gift will find a fitting place.*

—Margaret Mead (2003)

The growing diversity of students in the public school systems is occurring in every corner of our nation. The need for a teaching force that reflects this demographic student profile is evident, (Darling-Hammond and Sykes, 1999; Irvine, 2003; Ladson-Billings, 1999; Scheetz, 1995). The challenges for identifying, supporting, and preparing individuals from diverse backgrounds to become teachers are numerous. In an era of rapid educational reform, ensuring the successful transition of diverse teachers into the classroom is challenging.

This chapter reports on a teacher preparation program, in a northern New England city, that is targeting recent immigrant and refugees to become certified teachers. The city is experiencing rapid demographic changes as a federally designated immigrant and refugee resettlement community. The Newcomer ETEP program is an adaptation of the existing Extended Teacher Education Program (ETEP) graduate-level program. Both programs were built through school and university partnerships and are based on the core principles of professional development schools (Holmes Group, 1990).

# Literature Review

This research is framed by the theory of sociotransformative constructivism (Rodriguez, 2002). I use sociotransformative constructivism to examine the program structures that promote a shift in educational philosophy of students schooled in other nations as they prepare to teach in learning-centered classrooms (Darling-Hammond, 1992; Darling-Hammond et al., 1993; Lambert and McCombs, 1998). The program's goal is to prepare a teaching force that reflects the growing diversity of the student population seen in many, if not most, communities in the United States. The program also seeks to prepare students to teach in progressive, constructivist classrooms. The literature review looks at recruitment of minority teachers and program development for retention and success of minority teachers. In this literature 'minority teachers' most frequently refers to African American and Hispanic teachers who were born and raised in the public school system in the United States. The experiences of the Newcomer ETEP students are unique because they were not born and raised in the United States, but they provide much of the same richness of experience of other minority groups. They also experience many of the challenges and barriers experienced by other minority groups in the United States.

## SOCIOTRANSFORMATIVE CONSTRUCTIVISM

Teacher education is widely recognized as a process of socialization into the profession (Richardson, 1996; Zeichner and Gore, 1990). This is particularly true when preparing immigrants and refugees, who were raised in authoritarian societies in which the governments controlled the curriculum and dictated what teachers were to transmit to their students (Weintroub, 1996), to teach in progressive, constructivist classrooms. The life experiences of being schooled in one educational system and the influence of the "apprenticeship of observation" (Lortie, 1975) are recognized to have a strong influence on potential teachers. The theory of sociotransformative constructivism merges multicultural education with social constructivism (Gergen, 1995) and provides for a sense of agency that allows for the conscious and intentional transformation of philosophical beliefs by students. "Agency is defined here as the conscious role that we choose to play in helping to bring about change for the benefit of all and especially for the benefit of those who occupy disadvantaged positions in comparison with ours" (Rodriguez, 2002, p. 1020). In the context of the Newcomer ETEP program the impetus for the program creation was a social justice agenda of providing opportunities for under-served communities.

The notion of agency also frames the power of the students in the program to be active constructors of their learning through intentional reflection and their interaction with their newly found social context in their adopted country. There are many structures of the Newcomer ETEP program design that promote the socialization process. The program is cohort based and provides substantial time in the schools with mentor teachers, and course assignments encourage reflection on the classroom experiences.

## NEED FOR A DIVERSE TEACHING FORCE

Many researchers, practitioners, policy makers, and parents are calling for a teaching force that reflects the growing diversity of the student population (Darling-Hammond and Sykes, 1999; Scheetz, 1995; Shure, 2001; Stephens, 1999). Minority teachers are thought to be able to serve as role models for minority students (Irvine, 2003; Sheets, 2000; Sleeter, 1992). Minority teachers also are thought to bring sociocultural life experiences to the classroom that, "make them more aware of the elements of racism embedd(ed) within school . . . and more willing to enact a socially just agenda for society and schooling" (Quiocho and Rios, 2000, p. 487). Those minority teachers who have been successful in the mainstream society are thought to be "skilled in crossing cultural and linguistic boundaries in school contexts" (Quiocho and Rios, p. 488). Teachers who live bi- or multicultural lives because their home culture is not the mainstream, middle-class culture of the professionals in schools, may be able to model and guide students in how to be border crossers in bicultural contexts (Giroux, 1997; Hones, 1999).

It is proposed that all children may benefit from ethnically and linguistically diverse teachers, not just children who see their own diversity reflected (Quiocho and Rios, 2000) The influence of minority teachers on Caucasian students has not been well researched or documented but the benefits of teachers who bring a global perspective to the classroom may be assumed by many. Parents and teachers in a community that has been homogenous and is now experiencing a rapid change of demographics could be less enthusiastic about the possible benefits.

## RECRUITMENT EFFORTS

The need to recruit minority teachers to reflect the diversity of the student population has resulted in the creation of numerous programs and policies. One of the successful strategies has been to develop programs that support paraeducators (educational technicians, teacher assistants) to pursue their college education and teacher certification (Dandy, 1998; Genzuk and Reynaldo, 1998). In their study *Breaking the Class Ceiling: Paraeducator Pathways to Teaching*, Haselkorn and Fideler (1996) reviewed 146 programs nationwide that represented 43 colleges and 2,200 teacher candidates. The Newcomer ETEP program is founded on tapping the human resource of paraeducators in the Portland Public Schools.

In designing programs to support minority candidates to enter the teaching profession, several factors are identified related to success: peer group support, financial aid, faculty mentorships, and working for social justice through multicultural education (Bennett, Cole, and Thompson, 2000; Yopp, Yopp, and Taylor, 1992). The teaching candidates in the Newcomer ETEP program require many of the same comprehensive supports. There are some differences that arise from their status as recent immigrants and refugees. They have a need for English language supports in both oral and written communication as well as support in negotiating the bureaucratic hurdles of international transcript analysis and university admissions.

## DESIGNS OF PROGRAMS FOR CULTURALLY AND LINGUISTICALLY DIVERSE TEACHERS

The ETEP program is designed around several core commitments that the faculty believe are essential to preserving a quality teacher preparation program. These core commitments are: school/university partnerships for linking theory and practice, an extended mentored internship, an embedded assessment system, and a cohort structure (Canniff, Fallona, and Shank, 2004). The research on design of teacher education programs for minority teachers also supports the use of a cohort structure and mentors but offers some cautions (Quiocho and Rios, 2000; Yopp, et. al., 1992). The cohort structure is important for all teacher education students (Fallona, Shank, Canniff, and Hanley, 2002; Pritchard Ross, 2000) but has been reported to be particularly important for minority teacher candidates to "persist, minimize burnout, overcome feelings of isolation, and minimize feelings of being overwhelmed" (Quiocho and Rios, 2000, p. 503).

The cohort structure supports the "dialogic conversation" that is part of the sociotransformative constructivism (Rodriguez, 2002, p. 1020). It allows students to know each other as individuals, build trust, have conversations reflecting on their school experiences, and be able to speak and listen as individuals situated in their social contexts. The cohort structure also creates a sense of critical mass even when actual numbers and percentages of minority students compared to majority students are very small.

Another issue widely considered vital to the success of teacher education students is identifying high-quality, veteran teachers to serve as mentors (Holloway, 2002; Meyers and Smith, 1999; Torres-Guzman and Goodwin, 1995). However, the research cautions that the relationship between the minority teacher candidates and their mentors are especially sensitive to the cross-cultural communication and expectations that are inherent in our diverse society. The Newcomer ETEP program also has found this to be true as will be discussed later in this chapter.

In contrast, when teachers and schools value the experiences of the ethnically diverse teacher candidates as a resource for their schools everyone involved is strengthened. Jones, Maguire, and Watson, reported that 'When schools responded by . . . looking to them for the cultural capital that they brought, their experience was positive" (As cited in Quiocho and Rios, 2000, p. 503). This is also found to be true in the Newcomer ETEP program. For example, the students in a middle school classroom, when studying immigration through Ellis Island, were able to compare history with the present-day experiences of their class intern who was himself a recent immigrant.

# Design of the Newcomer ETEP Program

The development and daily operation of the Newcomer ETEP program is guided by the Steering Committee made up of university faculty, administrators, school district teachers and administrators, and representatives of the ethic communities who have contributed graduates of the program. The Newcomer ETEP program design has evolved over the five years of existence from 1999–2004. The program has adapted to fit the specific needs of each individual; however, there are several basic components of the design that are similar for most of the participants including admissions and course configuration.

The program coordinator has several responsibilities including identifying potential Newcomer ETEP participants and providing advising to meet the program admissions criteria. Coordinator supports includes paying for international transcripts to be analyzed, and identifying and registering for prerequisite content courses for the area of certification. Tutoring for PRAXIS I and ESL college writing courses are paid for by the program. The coordinator also advises candidates on how to gain access to the schools by applying for paraeducator positions. Most of the candidates thus far are employed by the partner school district as language facilitators, educational technicians, or parent/community specialists.

Admission is a two-stage process. Candidates are admitted first to the Newcomer ETEP program and later to the ETEP program. For admission to the Newcomer ETEP program candidates must: (1) hold a bachelor's degree; (2) demonstrate competency in conversational and academic English, both spoken and written; (3) meet most of the prerequisite content area courses for the desired area of teacher certification as designated by the state department of education; and (4) demonstrate a commitment to teaching and working with children and adolescents. To be fully admitted to the ETEP program, the Newcomer ETEP participants must meet the same entry criteria as all other applicants to the graduate-level program. They must hold a bachelor's degree, have completed the required subject area courses for their area of certification as designated by the Maine State Department of Education, pass the PRAXIS I exam, demonstrate commitment to teaching, and complete the ETEP program application, which requires an essay and annotated resume (http://www.usm.maine.edu/cehd/etep).

The Newcomer ETEP program is a modification of the nationally recognized ETEP program. It maintains the 33 graduate credits combined with extensive time in a mentored internship setting. The 12 teaching standards and 6 performance assessments remain the same.[1] The primary modification has been to extend the program over two years. The two-year plan allows Newcomer ETEP students to continue to work in the public schools as language facilitators and educational technicians (paraprofessionals), while taking courses with the ETEP cohort after school. The Newcomer ETEP students take university courses part-time for three semesters and full-time along with the internship for the fourth semester (see table 1.1).

The Newcomer ETEP program culminates in a full-time, 15-week internship, combined with 9–12 credits of university coursework. The 12 weeks of fieldwork required of the ETEP students in the fall semester is modified for Newcomers to fit the contexts in which they are already working in the schools.

# Data Collection and Analysis

Data regarding the program successes and challenges were collected through several methods. University-based course instructors were e-mailed a set of five questions regarding the benefits and challenges of having Newcomer ETEP students in their graduate courses. All five instructors provided e-mail responses. Three out of eleven mentor teachers who hosted Newcomer ETEP students in

**Table 1.1   Elementary Teacher Certification Newcomer ETEP Two-Year Program**

| Fall Term | Spring Term | Fall Term | Spring Term |
|---|---|---|---|
| Life Span Dev. | Science Methods | Seminar I | Seminar II |
| **Coursework** | | | |
| Exceptionality | | Math Methods | Social Studies Methods |
| | | Writing Dev. | Internship in Elem. Ed. |
| | | Reading Dev. | |
| **Assessments** | | | |
| Case Study | | Journal | Curriculum Unit |
| | | Philosophy | Portfolio |
| Praxis 1 test | | Statement | Video taped lessons |

1. The 12 teaching standards are: knowledge of adolescent and child development and principles of learning, knowledge of subject area and inquiry, instructional planning, instructional strategies, technology, assessment, culturally responsive practices, beliefs about teaching and learning, citizenship, collaboration and professionalism, professional development, and classroom management. The 6 performance assessments are: case study, journal, analysis of video of teaching, portfolio, curriculum unit, and a philosophy of teaching.

their classrooms were also asked questions about the benefits and challenges of having Newcomer ETEP students in classrooms. The three mentors were identified by the faculty coordinator as most likely to respond and able to be contacted during the summer months for interviews. Two mentor teachers were interviewed by telephone and one responded by e-mail. A focus group meeting of graduates of the program was held by the school district Assistant to the Superintendent for Multicultural Affairs and the results of that focus group framed data analysis.

The primary source of data was the author's firsthand experience. As the coordinator of the ETEP program, I worked in connection with the Newcomers ETEP program as advisor, field supervisor, course instructor, and as a member of the Steering Committee. In addition, two graduates of the program contributed e-mail and read and responded to this chapter. There were benefits and limitations to being a participant researcher. I brought to the research the insights and perspectives of an "insider" who understands many of the complexity and subtleties of structures and relationships within the program over time. The limitation was that I may be unable to identify assumptions that we as participants in the program make in the ways that an "outside" researcher might be able to. Participant member checks and collection of data from a variety of sources helped address some of these issues.

Program successes and challenges were identified in steering committee meetings in which results from the focus group with graduates and interviews with mentor teachers were presented. Most of the program challenges were supported in the literature on programs developed for the recruitment and preparation of minority teachers. Many of the program successes need to be more widely elaborated and substantiated to strengthen the support of development of similar programs. Many of the challenges in the program resulted in identifying questions for further research.

# Program Successes

The Newcomer ETEP program has had a number of successes including having had graduates hired to teach full-time in the public schools. Other successes include benefits to the K–12 classrooms in which they taught, and benefits to the graduate school classrooms in which they were students.

## GRADUATES

The Newcomer ETEP program has supported fifteen candidates as of 2004 to pursue teacher certification. Of these five are in the first year of the program.

Six have graduated from the program; of these, two graduates are in their third year as full-time classroom teachers in ESL classrooms. Another graduate has been hired to coordinate the Project Safe and Smart afterschool program at one of the elementary schools. Two other graduates returned to their jobs as parent-liaisons at the Multilingual Center with the school district and a third graduate returned to her job as a language facilitator at the high school. One student is in the second year of the program, one student left the program for family reasons, and two others completed the first year but did not pass the PRAXIS exam and so are retaking the exam before beginning their internship year.

## BENEFITS TO THE K–12 CLASSROOMS

In interviews and e-mail questionnaires the mentors identified numerous benefits and challenges to having the Newcomer ETEP students in their classrooms. The benefits included connections with individual students, enrichment of curriculum, and education of veteran teachers about cross-cultural communication and student needs. Mentor teachers identified a number of strengths of the Newcomer ETEP students including their high motivation, sophistication, awareness of world issues, and literacy in three to five languages.

## BENEFITS TO THE GRADUATE-LEVEL CLASSROOMS

Course instructors reported that the Newcomer ETEP students brought a richness of understanding to the graduate level classroom discussions. "We wouldn't be able to have the discussions we do without the Newcomer ETEP students. It gives us a deeper understanding of our own system as we reinvent American education" (instructor interview, July 30, 2002). In the integrative seminar teaching interns raised in the United States have had questions about working with students for whom English was not their native language and working with the parents of these students. Students reported informally that it was a tremendous asset for these beginning teachers to turn to their classmates who are themselves English speakers of other languages and parents of children in the school system. The open dialogue in a trusting environment allowed these beginning teachers to ask questions about discipline expectations, communication with parents, cultural expectations for gender roles, religious differences, and many other often undiscussed issues. Having students in the graduate classroom who are members of cultural and linguistic minority groups changes the discussion. The graduate students can no longer talk about "them" or "those students" when they are physically present in the classroom embodied in their peers.

# Challenges

The Newcomer ETEP program, its students, coordinators, and mentors have all met informally and formally at steering committee meetings and observations to struggle with many challenges. The challenges that were identified are passing standardized tests, meeting the demands of university coursework, cultural differences in educational philosophy, preparation of mentor teachers for working with non-traditional teaching candidates, and employment, interviewing, and education of hiring boards.

### STANDARDIZED TESTS

One of the most clear cut and well-documented challenges for minority teaching candidates was to pass standardized tests including PRAXIS I (Fields, 1988; Ladson-Billings, 1999; Memory, Coleman, and Watkins, 2003; Quiocho and Rios, 2000). In the Newcomer ETEP program, of ten candidates who have taken the exam, two passed PRAXIS I on the first attempt. Five have completed every other part of their certification and are still considered "conditionally certified" because they have not yet passed PRAXIS on the first and second attempts despite tutoring. Three retook sections of PRAXIS, one for admission to the internship year of ETEP.

### EDUCATIONAL PHILOSOPHIES—CULTURAL DIFFERENCES

There were many issues related to cultural differences which were identified by mentor teachers, the program coordinator, and course instructors. As has been previously mentioned, there were cultural differences in educational philosophies that played out in the classroom. Gender roles are culturally conditioned in different ways across various cultures. The immigrant students tended to be uncomfortable with having a "voice" and representing their opinions in writing and orally in a program that emphasizes reflective practice. Many mentor teachers expected interns to take initiative in the internship, which some Newcomers find disrespectful because of the perception of the hierarchical relationship of intern and mentor.

## UNIVERSITY TEACHER EDUCATORS—COURSEWORK

Instructors have consistently said that writing academically in English, comprehension of extensive reading assignments, and use of technology were challenges for each of the Newcomer ETEP students. Suggested solutions included more preparation with technology, more preparation for academic writing, more time for reading the texts, and possibly identifying translators for difficult concepts.

There were also more subtle challenges that are culturally based. One instructor said that Newcomer ETEP students, "Aren't familiar with the give and take of discussion (I'm not sure how they felt in small group discussions—I need to get feedback in the future because I don't know how they felt)" (instructor interview July 30, 2002). The structures of the constructivist classroom in a program designed to prepare "reflective practitioners" was very different from the delivery model of teacher training that some of the Newcomer ETEP students experienced in their home nations. Previous research has shown that this adaptation to a new cultural philosophy may be very difficult (Carter and Doyle, 1996; Hollingsworth, 1989; Lortie, 1975; Richardson, 1996; Zeichner and Gore, 1990). However, strategies such as reflective journaling and discussion, along with firsthand experience in progressive classrooms, appeared to have made a difference at least intellectually for the Newcomer ETEP students.

## PREPARATION OF MENTOR TEACHERS FOR WORKING WITH NON-TRADITIONAL TEACHING CANDIDATES

In interviews and e-mail surveys with three of the mentor teachers, they identified the following challenges working with Newcomer ETEP interns: language, educational philosophy, classroom management, and balancing coursework and teaching.

*Language*: Mentor teachers reported that, "It is more work having a Newcomer ETEP intern because their first language is not English." "Some students reported difficulty understanding the interns." Some teachers have raised the concern that it is important to have a native English speaker for students, especially in the primary grades where students are learning letter/sound relationships like various consonant blends. This is an area in which we need more research and evidence and even then it may be a very individualized situation depending upon the degree of accent of the Newcomer ETEP intern and on the receptive language skills of the students.

*Educational Philosophy:* The mentor teachers reported that, "Sometimes it can be frustrating because they (Newcomer ETEP interns) don't see it the same way as American educated teachers. I see education as a process while the intern is more concerned with the product; we help each other to understand another way of thinking and doing, but it takes time." The Newcomer ETEP students all experienced traditional, didactic, drill and skill education in their own K–12 schooling. They intellectually could talk and write about the benefits of a constructivist curriculum in which students have freedom to think and question, however the influence of their own schooling still appeared to be strong. Many studies document the strong, persistent influence of pre-training experiences on beginning teachers (Carter and Doyle, 1996; Hollingsworth, 1989; Lortie, 1975; Richardson, 1996; Zeichner and Gore, 1990). Prior beliefs and attitudes provided the schemata through which prospective teachers experienced their teacher preparation programs (Aitken and Mildon, 1991; Calderhead and Robson, 1991; Weinstein, 1990).

*Classroom Management*: Most teaching interns and beginning teachers struggle with classroom management. However, as the coordinator I have observed that the Newcomer ETEP interns, as a group, have had a greater challenge with democratic classroom management than the ETEP interns in general. Mentor teachers who have mentored both Newcomer ETEP and ETEP interns report that Newcomer ETEP interns, "Experience some difficulty with classroom management." This varies by individual personality, gender, and cultural background.

## EMPLOYMENT, INTERVIEWING, AND HIRING BOARDS

Finding employment as full-time classroom teachers was a challenge for graduates of the Newcomer ETEP program. The two graduates from 1999–2000 worked for a year as para-professionals and then received lead teaching positions in ESOL classrooms. Of the two graduates from 2001, one returned to his position as a parent/community liaison through the grant funded Multilingual Center with the school district. The other worked for a year and a half as a para-professional before earning the position of coordinator of Project Safe and Smart, a federally funded after-school program. The graduate from 2002 also returned to his position as a parent/community liaison through the multilingual center. None of the graduates have found teaching jobs in the mainstream classrooms for which they were prepared. This may be in part because only one of the graduates from 2001 held a provisional teaching certification because of passing Praxis I. The other four graduates all held a conditional teaching certificate, which is less marketable as school accreditation is linked to the certification levels of teachers.

The challenges for minority candidates for being hired are well documented in the research (Barr, 1991; Quiocho and Rios, 2000). Preparation for interviewing included the understanding that graduates needed to learn "flagrant self-promotion" which is culturally distinctive to the interview expectations for schools in the United States. Another need identified by the Steering Committee, was for review of the hiring process for sources of bias and education of hiring boards to broaden the perspective of what quality teaching to reach all students may include and to be aware of their own possible biases in the interview process.

# Conclusions and Implications for Future Research

This chapter offers a program model of how to recruit, prepare, and retain minority teachers that shows promise and hopefully has inspired those working for educational equity. The successes and challenges of the Newcomer ETEP students contribute to the research on minority teachers by confirming the struggle to pass standardized tests, the potential strength of influence on students, and the challenge of getting hired after training. The results are also unique because ETEP works with immigrants and refugees. They come from cultures not usually considered in studies that emphasize minorities who are African American or Hispanic. The teacher candidates from the immigrant and refugee communities tend to hold teaching as a profession in high regard. They tend to have great faith in the promise of education for a better way of life and the American dream. They tend to have confidence in their ability to work hard and master university courses.

When examining the discussion of the program's successes a couple of topics for future research arise. These include investigating the nature of influence of culturally and linguistically diverse teachers on Caucasian students in the K–12 setting and the nature of influence of minority teaching candidates on their Caucasian peers in a cohort and on teacher education faculty.

The discussion of the program's challenges leads to possible topics for future research in areas that highlight what may be institutional and systemic challenges that need to be addressed by teacher educators and policy makers. These systemic challenges clearly include the obstacle of standardized teacher tests like Praxis I, as well as hiring practices and possible biases of interview committees.

Some of the other challenges are embedded in the interactions of individuals and may be more clearly addressed through the understanding of sociotransformative constructivism and the design of the program curriculum. These include the expectations and cross-cultural communication needed between mentors and interns. Classroom management is another area particularly influenced by individual experience and beliefs in social contexts. Classroom management is an area that is filled with the implicit expectations of teachers and every student in the classroom. Future research could investigate whether discussions facilitated in the university coursework and in reflective conferencing with the mentor teacher, supervisor, and interns framed with the goal of social justice may be able to transform classroom management practices of individuals who were schooled in authoritarian classrooms.

It will be interesting to follow the graduates of the Newcomer ETEP program into their own classrooms to see how they blend their life experiences with the models of their teacher preparation program and to see how they respond to the growing diversity of the student population.

# References

Aitken, J. L., and Mildon, D. (1991). The dynamics of personal knowledge and teacher education. *Curriculum Inquiry, 21*, 141–62.

Barr, H. S. (1991). Unequal opportunities: The recruitment, selection, and promotion prospects of Black teachers. *Evaluation and Research in Education, 5*, 35–47.

Bennett, C., Cole, D., and Thompson, J. (2000). Preparing teachers of color at a predominantly white university: A case study of project TEAM. *Teaching and Teacher Education, 16*(4), 445–64.

Calderhead, J. and Robson, M. (1991). Images of teaching: Student teachers' early conceptions of classroom practice. *Teachers and Teacher Education, 7*(1) 1–8.

Canniff, J., Fallona, C. and Shank, M. (2004). *Strengthening and sustaining teachers, Portland, Maine. Project Report 2002–2003.* Gorham: University of Southern Maine.

Carter, K., and Doyle, W. (1996). Personal narrative and life history in learning to teach. In J. Sikula, T. Buttery, and E. Guyton, (Eds.). *Handbook of research on teacher education,* 2nd edition. New York: Macmillan.

Dandy, E. B. (1998). Increasing the number of minority teachers: Tapping the paraprofessional pool. *Education and Urban Society, 31*(1), 89–103

Darling-Hammond, L. (1992). *Standards of practice for learner-centered schools.* New York: National Center for Restructuring Education, School, and Teaching.

Darling-Hammond, L., Snyder, J., Ancess, J., Einbender, L., Goodwin, A. L., and Macdonald, M. B. (1993). *Creating learner-centered accountability.* New York: National Center for Restructuring Education, Schools, and Teaching.

Darling-Hammond, L. and Sykes, G. (1999). *Teaching as the learning profession: Handbook of policy and practice.* San Francisco, CA: Jossey-Bass, Inc.

Fallona, C., Shank, M., Canniff, J., and Hanley, S. (2002, October). The use of cohorts in teacher education. A presentation at the annual conference of National Network for Educational Renewal, Montclair, New Jersey.

Fields, C. (1988). Poor test scores by many minority students from teacher training. *Chronicle of Higher Education, 35*(10), A1, A32.

Genzuk, M., and Reynaldo, B. (1998). The paraeducator-to-teacher pipeline: A 5-year retrospective on innovative teacher preparation programs for Latinas(os). *Education and Urban Society*, *31*(1), 73–88.

Gergen, K. J. (1995). Social construction and the educational process. In L. P. Steffe and J. Gale (Eds.), *Constructivism in education*. Hillsdale, NJ: Lawrence Erlbaum.

Giroux, H. (1997). *Pedagogy and the politics of hope: Theory, culture and schooling*. Boulder, CO: Westview.

Haney, W., Madaus, G., and Kreitzer, A. (1987). Charms Talismanic: Testing teachers for the improvement of American education. 169–238. In *Review of research in education*, *14*, ed. E. Rothkopf. American Educational Research Association.

Haselkorn, D., and Fideler, E. (1996). *Breaking the class ceiling: Paraeducator pathways to teaching*. Belmont, MA: Recruiting New Teachers, Inc.

Heger, H., and Engelhart, J. (1991). Using predictor tests to strengthen ethnic diversity in teacher education. *Teacher Education and Practice*, *6*(2), 69–70.

Hollingsworth, S. (1989). Prior beliefs and cognitive change in learning to teach. *American Educational Research Journal*, *26*(2), 160–89.

Holloway, J. H. (2002). Mentoring for diversity. *Educational Leadership*, *59*(6), 88–89.

Holmes Group, (1990). *Tomorrow's schools of education*. East Lansing, MI: Holmes Group.

Hones, D. F. (1999). Making peace: A narrative study of a bilingual liaison, a school, and a community. *Teachers College Record*, *101*(1), 106–34.

Hood, S., and Parker, L. J. (1989). Minority bias review panels and teacher testing for initial certification: A comparison of two states' efforts. *Journal of Negro Education* 58, 511–19.

Irvine, J. J. (2003). *Educating teachers for diversity: Seeing with a cultural eye*. New York: Teachers College Press.

Ladson-Billings, G. (1999). Preparing teachers for diversity: Historical perspectives, current trends and future directions. 86–123. In *Teaching as the learning profession: Handbook of policy and practice*, ed. L. Darling-Hammond and G. Sykes. San Francisco, CA: Jossey-Bass Inc.

Lambert, N. M., and McCombs, B. L. (Eds.) (1998). *How students learn: Reforming schools through learner-centered education*. Washington, DC: American Psychological Association.

Lortie, D. (1975). *Schoolteacher*. Chicago: University of Chicago Press.

Mead, M. (1963). *Sex and temperament: In three primitive societies*. New York: HarperCollins Publishers, Inc.

Memory, D.M., Coleman, C. L. and Watkins, S. D. (2003). Possible tradeoffs in raising basic skills cutoff scores for teacher licensure: A study with implications for participation of African Americans in teaching. *Journal of Teacher Education*, *54*(3), 217–27.

Meyers, H. W., and Smith, S. (1999). Coming home—Mentoring new teachers: A school–university partnership to support the development of teachers from diverse ethnic backgrounds. *Peabody Journal of Education*, *74*(2), 75–89.

Pritchard Ross, F. (2000). Developing professionals: Graduates of a professional development school teacher preparation program. Dissertation, Teachers College Columbia University.

Quiocho, A., and Rios, F. (2000). The power of their presence: Minority group teachers and schooling. *Review of Educational Research*, *70*(4), 485–528.

Richardson, V. (1996). The role of attitudes and beliefs in learning to teach. 102–19. In *Handbook of research on teacher education*, second edition., ed. J. Sikula, T. Buttery, and E. Guyton. New York: Simon & Schuster/Macmillan.

Rodriguez, A. J. (2002). Using sociotransformative constructivism to teach for understanding in diverse classrooms: A beginning teacher's journey. *American Educational Research Journal, 39*(4), 1017–45.

Scheetz, P. L. (July, 1995). *Recruiting Trends 1995–1996, Educational Supplement.* East Lansing: Michigan State University, Career Services and Placement.

Sheets, R. H. (2000, April). Trends in the scholarship on teachers of color for diverse populations: Implications for multicultural education. Paper presented at the annual meeting of the American Educational Research Association, New Orleans.

Shure, J. L. (2001). Minority teachers are few and far between. *Techniques: Connecting Education and Careers, 76*(5), 32.

Sleeter, C. E. (1992). *Keepers of the American dream.* Washington, DC: Falmer Press.

Stephens, J. E. (1999). Wanted: Minority educators for U.S. Schools. *School Business Affairs, 65*(5), 37–42.

Torres-Guzman, M., and Goodwin, A. (1995). Urban bilingual teachers and mentoring for the future. *Education and Urban Society, 28*(1), 48–66.

Weinstein, C. S. (1990). Prospective elementary teachers' beliefs about teaching: Implications for teacher education. *Teaching and Teacher Education, 6,* 279–90.

Weintroub, E. (1996). Breaking down barriers: The adjustment of immigrant teachers to new educational frameworks. *Teacher Trainer, 10*(1-3), 20–22.

Yopp, R. H., Yopp, H. K., and Taylor, H. P. (1992). Profiles and viewpoints of minority candidates in a teacher diversity project. *Teacher Education Quarterly, 19*(3), 29–48.

Zeichner, K., and Gore, J. (1990). Teacher socialization. 329–48. In *Handbook of research on teacher education*, ed. W. R. Houston. New York: Macmillan.

CHAPTER 2

# A "Traditional" Alternative Route to Certification: Narrative Research and Implications for Teacher Education and Teacher Retention

*Arthur Costigan*
Queens College, CUNY

> Arthur Costigan is an Assistant Professor and Co-Director of English Edu-
> cation Programs at Queens College, CUNY. His interests are urban teach-
> ing and the autobiographical ways new teachers develop into the profession
> in poor urban school districts, particularly in an era of high-stakes testing
> and increased accountability.

ABSTRACT

As the majority of states now have alternative routes to certification,
such programs may be thought of as "traditional." Like many programs based on the Teach for America model, the New York City
Teaching Fellows program is a particularly substantial example of
current practices in teacher induction. Using interviews, journals,
and group discussions, researchers followed a cohort of Fellows for
three years seeking to realize how they came to understand themselves as teachers and develop a satisfactory teaching practice, as well
as what factors would lead them to remain teaching in urban
schools, to leave for wealthier suburbs, or to leave teaching altogether. Although they entered urban teaching with high ideals and
a strong desire to teach, the Fellows were faced with high-stakes
testing, scripted curricula, and a lack of autonomy. This led many
Fellows to strongly consider leaving urban teaching for the wealthier
suburbs.

# Objectives

Due to a shortage of teachers in the United States, one that is particularly acute in poor urban areas, the overwhelming majority of states now have alternative routes to teacher certification (Park, 2003). Many of these are based on the Teach for America (TFA) model and include a sign-on bonus, financial incentives, summer intensive immersion training, immediate full-time teaching, and reduced-credit educational coursework. So common have these programs become that they can be thought of as "traditional" alternative routes to certification (Michelli, 2003). These programs maintain that people with strong college backgrounds and solid work experience are best suited to teach, and such programs support the idea that smart people with solid backgrounds can become "urban pioneers" (Costigan, Crocco, and Zumwalt, 2004), and become teachers who are as effective as teachers from traditional programs. This "urban pioneer" philosophy devalues traditional teacher education programs (U.S. Department of Education, 2002) and sees teaching as a set of learned teaching behaviors, an understanding which is seen by policy makers as particularly appropriate to the current era of high-stakes testing and increased accountability.

The New York City Teaching Fellow (NYCTF) program, now in its fourth year, is a particularly substantial experiment in alternative teacher recruitment. Thousands of people divided into six cohorts have entered the program since 2000 to teach in troubled New York City Public schools which are "hard to staff." This program invites inquiry in several ways. First, programs such as the NYCTF program address teacher recruitment, not retention, even when the so-called shortage of teachers is actually an exodus of new teachers, half of whom leave within the first three years of teaching (Ingersoll, 2002). Second, the educational research community has come to see learning to teach as an autobiographically grounded process (Clark, 2001; Hubermann, 1993; Levin, 2003). Put simply, who teachers are, and how they develop, matters, particularly in the first few years of teaching (Rust and Orland, 2001). This autobiographical understanding of teaching seeks to understand the development of teachers through their voices and narratives as they grapple with the complexities of teaching (Connelly and Clandinin, 1987; Hollingsworth, 1989; Zeichner and Tabachnick, 1985). As a result, it contrasts sharply with a market-driven, supply-side behaviorist conception found in such programs as TFA and the NYCTF program. The research presented in this chapter is a three-year attempt to understand the NYCTF program by listening to the Fellows themselves, to explore why they choose to become teachers, to see how their thinking changed during their first few years of teaching, and to understand why they eventually choose to remain teaching in poor urban areas, to leave for more attractive teaching positions in the suburbs, or to leave teaching altogether.

# Educational Perspectives on Alternatively Certified Teachers

Studies of alternative routes to certification are situated in the political debate about the effectiveness of traditional teacher education programs, as well as within the public discussion of whether any teacher preparation, other than content-area mastery, is necessary at all (U.S. Department of Education, 2002). The educational research community maintains that teacher effectiveness is due as much to teacher education and preparation as to teachers' content knowledge (Cochran-Smith, 2003). Most recently Darling-Hammond and Youngs (2002) challenge the validity of the findings of the U.S. Secretary of Education, Rod Paige (U.S. Department of Education, 2002), and maintain that teachers prepared through quality teacher preparation program are essential for high student achievement. Similarly, Laczko-Kerr and Berliner (2002) maintain that the students of teachers from alternative programs academically perform lower than those taught by traditionally certified teachers. In fact, students of TFA teachers performed only as well as teachers labeled "under-qualified" (Cochran-Smith, 2003, p. 186; Lackzo-Kerr and Berliner, 2002). However, there is much less knowledge about what specific factors influence teacher effectiveness (King, 2003). According to King (2003), the educational research community is unclear about the level of teaching effectiveness of those who pursue non-traditional routes to certification.

The so-called teacher shortage is actually an exodus of certified teachers (AACTE, 2002; Ingersoll, 2002; Voke, 2002), and nationwide, schools of education, with a few exceptions, graduate enough teachers to meet vacancies due to teacher retirement (NCTAF, 2003). Yet, despite the adequate supply of teachers from traditional programs, teaching has become a "revolving door profession." New teachers leave at five times the rate as professors, lawyers, and nurses, with 35 percent of teachers leaving in their first three years, and 46 percent leaving within five years (Ingersoll, 2002). By the turn of the twenty-first century, there were 130 bills pending nationwide to implement programs to recruit teachers through alternative routes to certification; by 2003, 45 states had adopted such alternative routs, and 25 of these are "structured" programs. Currently all but six states have some kind of alternative route to certification (Blair, 2003).

The reason for teachers leaving the profession is not due primarily to low salaries, but rather because of "quality of life" issues (Park, 2003), such as poor working conditions, lack of autonomy in teaching (Claycomb, 2002), limited input into school decision-making (Gordon, 2003), increased accountability and high-stakes testing (Wright, 2002), chaotic teaching environments (Johnson, et al., 2001) and student resistances to schooling and instruction (Ingersoll, 2002). Other factors include inadequate teacher preparation, lack of support (AACTE, 2002), and the low status that teaching as a career carries among family and friends (Costigan, Crocco and Zumwalt, 2004; Hartocollis, 2003).

# Methodology

Using a layered approach of individual interviews, group discussions, and journal reading, a principal investigator and several co-researchers followed a cohort of New York City Teaching Fellows since the summer of 2000. Typically, a cohort is composed of several thousand teaching candidates who attend over 15 local colleges. The average age is 32, and the candidates entered the program from business and industry, their backgrounds ranging from middle to professional classes. The researchers attempted to understand how the Fellows developed during their first and second years of commitment to the program. As new teachers had fluctuating areas of focus (Rust and Orland, 2001), researchers sought to understand the Fellows' thinking processes as they focused on career choices, problematic students, and control and management issues (Costigan, 2004). In the second year of teaching, as they began to complete their two-year commitment to the program, the researchers sought to comprehend how they continued to develop in their understanding of themselves as teachers, as well as what experiences would lead them to chose to remain teaching in poor urban schools, to leave to teach in suburban school systems, or to leave the teaching profession.

Research began in the summer of 2000 by focusing on 38 Fellows out of a cohort of 130; these Fellows were all enrolled in the same classes and would teach literacy programs in elementary and middle schools in adjacent poor, culturally diverse urban areas in New York City. Over that summer and the first year, researchers read the journals of these 38 Fellows several times. The journals contained both guided entries about teaching and unguided diary entries about their experiences. Researchers noted themes or "process codes" (Bogdan and Biklen, 1992) common in the journals, and, over the first year of the study, researchers conducted nine hour-long individual interviews with Fellows whose journals were considered particularly rich in emerging themes. Following Rust's (1999) methodology researchers additionally used five-hour-long "brown bag" discussions with five to seven Fellows during the first two semesters of full-time teaching. These discussions were voluntary and a total of 25 Fellows participated in groups of four to six. All interviews and discussions were taped and transcribed.

In the second year, interviews of roughly one hour were conducted with seven second-year Fellows. Emerging understandings, themes, and issues relevant to these Fellows were discussed in a two-hour focus discussion to ascertain if the researchers' emerging understandings were trustworthy (Ely, Anzul, Freidman, Garner, and Steinmetz, 1991). Further research was conducted in the spring and summer of 2003 through an additional 14 interviews with some of the original 38 Fellows who now were ending their two-year commitment to the Fellows program. Also, seven additional summative interviews of roughly one-and-a-half hours were taped and transcribed to check the trustworthiness of the researchers' understandings. In all of the second-year interviews, the participants were asked about what factors induced them to remain teaching in the city, to leave for the suburbs, or to leave the teaching profession, as well as other issues effecting their understanding of themselves as teachers and of the teaching craft.

As Costigan (2004) noted, in all of the various research conversations, group discussions and interviews, researchers found that the Fellows were very willing to talk openly, freely, and without constraints. This gave the researchers access to what Clandinin and Connelly (1996) called "secret stories," the understandings and attitudes which are not typically shared in public forums such as the politicized environments of local schools and in college classrooms (Clandinin and Connelly).

## Program Description

While the NYCTF program has evolved since 2000, it continues to feature basic elements such as: (1) a detailed application process that involves intensive interviews and teaching a sample lesson, as well as a careful review of the candidates' academic backgrounds and employment histories; (2) participation in an intensive summer program which included coursework, student teaching, mentoring, and test preparation; (3) full-time teaching for a contracted two-year period in the following fall; and (4) matriculation into an alternative free or reduced cost two-year 36-credit masters program (MSEd) leading to full certification (Resource Guide, 2001).

Quantitative data about the Fellows has been relatively meager, but recently the statistics of retention have emerged. By April 4, 2003, 62 percent of the 323 Fellows who began in the summer of 2000, and 74 percent of the 1096 Fellows who began in the summer of 2001, were still teaching (Duncan-Poitier, 2003). However, although the program formally asks for only a two-year commitment, Fellows were allowed to take three years to complete their MSEd and must teach during their fourth year to gain permanent state certification. There was evidence that by the end of their commitment to the NYCTF program, at least

90 percent were considering leaving for suburban schools or leaving teaching altogether (Stein, 2002).

An ongoing, online, voluntary exit survey of 75 Fellows who chose to withdraw from the program before their two-year formal commitment had ended (Office of Alternative Certification, 2003) revealed that most Fellows were relatively happy with the program, reported high degrees of collegiality with other new teachers, and felt they were getting adequate support. However, respondents reported the chief reasons they chose to withdraw from the program were "student discipline problems" (50%) and "lack of student motivation" (29%). Roughly 20–30 percent of respondents also reported "lack of teacher influence on school policy," "unsafe environments," and "[low] quality of school leadership." Of those who have left the program, 19.4 percent will look for another job in "teaching," and 80.6 percent are looking for "something other than teaching" (Office of Alternative Certification, 2003).

# Results

## THE FELLOWS IN THE FIRST YEAR

In their first year of teaching, the Fellows went through a number of clear transitions in thinking about themselves as teachers and in their thinking about the teaching craft (Costigan, 2004). The Fellows entered the program because of their high ideals and were highly conscious of their "vocational leap of faith" in leaving business and industry to teach in troubled schools. Furthermore, the Fellows entered with initial theories about teaching and their students. These were not merely "lay theories," long-established, commonsense, and well-worn images and archetypes of teachers' work that would remain consistent and be resistant to change in teachers' early years (Britzman, 1986; Holt-Reynolds, 1992; Lortie, 1975; Sugrue, 1996); rather, researchers came to call these thoughts *initial* theories, concepts about students and teaching that were capable of being developed, and that were based on thoughtful consideration of the teaching vocation. These initial theories involved thoughts about how teachers relate to students, the potential ways of imparting an official curriculum, situating learning within the context of the lives of their students, and the creation of a healthy classroom community.

When the Fellows entered the classroom, though, they tended to drop these ideas because of the need for daily survival (Costigan, 2004). The Fellows program does not have as its purpose to take into consideration these initial theories about teaching, nor does it seek to continue to assist the Fellows in developing them. Thus, Fellows tended to put aside consideration of "teaching as a vocation" for the immediate necessity to develop basic competencies in "delivering a lesson" on a daily basis. The Fellows were primarily concerned with classroom "management" and student "control." Initially, the researchers saw these terms as limiting, perhaps something that the Fellows should "unlearn," yet, on reflection, the researchers found that the Fellows were using terms of "management" and "control" in the larger sense of attempting to create safe, orderly, and welcoming environments for their students. The researchers came to see the "management" and "control" language as initial theories of teaching that could be developed through reflective practice. When talking of "management" and "control," the Fellows increasingly through their first year focused on what researchers came to call "bellwether students," the handful of students in their classes which they found disruptive, disengaged, or otherwise problematic. Throughout their first year of teaching, the Fellows tended to use these problematic students as the gauge of their teaching effectiveness (Costigan, 2004).

By the end of the first year of teaching, many Fellows expressed frustration with a curriculum in their schools that was increasingly driven by high-stakes testing, test preparation, mandated curricula, and scripted lessons. The first year of teaching is often chaotic (Rust, 1999), but afterwards, when new teachers had begun to understand the rhythms of the school year (Clandinin and Connelly, 1986), they frequently began to pay attention to other factors which influenced them to stay in or leave the profession (Rust and Orland, 2001). Overwhelmingly, the Fellows reported that they had built strong positive relationships with their students, but that they continued to confront the serious issue of how best to learn a teaching practice that could serve a significant minority of students who they felt were unprepared for traditional schooling. The Fellows felt that their inability to deal with a handful of disruptive students was exacerbated by their experience of the authoritarian culture of schooling, increasingly driven by high-stakes testing, excessive accountability, and mandated curricula. They felt that these factors had intensified (Hargreaves, 2000) their teaching experience to such a degree that leaving the profession was a realistic option.

## THE FELLOWS IN THE SECOND YEAR

Throughout the second year, the Fellows struggled with several issues and began to consider seriously whether or not to remain teaching in urban schools, to leave to teach in the wealthier suburbs, or to leave teaching all together. Researchers identified four themes, or "process codes" (Bogdan and Biklen, 1992), in the way they talked about themselves as teachers and how they were learning the teaching craft: (1) "Culture and Continuity," the relationship between the Fellows' understanding and expectations about schooling and the home cultures and academic beliefs of their students; (2) "Authority and Autonomy," the degree of autonomy they were given by educational authorities to develop teaching strategies which were personally gratifying and seen as beneficial for students; (3) "Autobiography and the Professional Self," the degree to which the Fellows could see their future development as "self" and "teacher" in their current urban setting; and (4) "Students and Relationship," the quality of personal relationships the Fellows were able to develop with a diverse body of students from poor urban communities.

For the researchers, the most troubling issues were the discontinuity between the Fellows' expectations about students' educational attitudes and those of a significant minority of their students (Costigan, 2004). The Fellows, who were primarily white and middle class, had trouble understanding the students who came from areas of high poverty, gang violence, and crime. They were particularly bothered by a lack of educational values in some of their students, an attitude which was reflected in perceived parental indifference. Roughly half of the Fellows came to understand that overworked parents just "didn't have time" to become involved in their children's schooling. A handful of Fellows reported that they felt the local community to be so problematic that it was "broken." As one Fellow stated, "How do you go and tell a community that you're not raising your kids right?" Although the Fellows typically did attempt to understand community issues and students' preparedness to learn a traditional curriculum, they felt that a handful of students consistently created such serious disruptions that none of the teachers, deans, or administrators were able to handle them.

By the middle of the second year, the participants in this study were considering leaving because of a lack of autonomy. In New York City, the current solution to schools that are under state review, labeled "hard to staff," or otherwise seen as troubled, is to increase the use of mandated curricula and scripted lessons, which creates a general lack of autonomy that extends to formal classroom arrangements and the format of bulletin boards. By the fall of 2003, this lack of autonomy was so troublesome to teachers that the issue caused public demonstrations in New York City. By the participants' second year of teaching, these mandated curricula were coming fully into force, and the Fellows felt that they in particular were being singled out and mistrusted by the educational bureaucracy. As the Fellows had entered urban teaching as a deliberate choice and with high ideals, this lack of autonomy created an inability to see themselves developing a personally gratifying teaching practice in city schools. The Fellows told the researchers many stories of attempting to develop a personal and innovative student-centered curriculum based on such things as dramatic activities, research projects based on students' home communities, and various writing activities of high interest which included student-generated stories, newspaper articles, and books. Yet because of a mandated curriculum, they felt prohibited from exploring the possibilities for innovation based on their students' needs and interests. All of the Fellows reported that this lack of autonomy in teaching was a highly significant factor in wanting to leave for the suburbs, where they felt they could develop a curriculum that was both personally rewarding and beneficial for students (Costigan, 2004).

Despite continuing problems with a minority of disengaged and disruptive students, most of the Fellows reported that they had developed strong relationships with almost all of their students and felt guilty about considering leaving for other teaching positions. Researchers initially felt that there was a paradox to the Fellows' stated personal relationship with the students and the fact that they found that a handful of students troublesome and disruptive of classroom and school life. Yet one Fellow told us, "Though one or two students continue to be a pain, I like them. I just don't know what to *do* with them. The school doesn't know what to do with them, and, obviously the chancellor and those people don't know what to do with them." The researchers came to understand that the Fellows' teaching experiences were severely at odds with state and local mandates, and they asked the researchers for more assistance than they had been provided in order to develop a personally gratifying teaching practice in a era of high stakes testing and increased accountability.

# Implications: What the Fellows Are Telling Researchers and Teacher Educators

"Traditional" alternative routes to certification are primarily *instrumental*. The autobiographical development of new teachers is simply not a consideration in such alternative programs. The Fellows are recruited to perform a behavior called "teaching." This instrumental conception does not value the personal, developmental, and relational aspects of becoming a teacher. As one Fellow who was leaving to teach in the suburbs stated, "You know, there's an irony surely— here is an 'urban pioneer' program and I am not trusted to teach the way I want. I have to teach three different scripted lesson programs—*or else!*" The narratives of the Fellows stand in stark contrast to the instrumentalism, standardization, and objectification of the teaching practice in alternative routes to certification.

Programs such as NYCTF exist to address a perceived teacher shortage, one that is in reality an issue of retention. The unintended result is that newly recruited Fellows are merely filling the vacancies being created by previous Fellows who are leaving city teaching at rates from 50 to 90 percent (Stein, 2002). In this sense, the NYCTF program fails to meet its own goals of recruiting large numbers of teachers willing to teach beyond a two-year commitment. The reason for this is the discontinuity between an instrumental program that accepts educational reform through standardization and accountability and the intensely personal and autobiographical ways in which teachers develop and come to understand the profession. The Fellows indicate clearly that the autobiographical and personal aspects of becoming a teacher are central to their choice to remain teaching in urban schools and that these autobiographical considerations of teacher retention are ignored at the peril of losing those same people who have consciously chosen to teach in urban schools in poor neighborhoods.

The journey of the Fellows through their two-year commitment to the NYCTF program demonstrates that becoming a teacher and learning the teaching craft is a developmental and autobiographical process. The initial ideals and noble goals in wanting to become a teacher, the struggles with difficult students, the frustration in working without autonomy, and the relationships established with students are central to the way in which these Fellows come to understand themselves as teachers and come to understand the teaching craft. Teacher educators and educational researchers can be challenged to use these autobiographical processes to assist new teachers in coming to an understanding of themselves and to assist them in negotiating a meaningful teaching practice within the complexities of high-stakes testing and increased accountability. It seems clear, however, that the NYCTF program, a "traditional" alternative route to certification, will not succeed until it takes seriously the autobiographical understandings of those people it has recruited to teach.

The Fellows raise several questions, not only about alternative routes to certification, but about teacher education in general. The largest question arises from the Fellows' conception of teaching as relational and autobiographical. A significant factor in what keeps them in the profession is their request for a balance of support and autonomy, as well as their relationship with their students. This reality begs the question of how teacher education programs can build upon the profoundly autobiographical and personal process it takes to become a teacher and to assist new teachers in incorporating their developing relationships with their students into their emerging understanding of how best to teach.

# References

American Association of Colleges for Teacher Education. (2002, September 9). NCTAF shifts focus from supply to retention: Symposium paves way for new report. *AACTE Briefs, 23*(11), 1, 3.

Blair, J. (2003, January 9). Skirting tradition. *Education Week, 23*(17), 35–39.

Bogdan, R. C., and Biklen, S. K. (1992). *Qualitative research for education: An introduction to theory and methods,* second edition. Needham Heights, MA: Allyn and Bacon.

Britzman, D. P. (1986). Cultural myths in the making of a teacher: Biography and social structure in teacher education. *Harvard Educational Review, 56*(4), 442–56.

Clandinin, D. J. and Connelly, F. M. (1986). Rhythms in teaching: The narrative study of teachers' personal practical knowledge of classrooms. *Teaching and Teacher Education, 2*(4), 377–87.

Clandinin, D. J., and Connelly, F. M. (1996). Teachers' professional knowledge landscapes: Teacher stories—stories of teachers—school stories—stories of schools. *Educational Researcher, 25*(3), 24–30.

Clark, C. M. (Ed.) (2001). *Talking shop.* New York: Teachers College Press.

Claycomb, C. (2002, Winter). High-quality urban school teachers: What they need to enter and to remain in hard-to-staff schools. *The State Education Standard, 1*(1), 17–21.

Cochran-Smith, M. (2003). Assessing assessment in teacher education. *Journal of Teacher Education, 54*(3), 187–91.

Connelly, F. M., and Clandinin, D. J. (1987). On narrative method, biography and narrative: Universities in the study of teaching. *Journal of Educational Thought, 21*(3), 130–39.

Costigan, A. (2004). Finding a name for what they want: A study of New York City's Teaching Fellows. *Teaching and Teacher Education, 20*(2), 129–43.

Costigan, A., Crocco, M., and Zumwalt, K. (2004). *Learning to teach in an age of accountability.* Mahwah, NJ: Lawrence Erlbaum Associates, Inc.

Darling-Hammond, L. and Youngs, P. (2002). Defining "highly qualified teachers": What does "scientifically-based research" actually tell us? *Educational Researcher, 31*(9), 12–25.

Duncan-Poitier, J. (2003). [Memorandum to] The Honorable the Members [sic] of the Board of Regents. New York: State Department of Education. Retrieved from http://www.regents.nysed.gov/June2003/0603hpd3.htm

Ely, M., Anzul, M., Freidman, T., Garner, D., and Steinmetz, A. M. (1991). *Doing qualitative research: Circles within circles.* New York: Falmer.

Gordon, D. T. (Ed.). (2003). *A nation reformed? American education 20 years after "A nation at risk."* Cambridge, MA: Harvard Education Press.

Hargreaves, A. (2000). *Changing teachers, changing times: Teachers' work and culture in the postmodern age.* New York: Teachers College Press.

Hartocollis, A. (2003, April 17). As social status sags, teachers call it a career. *The New York Times,* B3.

Hollingsworth, S. (1989). Prior beliefs and cognitive change in learning to teach. *American Educational Research Journal, 26*(2), 160–89.

Holt-Reynolds, D. (1992). Personal history-based beliefs as relevant prior knowledge in coursework: Can researchers practice what researchers teach? *American Educational Research Journal, 29*(2), 325–49.

Huberman, M. (1993). *The lives of teachers.* (J. Neufeld, Trans.). New York: Teachers College Press. (Original work published 1989).

Ingersoll, R. M. (2002). The teacher shortage: A case of wrong diagnosis and wrong prescription. *NASSP Bulletin, 86*, 16-31. Retrieved from www.principals.org/new/bltn_teachshort 0602.html.

Johnson, S. M., Birkeland, S., Kardos, S., Kauffman, D., Liu, E., and Peske, H. G. (2001, July–August). Retaining the next generation of teachers: The importance of school-based support. *Harvard Educational Letter*.

King, J. R. (2003, August). Understanding the effectiveness of teacher attributes. Economic Policy Institute. Washington, DC: Educational Policy Institute.

Laczko-Kerr, I. and Berliner, D. C. (2002). The effectiveness of "Teach for America" and other under-certified teachers on student academic achievement: A case of harmful public policy. *Educational Policy Analysis Archives, 10*(37). Retrieved from www.epaa.asu.edu/epaa/v10n37

Levin, B. B. (2003). *Case studies of teacher development: An in-depth look at how thinking about pedagogy develops over time*. Mahwah, NJ: Lawrence Erlbaum Associates, Inc.

Lortie, D. (1975). *Schoolteacher: A sociological perspective*. Chicago: University of Chicago Press.

Michelli, N. (2003, April 28). The vision for teacher education at CUNY: Developing a moral agenda for the education of educators and the renewal of schools in difficult times. Address to The Policy Context for Teacher Education: Putting New York in Perspective. New York: The CUNY Office of Academic Affairs.

National Council for Teaching and America's Future. (2003). *No dream denied: A pledge to America's children*. Washington, DC: National Council for Teaching and America's Future.

Office of Alternative Certification. (2003). [Survey summary/Results Summary/Filter Summary]. Unpublished raw data.

Park, J. (2003, January 9). Deciding factors. *Education Week, 22*(17), 17–19.

Resource guide for the New York City Teaching Fellows. (2001, May). New York: The New York City Board of Education.

Rust. F. O. (1999). Professional conversations: New teachers explore teaching through conversation, story and narrative. *Teaching and Teacher Education 15*, 367–80.

Rust, F. and Orland, L. (2001). 82–117. In *Talking shop*, ed. C. M. Clark. New York: Teachers College Press.

Stein, J. (2002). Evaluation of the NYCTF program as an alternative certification program. New York: New York City Board of Education.

Sugrue, C. (1996). Student teachers' lay theories: Implications for professional development. 154–77. In *Teachers' professional lives*, ed. I. F. Goodson and A. Hargreaves. Washington, DC: Falmer Press.

U.S. Department of Education. (2002). *Meeting the highly qualified teachers challenge: The Secretary's annual report of teacher quality*. Washington, DC: USDOE.

Voke, H. (2002, May). Understanding and responding to the teacher shortage. Association for Supervision and Curriculum Development, 29. Retrieved from http://www.ascd.org/readingroom/infobrief/issue29.html

Wright, W. E. (2002, June 5). The effects of high stakes testing in an inner-city elementary school: The curriculum, the teachers and the English language learners. *Current Issues in Education, 5*(5). Retrieved from http://cie.ed.asu.edu/volume5/number5

Zeichner, B., and Tabachnick, R. (1985). The impact of the student teaching experience on the development of teacher perspectives. *Journal of Teacher Education, 31*(6), 28–36.

# CHAPTER 3

# Project TEAM Expansions at Indiana University: A Cross-Campus Analysis

*Christine Bennett*
Indiana University

*Paulette Dilworth*
Indiana University

*John Kuykendall*
Indiana University

*Raquel Barrera*
Indiana University

Christine Bennett is Professor of Social Studies and Multicultural Education at Indiana University–Bloomington where she also directs Project TEAM. Her research includes studies of the impact of multicultural social studies, classroom climates in desegregated middle schools, racial inequities in school suspensions and expulsions, racial issues in higher education, multicultural teacher education, and African American and Latino perspectives on PRAXIS I.

Paulette Patterson Dilworth is Assistant Professor of Social Studies and Curriculum Studies at Indiana University–Bloomington where she co-directs Project TEAM. Her research interests include studies of multicultural content integration, curriculum access and equity in middle and high school classrooms, multicultural citizenship education, and intersections between historical and contemporary approaches to civic education for social justice.

John Kuykendall is a doctoral student in Higher Education Administration at Indiana University–Bloomington and a graduate assistant with Project TEAM. His research examines racial and gender equity in higher education,

African American student persistence in higher education, and the impact of students of color persisting in teacher education programs.

Raquel Barrera is a doctoral student in Curriculum and Instruction at the University of Texas at Austin. At the time of this research she was a graduate assistant with Project TEAM while she completed her Masters Degree in Instructional Systems Technology at Indiana University–Bloomington. Her current research focuses on Latino alternative health at the University of Texas at Brownsville, minority access to higher education, and the creation of new learning environments.

## ABSTRACT

In this chapter we present a cross-case description and analysis of Project TEAM at five very different campus sites that range from small-town residential to highly urban and inner-city commuter-college settings. We provide an overview of the original Project TEAM program that serves as a model for the new sites, including the conceptual framework and longitudinal research design; we also develop cross-campus comparisons and contrasts among Project TEAM students on each campus, particularly their perspectives on teaching, ethnic identity development, and the Project TEAM experience. We hope to create a context for examining best practices at various types of predominantly white colleges and universities that seek to increase ethnic diversity in their teacher education programs.

# Introduction

Project Transformative Educational Achievement Model (TEAM) is an instructional initiative designed to increase the number of students from underrepresented minorities at Indiana University who enter a teacher education program (P–12), complete their baccalaureate degree, and obtain teaching licensure in Indiana (Bennett, 1996). TEAM recruits talented students of color into teacher education, as well as students planning to teach in urban and/or ethnically diverse schools, provides them with honors work beyond the regular teacher education courses they take, and provides them with additional academic, social, and financial support from acceptance into the program through graduation (typically 3 years).

Two years ago Project TEAM expanded from Bloomington to Gary and Indianapolis; last year the program expanded to Fort Wayne and South Bend as well. The Project TEAM coordinators on all campuses agreed to follow the established Bloomington model during the first two years of start-up on partner campuses. We all wondered to what extent the original model would be appropriate in other settings and agreed that we needed to better understand the similarities and differences among our students across the campuses to answer this question. We assumed that students on the Bloomington campus, the only residential campus where students lived far from their home communities, would have different needs and privileges than students on the other campuses. We felt our findings could have implications for predominantly white colleges and universities elsewhere where there exists a core campus and regional campuses all working to increase the number of teachers of color as well as teachers committed to work in urban and multicultural school settings.

# Educational Importance

Project TEAM was designed to address the national and state shortage of teachers of color, as well as the need for teachers who are motivated and prepared to teach in urban and multicultural schools. TEAM also strives to address the broader urgent need to provide evidence of the benefits of student diversity on college campuses (Milem and Hakuta, 2000). When Project TEAM was initiated in 1996, our goal was to address the nation's need for competent teachers who are caring advocates for children and youth from all racial, cultural, and socioeconomic backgrounds. Initially we focused on the recruitment of teachers of color to address changing national demographics that reveal an increasingly diverse school-age population, while the teaching force remains predominantly white, middle class, and female. For example in 2002, 10 percent of the nation's teachers were minorities, 6 percent African American and 4 percent other teachers of color, and almost 75 percent were female (National Education Association, 2003). However, students of color comprise nearly 39 percent of the school-age population nationally, with about 17 percent speaking a language other than English at home (National Center for Education Statistics, 2003). And in the state of Indiana, the percentage of public school children of color increased from 11.1 percent in 1974–1975 to 17 percent in 2001-02, while the percent of teachers of color during this time period declined from 6.1 to 4.8 percent (National Center for Education Statistics, 2003).

The mission of Project TEAM connects with education in P–12 classrooms as well, with an emphasis on preparing teachers for work in urban and ethnically diverse schools. Our work aims to help mediate disproportionately low high school completion rates among African American, American Indian, and Latino youth, especially in urban areas (Harvey, 2001). The latest national "report card" from National Assessment of Educational Progress (NCES, 2003) reveals persistent disparities in the academic achievement among ethnic groups, even when socioeconomic level is held constant. Although there have been overall improvements in the achievement gains for all groups in most content areas, Anglo and Asian students in grades 4, 8, and 12 score significantly higher than African American, Latino, and American Indian students in mathematics, writing, science, reading, U.S History, Civics, and Geography (NCES, 2003). Unequal school conditions, such as high numbers of teachers who teach without a license in urban and rural schools, and lower teacher expectations of racial and language minority students, contribute to these disparities in student achievement (Irvine, 2003). Teachers of color with the knowledge, understanding, and dispositions needed to reverse these trends can serve as role models for all teachers who wish to be successful with students of color and others who are poorly served by our schools (e.g., Delpit, 1995; Ladson-Billings, 1994). Programs like Project TEAM strive to help make this happen.

# Conceptual Framework

A conceptual framework based on theories of campus climate and integrated pluralism, ethnic identity development, and teaching for social justice, as well as longitudinal action research using primarily a qualitative case study methodology (Stake, 1995) guides program development and inquiry at all five sites (Bennett, 2002). *Integrated pluralism* refers to a campus climate characterized by equity and mutual respect among diverse racial and cultural groups on campus. It affirms the value of a school's various ethnic groups and encourages their participation in a climate that (1) includes contributions from all groups; (2) avoids "business as usual" policies and practices rooted in expectations of assimilation into the predominantly white cultural milieu; (3) supports opportunities for inter and intra minority group social interactions along with social interactions with non-minority peers; and (4) fosters and expects high levels of academic learning among all students on campus. Over thirty years of research on ethnic minority students' experiences at predominantly white colleges and universities has confirmed that many college students of color feel alienated, experience culture shock, and have a difficult time academically and socially at these institutions (Allen, 1988; Allen, Epps, and Haniff, 1991; Fleming, 1984; Nora and Cabrera, 1996). More recent research in higher education underscores the importance of a campus climate where *all* students feel comfortable and respected, as well as the benefits of racial and ethnic diversity on college campuses in terms of student learning and career success (Hurtado, Milem, Clayton-Pederson, and Allen, 1999; Wilds, 2000). Cognizant of this research, Project TEAM attempts to help students mediate the campus climate at Indiana University.

*Ethnic Identity* refers to the degree to which a person feels connected with a racial and/or culture group that is important to one's family and early peers. It is a complex cluster of factors that include "self-labeling, a sense of belonging, positive evaluation, preference for the group, ethnic interest and knowledge, and involvement in activities associated with the group" (Phinney, 1996, p. 923). Researchers in higher education argue that a strong sense of ethnic identity held by college students of color at Predominantly White Institutions (PWIs) is related to positive academic experiences and social actions on campus (Sedlacek, 1987). And multicultural teacher educators argue that a strong sense of ethnic identity is necessary for a positive and confident sense of self and teacher efficacy, especially in culturally and racially diverse classrooms where most Project TEAM students hope to teach. Thus, an important goal of Project TEAM is self-examination of ethnic identity development.

*Teaching for Social Justice* is conceptualized in terms of core values, dimensions, and themes of multicultural education (Banks, 1991; Bennett, 2001 and 2003; Gay, 2000). The core values are to prepare teachers who (1) are caring advocates for children and youth from all cultural, racial, linguistic, and socioeconomic backgrounds; (2) regard teaching as a form of inquiry and reflection on practice; (3) see themselves as thoughtful, creative change agents working for social justice in their schools and communities; and (4) are competent in creating multicultural curriculum and pedagogy.

## PROJECT TEAM AND THE HONORS SEMINAR

Our research is associated with Project TEAM, a program designed to create a supportive teaching-learning community for selected students of color in the School of Education at a Big Ten university. Based on the theme of "strengthening social justice through education," Project TEAM is a research and development initiative designed to increase the number of students from underrepresented minorities who complete their baccalaureate degree and enter the teaching profession. A maximum of 15 students are recruited into TEAM each year, based on their record of community service, academic success (the majority has a GPA greater than 3.0, well above our required 2.5 minimum), and commitment to a career in education. Together we are striving to develop a supportive teaching-learning community in the School of Education as well as provide outreach and networking opportunities to work with middle and secondary school students of color in Indiana public schools.

An important aspect of Project TEAM is the honors seminar students enroll in each semester. These seminars focus on issues of social justice in education, multicultural teaching, collaborative inquiry, and leadership and professional development in connection with a summer camp for middle school students of color. Only TEAM students may enroll in the Honors Seminar; the seminar provides enrichment work and is not required for the students' teacher preparation program. Our research since 1996 explores the benefits, challenges, and potential problems of an all-minority multicultural education seminar for preservice teachers of color (Bennett, Cole and Thompson, 2000).

# Methodology

## RESEARCH QUESTIONS

To date, the primary research question that underlies our inquiry is: What is the nature of students' experience in Project TEAM? Longitudinal research findings on the Bloomington campus since 1996 identify four main themes that help answer this question (Bennett, 2002): (1) the creation of community among students of color to mediate an alienating campus climate; (2) a strengthened ethnic identity among our TEAM students, as well as a stronger understanding of and ability to deal with racism; (3) an increased desire and ability to work for social justice through multicultural education; and (4) professional development and commitment to teaching as a profession.

Now that the program has expanded to four additional sites our questions also include: What recruitment and support practices are most effective at each site? How are the students similar and different at each site, in terms of personal histories, motivations, teaching perspectives, program support needs, sense of ethnic identity, and conceptions of teaching for social justice? What evidence, if any, supports affirmative efforts to increase student diversity on campus? What are the major benefits and challenges experienced by students and staff at each site? In this paper we will address questions about similarities and differences in students' background characteristics, teacher perspectives, ethnic identity, and views of Project TEAM on their campus.

## DATA SOURCES

For this study, an identical case study methodology using both quantitative and qualitative data collection techniques was employed on each campus to study the 81 new students recruited into TEAM in 2001 and 2002. Data collection at each site included a questionnaire comprised of ethnic identity and multicultural competence scales, as well as items on career choice, career certainty, and parents' educational background; focus group interviews about the Project TEAM experience; and detailed analysis of the student applications, including the essay on reasons for wanting to teach.

## THE SURVEY

A paper-pencil questionnaire containing measures of ethnic identity, multicultural competence, multicultural knowledge, and background questions related to parents' level of education, personal goals and educational history, was administered at all sites during the orientation of new students in Project TEAM. The questionnaire's measure of ethnic identity was an adaptation of the Teacher Student Interaction (TSI) scale developed by Margaret Ford and H. Prentice Baptiste to measure teachers' stages of ethnic identity according to a five-stage typology of ethnic identity developed by James A. Banks (Ford, 1979). Our adaptation of the TSI was a 24-item likert scale, with a five-choice response ranging from Strongly Agree (1 point) to Strongly Disagree (5 points), with individual averages ranging from a lowest possible score of 1.0 (Stage One, Psychological Captivity) to the highest possible score of 5.0 (Stage Five, Multiethnicity).

Ford's original research with the TSI concluded that teachers who are at a level of *Multiethnicity*, Banks's fifth stage, were more effective teachers with culturally diverse students than were teachers at any of the lower four stages. Outliers on the TSI (four students who scored highest and four who scored lowest on each campus) were selected for focus group interviews.

## FOCUS GROUP INTERVIEWS

A total of 81 students (see table 3.1) of color were recruited into Project TEAM across the campus sites in 2001 and 2002: 31 in Bloomington (IUB), where the program was in its seventh year; 24 in Gary (IUN) and 14 in Indianapolis (IUPUI), where the program was in its second year; and 7 in Fort Wayne (IPUFW), and 5 in South Bend (IUSB) where the program was in its first year. Eight students from both cohorts on the IUB, IUN, and IUPUI campuses were selected for the focus group interviews. All available students at the IPFW and IUSB campuses were interviewed, or six and three at the respective sites. Inter-

**Table 3.1    Student Background Characteristics across the Sites, 2001–2003**

|  | IUB N=31 | IUN N=24 | IUPUI N=14 | IPFW N=7 | IUSB N=5 | Total N=81 |
|---|---|---|---|---|---|---|
| Percentages in TEP | 31% | 100% | 71% | 71% | 60% | 67% |
| Average GPA | 3.16 | 3.05 | 3.04 | 2.88 | 3.05 | |
| **Classification** | | | | | | |
| Graduate Student | 0 | 4 | 4 | 0 | 2 | 8 |
| Senior | 4 | 5 | 6 | 1 | 0 | 16 |
| Junior | 15 | 11 | 0 | 2 | 0 | 28 |
| Sophomore | 14 | 4 | 3 | 3 | 1 | 25 |
| Freshman | 0 | 0 | 1 | 1 | 2 | 4 |
| **Ethnicity** | | | | | | |
| African American | 22 | 17 | 11 | 5 | 4 | 59 |
| Latino/a | 8 | 7 | 1 | 2 | 1 | 19 |
| Native American | 1 | 0 | 0 | 0 | 0 | 1 |
| Caucasian | 0 | 0 | 0 | 0 | 0 | 0 |
| Other | 0 | 0 | 2 | 0 | 0 | 2 |
| **Gender** | | | | | | |
| Male | 8 | 2 | 1 | 4 | 1 | 16 |
| Female | 23 | 22 | 13 | 3 | 4 | 65 |
| **Financial Aid** | | | | | | |
| Grants | 72% | 29% | 29% | 14% | 40% | |
| Loans | 68% | 54% | 64% | 14% | 60% | |
| Scholar | 58% | 42% | 21% | 57% | 40% | |
| Other | 3.4% | 0% | 7% | 43% | 20% | |
| None | 3.4% | 25% | 0% | 0% | 0% | |
| **Mother's Education** | | | | | | |
| M | 4.10 | 3.58 | 3.50 | 3.00 | 5.00 | |
| Mode | 3.00 | 3.00 | 3.00 | 2.00 | 6.00 | |
| Mdn | 4.50 | 3.00 | 3.00 | 2.00 | 5.50 | |
| **Father's Education** | | | | | | |
| M | 3.90 | 3.08 | 3.67 | 2.60 | 4.75 | |
| Mode | 3.00 | 3.00 | 2.00 | 4.00 | 3.00 | |
| Mdn | 3.00 | 3.00 | 3.00 | 3.00 | 4.50 | |
| Mean Certainty of Career Goals | 3.10 | 3.12 | 2.28 | 2.00 | 1.75 | |

Key: Educational Level
1.00- Did not go beyond the 8th grade
2.00- 8th–11th grade
3.00- Graduated from high school
4.00- Schooling other than college
5.00- Attended but did not complete college
6.00- Graduated from college
7.00- Graduate degree

Key: Certainty of Career Goals
1.00- Very uncertain
2.00- Somewhat uncertain
3.00- Somewhat certain
4.00- Very certain

views were conducted by one of the authors (John Kuykendall) at each campus and lasted from one to two hours, for a total of twelve interviews and 33 participants; all interviews were audiotaped and transcribed by John. Interviews were conducted during the spring semester, the second semester in TEAM for students recruited in 2002 and the third semester for students recruited in 2003. Data were analyzed in a retrieval chart for each campus that separated most open and least open participants, that coded participant responses for each guiding question, and that noted salient representative quotes.

Focus group interviews used the following guiding questions:

Teaching:

1. How are you feeling about your decision to become a teacher? What will you enjoy most about teaching? What will you find most difficult or challenging?
2. How are you feeling about your teacher education coursework thus far? What has proved to be most beneficial to you as a future teacher? What is lacking?
3. Briefly describe your ideal classroom setting. What do you hope your students will be like? What do you hope your school will be like?

Ethnic Identity and Social Justice:

4. How would you describe your ethnic identity? How important is racial and/or cultural identity to you personally? Do you discuss racial and cultural issues with your family and friends? To what extent, if at all, is a strong sense of ethnic identity necessary for effective teaching?
5. To what extent have you experienced racial or cultural issues in your own educational experiences (P–college)? Does Project TEAM deal too much with these issues, or not enough?
6. As you prepare to enter the classroom, how do you feel about our emphasis on teaching for social justice? How do you define it? Is it important, or just too idealistic?

Project TEAM:

7. How do you feel about TEAM's Honors Seminar? What are the strengths and weaknesses? What suggestions do you have?
8. To what extent, if at all, is Project TEAM having an influence on you to become a classroom teacher?
9. Now that you have experienced Project TEAM for a few months/over a year, do you think it has a place on your campus? Alternatively, is it necessary? Why not just have the scholarships?

In this chapter we focus primarily on questions related to section three, Project TEAM.

## APPLICATIONS AND APPLICANT ESSAYS

The basic application format originally developed for the Bloomington Campus was used at all sites and included: GPA, teaching level and/or content area, community service record, extracurricular activities, and an essay on *"Why I wish to become a teacher."* We used content analysis (Schwandt, 1997; Silverman, 1993) to examine the applications of 81 students accepted into Project TEAM in 2001 and 2002 to ascertain the backgrounds and motivations about teaching among Project TEAM students on the five campuses. Data was organized into a retrieval chart with twelve columns: Students' ID (included self-identified ethnic group), admission into teacher education (the TEP), GPA and credit hours, year in college, major, type of financial aid, mother's education, father's education, community service and extra curricular activities, essay word count, quality of writing, and reasons for wanting to teach. Selected findings are summarized in tables 3.1 and 3.2.

## LIMITATIONS IN THE DATA SOURCES

Although extensive and rich data has been gathered using research and evaluation procedures that have been refined since 1996, a number of important limitations in our research must be acknowledged. First, there is the possibility of student coercion, despite the many safeguards we have taken to guard against this. Project TEAM students are enrolled in the Honors Seminar taught by members of the research team, course assignments are used as data, and students may feel constrained to create projects and answer interview questions to gain instructor approval. Furthermore, since they receive a $4000 scholarship each year, students may hesitate to be critical of the program. Second, the survey instruments used were developed primarily with white teachers and may lack validity and reliability with teachers of color. And third, the primary project director, who also teaches the Honors Seminar on the Bloomington campus, is an Anglo; the coordinators and instructors at three other sites are African American, and the fifth coordinator is American Indian. We have yet to explore the impact the ethnicity of program leaders may have on the nature and effectiveness of the program, or on the data gathered. However, we recognize that there is ample evidence to show that a researcher's race can be a significant factor in the conceptualization of research as well as data analysis and interpretation.

**Table 3.2    Reasons for Wanting to Teach across All Campuses**

| Category | Definition | Overall Frequency | First Reason Frequency |
|---|---|---|---|
| Role Model | Make a positive difference in a child's potential, self-esteem, motivation, and shape a child's life in general through personal influence or mentoring. | 49 | 20 |
| Inspire Student Learning | Impact positively a student's academic ability, classroom experience or motivation toward learning in general or a specific content area through motivation, inspiration, and effective teaching. | 44 | 20 |
| Personal Rewards | The benefits of teaching at a personal and professional level as well as the self-satisfaction that is part of teaching. The focus is on self, not children or society. | 20 | 8 |
| Ethnic of Caring | General love of children and genuine concern for their life. Also, nurturing, encouraging, motivating and willingness to work with them. | 17 | 8 |
| Previous Positive Experience | Previous positive experience such as substituting, volunteering and/or personal experience with teaching or learning. Also, influence by other people such as role models and friends that turned them on to teaching. | 11 | 7 |
| Change Agent for Equity | A desire to change society and increase educational equity. | 10 | 5 |
| Give Back | A desire and commitment to give back to the community (family, friends, neighborhoods, schools). | 9 | 5 |
| Call to Teach | Expressed love for the profession and/or innate need/destiny to become a teacher. | 9 | 6 |

# Findings

## STUDENT BACKGROUND CHARACTERISTICS ACROSS THE SITES

Overall, there were 59 African Americans, 19 Latinos, 2 of mixed race, and 1 American Indian in the program; 16 were male and 65 were female (see table 3.1). Student grade point averages across all five sites exceeded the minimum 2.5 requirement with the overall average approximately 3.0 on a 4.0 scale; the average was slightly higher in Bloomington at 3.16 and slightly lower in Fort Wayne at 2.88. In Bloomington, where students are recruited in their Freshman year on campus, only 31 percent have been admitted into the Teacher Education Program (TEP) at the time of application, compared with 100 percent in Gary, 71 percent in Indianapolis and Fort Wayne, and 60 percent in South Bend. We found that mother's education tended to be higher than father's education across the campuses, with most graduating from high school and not continuing in school. This was especially true for African American students, the numerical majority in the program on all campuses, and less true for Latinos where father's education tends to be the same or higher than mother's education. Contrary to our assumption that parental education level might be higher for students on the Bloomington campus, the flagship university of the state, these modes were quite comparable across the sites, with the exception of the Gary campus where levels of parental education were lower. We also found that a large majority of students received financial aid, primarily through loans, with the exception of Fort Wayne (ranging from a high of 68 percent in Bloomington to a low of 54 percent in Gary), and scholarships beyond the TEAM scholarship (ranging from 58 percent in Bloomington to 21 percent in Indianapolis). In addition, 72% of the students in Bloomington received grants, while 29% in Gary and Indianapolis, 14% in Fort Wayne, and 60% in South Bend received grants.

In addition to the differing percentages of students in the TEP at time of acceptance, the other area of difference across the campuses was certainty of career goals. Career certainty was ascertained from the confidential pretest survey, not the application, and ranged from a low of 1 (very uncertain) to a high of 4 (very certain). Students in Bloomington and Gary appeared more certain of their desire to enter teaching, with an average response of 3.10 and 3.12, than did students on the Indianapolis, Fort Wayne, and South Bend campuses, whose average certainty scores were 2.28, 2.00, and 1.75 respectively. Therefore, acceptance into the TEP did not necessarily indicate a stronger commitment to teaching than students who had not yet been accepted. Whether or not commitment declines over time in some programs is a question to be explored. However, evidence from the number of Bloomington graduates who entered teaching, about 80 percent indicated that this was not the case on that campus.

## REASONS FOR WANTING TO TEACH

Data on reasons for wanting to teach (see table 3.2) were gathered from the 81 accepted student applications from the five campuses. Applicant essays were reviewed and the first reason, followed by any additional reasons, was listed per applicant. The number of reasons ranged from 1 to 4 per essay, with two essays containing no reasons. Reasons were mounted on index card and labeled with the student ID. Thirteen initial categories were generated using the constant comparative method; these categories with all reasons therein were later entered into Microsoft Excel and grouped by theme under campus and cohort. We continued to refine the categories through constant comparison and reduced the number of categories to eight. In table 3.2 we combine the data for all the campuses. The first frequency column shows the total number of reasons for teaching per category; the second frequency column shows only the first reasons given.

The primary categories in our analysis were *Role Model* and the desire to *Inspire Student Learning.* Over half of the first reasons listed, and 93 of the 169 total reasons fell into these two top categories. While both categories emphasized making a difference in the lives of children, the *Role Models* emphasized mentoring and personal influence to shape children's lives in general; many used the actual term *role model.* In contrast, reasons in the *Inspire Student Learning* category stressed classroom teaching. Related to both of these categories was what we called *Ethic of Caring,* where reasons for teaching included loving children and the desire to nurture. Eight applicants stated first reasons in this category and an additional nine included reasons related to *Ethic of Caring.* Seven applicants listed first reasons related to *Previous Positive Experience* and another five included secondary reasons in this category; no applicants cited the desire to mediate poor teachers or negative educational experience as a motivation for teaching. All the experiences were positive and seemingly powerful. Serving as a *Change Agent for Equity, Giving Back* to one's community, and feeling the *Call to Teach* were the remaining categories, with 5, 5, and 6 first reasons in each category respectively.

An eighth category, *Personal Rewards,* was a miscellaneous collection of reasons related to a range of benefits in teaching as a profession, or benefits of Project TEAM, that focused on the *self,* rather than children, youth, or society as seen in the other categories. For example, one applicant saw teaching as an opportunity to express her love of dance and theatre, another liked the job stability, and two mentioned the TEAM scholarships as their only reasons. Eight first reasons fell into this category, and another twelve secondary reasons related to *Personal Rewards.*

Since prior to this analysis we were familiar with student applications on our own campus, we are not surprised by the general motivations of wanting to be a role model, the strong ethic of caring and the desire to inspire students among Project TEAM pre-service teachers. Nor are we surprised that these motivations for teaching are prevalent across the campuses. What *is* surprising is the absence of motivation connected to issues of equity and social justice in education, even as secondary reasons, particularly since the main theme of Project TEAM is "working toward social justice in education." Given our students' initial dispositions, as revealed in this cross-campus analysis, we are developing a better understanding of Project TEAM's influence on pre-service teachers who experience the program for several years.

## STUDENT PERCEPTIONS OF THE PROJECT TEAM EXPERIENCE: THE FOCUS GROUP INTERVIEWS

The focus group interviews allowed us to explore similarities and differences in students' perceptions of Project TEAM, especially as they related to the earlier themes noted in student perceptions over a five-year period on the Bloomington campus: feelings of community, stronger sense of ethnic identity, and deeper awareness of and commitment to issues of social justice in teaching (Bennett, 2002). As noted above, students were asked about the Honors seminar, whether Project TEAM had any influence on their desire to become a teacher, and whether the program was really needed on campus, other than the scholarship. The focus group interviews also allowed us to explore these perceptions through a lens of stage of ethnic identity development (open and less open).

We examined TEAM students' perceptions in three selected areas of the focus group interviews on four of the five campuses, divided between students who are open and less open on the Ethnic Identity Scale with the exception of the IUPUI campus where outliers on the Scale were unavailable for interviews. On the Fort Wayne Campus all students interviewed, both open and less open, felt positive about the Honors Seminar, felt that TEAM had a positive influence on their becoming a teacher, and argued that TEAM was needed on their campus. One African American woman who was less open than her peers expressed these views in her interview with John,

> *I leave every day with food for thought and I can be dominant in discussions, but I really have learned to listen to people in the discussions. In a*

*short time I have learned just as much from others, based on their perspective. I thought when (an Asian woman guest speaker) came she shared with us how different yet similar our races were. It's not just a black/white thing. . . .*

*Financially, this program has driven me because I could not afford to take the classes at the cost per credit hour. The funding has allowed me to take the necessary classes to pursue my goal of being a teacher. And I think it is good to have classmates who care and we can share one another's thoughts and I can see what classes they have taken and follow up on those. . . .*

*I like our discussions because I can get experiences through someone else's lenses; it helps me have a different perspective. I am ready for TEAM and I get off work to come to this class. It is definitely key in us being successful in our field.*

The pattern was similar for open students on both the Gary and Bloomington campuses. However there was less agreement among less open students on the benefit of the Honors Seminar and TEAM's influence on their desire to teach. For example, one woman in Gary told us,

*No, (TEAM is not influencing me). I was already motivated. Some of our discussions turned the light on, like when we talked about some of the founders of education and the way they thought about it, but other than that I was already motivated.*

On the Gary campus less open students were divided in their opinion of the necessity of TEAM (besides the scholarship) but on the Bloomington campus all the less open students argued that TEAM was a necessity. In the words of one African American male who was skeptical about his experience in TEAM,

*I think it has a place here on campus. It would hinder minority students who want to be teachers if we did not meet. Truthfully, if there were not a scholarship I would probably still be in Project TEAM.*

On the Indianapolis campus where most students enter TEAM their junior year, after acceptance into the Teacher Education Program (TEP), three of the nine students interviewed felt the Honors Seminar was important, and five said the program had an influence on their desire to teach. However, all nine students interviewed at IUPUI felt the program was a necessity. One student told John,

*It would have been nice if I had this seminar a lot sooner in my educational program. I would like to see this (the Honors Seminar) extended to freshmen as a course. Then they might stay on in the education track*

*instead of changing majors simply because they cannot pass the PPST. Project TEAM could save more underrepresented people in the education profession that way.*

Another said,

*Project TEAM forms a mini family/network to help those who would otherwise drop out or change their major. Scholarships are good but they do not follow up on a student to see if their needs are being met. I feel that Claudette Lands has a personal stake in my education. She wants to see all of us succeed. She cares and that has made all the difference.*

And a third student summed up feelings about TEAM as follows,

*Yes, (we need Project TEAM) because IUPUI is predominantly a white university. Project TEAM is very badly needed on this campus because of that fact alone. The African American students who attend this school need to know that they have somewhere to turn for their problems and they don't need to feel isolated or different because we are all different in some way or another.*

Based on this data from the focus group interviews, with the exception of three students on the Gary campus, all of the interviewed students perceived the sense of community in their TEAM experience, a theme that emerged in 1997 and has continued ever since. Students commented that the Honors Seminar provided a sense of comfort for minority students in sharing teaching ideas, in motivating each other to teach and be able to relate to all kinds of students, and in discussing issues of culture and race. For example, an African American woman at IUB who was unhappy with many aspects of the Honors Seminar commented on the comfort level of being in TEAM as follows,

*It is nice networking. It is nice to see your faces because you will have classes that have no minorities in there. Therefore, I still feel that TEAM helps us get together and discuss issues that help us. I know that when I am in F400 I can just be myself and when I am in other classes I have to represent my race and everybody is looking at you. Here I can just be me. They (non-minority peers) already have perceptions of African Americans and they are not always positive. Therefore, I feel that I have to come correct when I speak and not look stupid. Especially when it is a Black issue, they look to me for all the answers.*

In addition to creating feelings of comfort and community, a number of students described TEAM's influence in motivating them to think about teaching for social justice. When we considered TEAM students' reasons for wanting to teach at the time of their application, where there was little to no evidence of such interest, the possibility that the program is making a difference in this regard is clear. For example, an African American woman at Fort Wayne said,

> *I have always been motivated to be a teacher but the TEAM program has brought out other ideas that I now see as important, such as the miscommunication between groups and the cultural barriers that exist.*

Two students at IUPUI said,

> *Team is making me realize how much of an issue social justice is even now. I am glad I am learning about this topic, because it will help me become a better teacher.*

> *Project TEAM has made me think long and hard about the need for African American representation in the classroom. We must deal with our own children. Our children must see us as role models and know that we can learn beyond high school and we can read and teach and invent.*

And at IUN a student shared a "classic example" of how the instructor

> *gave us information on how to teach in the urban setting. Nobody had ever done anything of that nature before, most of the stuff is cognitive learning styles and it gave me a lot of insight on the students I would be teaching.*

## SUMMARY AND CONCLUSIONS

This chapter provides a summary of what we discovered about student characteristics and selected perceptions of their Project TEAM experience on five of the eight Indiana University campuses. Our findings to date are limited by the small numbers of students recruited into TEAM the first year in Fort Wayne and South Bend, as well as missing applications from the first cohort on the IUPUI campus. Nevertheless, some preliminary conclusions are warranted.

First, students across the campuses are similar in ethnicity and gender balances, with African American students and women exceeding Latinos and men in all cohorts. They are similar in their grade point averages, well above the 2.5 required for admission to the TEP; and a high percentage of students on most campuses have student loans as well as grants and scholarships. Further, the overall average level of parental education is graduation from high school, although there are parents with advanced college degrees and less than a high school education on all the campuses.

Second, students on the Bloomington campus are different is some ways, but not in the ways we originally assumed, such as socioeconomic privilege. As a group, students who enter TEAM in Bloomington have not been accepted into the TEP, have a stronger history of community service, are more certain in their desire to become a teacher (along with the pre-service teachers in Gary), have a higher percentage of student loans as well as grants, and feel less open to ethnic diversity than their peers on the other campuses.

We conclude that overall students across the campuses are more similar than different. However, on the regional campuses students tend to be older, have families, and to date have entered TEAM relatively late in their teacher preparation. The constraints of family responsibilities, work, and student teaching all make it remarkable that most of these students find time to participate in the TEAM Honors Seminar that is not required for the TEP, despite some skepticism about the seminar's merits.

Finally, several implications seem evident in our work to date. First, the idea of *integrated pluralism* affirms the value of the all-minority student Honors Seminar at a predominantly white institution. Students of color across the campus sites agree that the sense of community and support they feel in TEAM makes a difference in their motivation to pursue a career in teaching. Second, dispositions of openness to ethnic diversity and a sense of one's own *ethnic identity* mediate students' experience on campus, including their experience in Project TEAM. Efforts must be made to provide challenges and supports that are compatible with a student's sense of ethnic identity; one Project TEAM experience does not fit all. And third, the idea of *teaching for social justice* does not come naturally to most students in Project TEAM, even though this is the main mission of the program and one might assume applicants would be predisposed to the idea. However, we do find that this idea resonates with most students during their first semester in TEAM, though this is less true with students who initially score lower on measures of ethnic identity. TEAM pre-service teachers' primary motivations to become teachers focus on an ethic of caring, the desire to serve as a role model, and to inspire learning in *all* students. To the extent that social justice in education requires high equitable expectations for *all* learners, we find a natural inclination among TEAM pre-service teachers to work toward this goal. On the other hand, when they enter the program most TEAM students lack awareness of our history of discrimination across the nation's ethnic minorities as well as societal and economic structures that create an unequal playing field for children who come from segregated and/or impoverished communities. Most know little about the civil rights movement or the possibilities of multicultural education. However, most Project TEAM pre-service teachers plan to work in urban, multicultural school settings. We wonder, is it necessary for them to act as change agents to make a difference? Will they bring with them the understanding and dispositions needed to ensure no child is left behind? Will they become leaders in their school settings who can help create more equitable school conditions and an inclusive curriculum? These are questions to be pursued as TEAM pre-service teachers enter the profession of teaching.

# Acknowledgment

We wish to thank Cynthia Jackson and Claudette Lands at IUPUI, Stacey Akeya and Vernon Smith at IUN, Joe Nichols at IPFW, and Robert Lewis at IUSB for their extraordinary efforts in helping us expand Project TEAM to these campuses. We also appreciate their support in helping us collect survey data and applications, as well as schedule the focus group interviews used in our cross campus analyses.

# References

Allen, W. R. (1988). Improving Black student access and achievement in higher education. *Review of Higher Education, 11*(4), 403–16.

Allen, W. R., Epps, E. G., and Haniff, N. Z. (Eds.). (1991). African American students in predominantly white and in historically black public universities. *College in black and white.* Albany: State University of New York Press.

Banks, J. A. (1991). Teaching multicultural literacy to teachers. *Teaching Education, 4*(1), 135–44.

Bennett, C. I. (1996). Project TEAM: An initiative to recruit and support students from underrepresented minorities into teaching. Proposal submitted to President Brand's strategic directions committee, Indiana University.

Bennett, C. I. (2001). Genres of research in multicultural education. *Review of Educational Research, 71*(2), 171–217.

Bennett, C. I. (2002). Enhancing ethnic diversity at a big ten university through Project TEAM: A case study in teacher education. *Educational Researcher. 31* (2), 21–29.

Bennett, C. I. (2003). *Comprehensive multicultural education: Theory and practice.* Boston: Allyn & Bacon.

Bennett, C. I., Cole, D., and Thompson, J. N. (2000). Preparing teachers of color at a predominantly white university: A case study of Project TEAM. *Teaching and Teacher Education, 16,* 445–464.

Delpit, L. (1995). *Other people's children.* New York: The New Press.

Fleming, J. (1984). *Blacks in college.* San Francisco: Jossey-Bass.

Ford, M. L. (1979). The Development of an Instrument for Assessing Levels of Ethnicity in Public School Teachers. Unpublished Ph.D. dissertation, University of Houston.

Gay, G. (2000). *Culturally responsive teaching: Theory, research, and practice.* New York: Teachers College Press.

Harvey, L. (2001). Defining measurable employability. *Quality in Higher Education,* 7(2) 97–109.

Hurtado, S., Milem, J. F., Clayton-Pedersen, A. R., and Allen, W. (1999). Enacting diverse learning environments: Improving the climate for racial/ethnic diversity in higher education. *Association for the Study of Higher Education, 26*(8) 1–140.

Irvine, J. J. (2003). *Educating teachers for diversity: Seeing with a cultural eye.* New York: Teacher College Press.

Ladson-Billings, G. (1994). *The dream keepers: Successful teachers of African American children.* San Francisco: Jossey-Bass.

Milem, J. F. and Hakuta, K. (2000) Special focus: The benefits of racial and ethnic diversity in higher education. In *Seventeenth annual status report: Minorities in higher education, 1999*–2000, ed. D. J. Wilds. Washington, DC: American Council on Education.

National Center for Education Statistics. (2003). *Student school characteristics: By community type and by state: School year 2001–2002.* Washington, DC: U.S. Office of Education.

National Education Association. (2003). *2002 Tomorrow's Teachers: Help Wanted: Minority Teachers.* Washington, DC: U.S. Office of Education

Nora, A. and Cabrera, A. (1996) The role and perceptions of prejudice and discrimination on the adjustment of minority students to college. *Journal of Higher Education, 67*(2), 119–48.

Phinney, J. (1996). When we talk about ethnic groups, what do we mean? *American Psychologist, 51*(9), 918–27.

Schwandt, T. A. (1997). *Qualitative inquiry: A dictionary of terms.* Thousand Oaks, CA: Sage Publications.

Sedlacek, W. E. (1987). Black students on white campuses: 20 years of research. *Journal of College Student Personnel, 28*(6), 84–495.

Silverman, D. (1993). *Interpreting qualitative data: Methods for analyzing talk, text, and interaction.* Thousand Oaks, CA: Sage Publications.

Stake, R. (1995). *The art of case study research.* Thousand Oaks, CA: Sage Publications.

Wilds, D. J. (2000). (Ed.), *Seventeenth annual status report: Minorities in higher education, 1999–2000.* Washington, DC: American Council on Education.

CHAPTER 4

# Innovation in Teacher Preparation: Creating Alternative Routes to Teacher Quality

*Bette S. Bergeron*
Arizona State University East

*Brenda Larson*
Chandler Gilbert Community College

*Alison Prest*
Arizona State University East

*Lee Ann Dumas-Hopper*
Arizona State University East

*James C. Wenhart*
Arizona State University East

Bette S. Bergeron is the Head of the Faculty of Education and Professor of Education at Arizona State University East. Her research interests focus on determining effective practices in teacher education programs. Her work in literacy includes a focus on developing effective strategies for supporting young learners' development as independent readers and writers.

Brenda Larson is a faculty member and Coordinator of Teacher Education Programs at Chandler Gilbert Community College. Her research focuses on the development of learning communities. Her areas of expertise include business and computer science and the integration of technology into effective practice.

Alison Prest is a Lecturer and the Coordinator of Evening Programs at Arizona State University East. Her area of study includes the development of best practices in elementary science instruction. She also is involved in a comparative study of alternative routes to certification for post-baccalaureate students.

Lee Ann Dumas-Hopper is a Lecturer and Coordinator of Advanced Studies at Arizona State University East. Her research focuses on assessment in higher education, the effective use of technologies in teacher preparation programs, and the development of tools to assess the effectiveness of teacher education programs.

James Wenhart is a Senior Lecturer and the Elementary Education Program Coordinator at Arizona State University East. His areas of expertise include early childhood and classroom management. He is also involved with creating effective assessment tools for interning and student teaching experiences.

## ABSTRACT

The purpose of this chapter is to share experiences related to the implementation of four distinctly different routes to teacher certification that have been developed to target diverse and non-traditional populations of teacher candidates. The cases include clearly defined partnerships with community colleges and school districts. The chapter addresses the following outcomes: (1) to describe effective, non-conventional models for preparing quality teachers; (2) to explore routes for bringing non-traditional candidates into the profession; and (3) to encourage teacher educators to think innovatively regarding program redesign. In analyzing the data from these four distinct cases, a number of common elements emerged. These elements include direct lines of communication among participants, the use of peer cohorts, intensive and directed field experiences, creative partnerships, and effective modeling of educational technologies.

# Objectives

The purpose of this chapter is to share experiences related to the implementation of four distinctly different routes to teacher certification. Each of these non-conventional routes has been developed for different populations of teacher candidates, including those who are considered non-traditional, who represent diverse populations, or who are pursuing a second career. The varied experiences of these candidates have the potential to enhance the academic lives of their students.

Currently, the United States is facing an unprecedented teacher shortage, particularly in urban and rural areas and with diverse student populations. Teacher educators are challenged to increase the number of program completers by creating innovative pathways to certification, while producing teachers of quality who can effectively foster the academic achievement of all students. The chapter intends to: (1) describe four effective, non-conventional models for preparing quality teachers; (2) explore routes for bringing nontraditional candidates of diverse backgrounds and experiences into the profession of teaching; and (3) encourage teacher educators to think innovatively in meeting challenges specific to their constituents and programs.

# Review of Literature

Concerns regarding quality practices and perceived inflexibility within teacher education have prompted Colleges of Education to consider new avenues for reforming their programs. Also prompting change are external pressures from competitors that offer alternative or accelerated programs to meet unprecedented demands of widespread teacher shortages, a crisis that demands an additional 500,000 K–12 teachers by 2006 (Imig, 1997). Routes to certification that specifically attract non-traditional teacher candidates have the potential to curb the crisis while bringing highly competent teachers into the classroom.

Included in the current political landscape is a drive for accelerated certification programs and the emergence of alternative providers (Imig, 1997). Nontraditional programs now include short-term alternatives, a variety of delivery modes, and emergency hiring practices. Many charter and private schools that hire both licensed and unlicensed teachers often are leading the charge to reduce tight certification requirements (Finn and Madigan, 2001). Also among the competitors are accelerated "fast-track" programs that include Teach for America and private companies working directly through states and districts. It is suggested that 80,000 teachers have entered the profession through these alternative routes (Berry, 2001).

Proponents of accelerated, alternative routes suggest that these programs produce teachers who are at least as effective as those prepared conventionally and are more apt to attract minorities into the profession (Finn and Madigan, 2001). Many of these programs target career changers and retirees who can be prepared to enter teaching more quickly than younger recruits. These non-

traditional candidates also can bring maturity, life experiences, and resourceful-
ness to their new profession (Resta, Huling, and Rainwater, 2001).

Professional consequences associated with alternative accelerated programs
also have been cited. Darling-Hammond (1994) suggests that some accelerated
certification programs are so inadequate in preparing teachers that they undermine the education of children. Candidates of accelerated programs often struggle with curriculum development, pedagogical content knowledge, classroom
management, and student motivation. Additionally, those involved with short-
cut programs often find themselves thrust into the most challenging classrooms,
without sufficient guidance from a mentor, and with limited knowledge and
skills demanded to teach today's children (Berry, 2001). It is estimated that the
attrition rate for these candidates is nearly twice that of more traditionally prepared teachers.

Those alternative programs that have been most effective include strong
content preparation aligned with professional standards, rigorous curriculum in
human growth and development, preparation in pedagogy and technology, and
support from peers and mentors (Berry, 2001; Resta et al., 2001). Also critical
to the success of these programs are structured, supervised, and intensive experiences in classrooms that lead up to student teaching (Berry). The most effective
programs culminate in initial certification *before* candidates are hired as teachers
(Resta et al., 2001).

Despite the increasing evidence that many of the solutions to teacher shortages proposed by outside competitors may not hold much promise for the young
learners they intend to serve, it is also recognized that alternative routes are
increasingly becoming the strategy for policy makers who continue to question
the effectiveness of traditional teacher education (Berry, 2001). Finn and Madigan (2001) contend that alternative certification programs make schools of education nervous because they "crack the cartel and create competition for the
monopoly" (p. 31). Teacher preparation units must take heed of these harsh
criticisms, and find solutions to today's teaching crisis through thoughtful partnerships and rigorous programs that account for quality and high professional
standards.

# Methods

The reported research utilized comparative case study methodology. As described by Merriam (1998), case studies include the rich description and analysis
of a focused phenomenon, which is anchored in a real-life situation. As a result,
case study methodology reveals a rich and holistic account of the phenomenon

and deep insight into future research. This methodology is particularly useful in studying educational innovations, evaluating programs, and informing policy.

The phenomenon that provided the focus for the reported study was the development of non-conventional teacher education programs that attract non-traditional students. Specifically, data from four distinct programs were ana-lyzed: a two year community college program that transitions into a university, an accelerated program for post-baccalaureate students, evening programs tar-geted for district employees, and a program specifically for emergency certified teachers. Each of these programs was based in the regional campus of a large southwestern university and included directed collaborative efforts with com-munity colleges and/or K–12 school districts.

The subjects for this study were the students who participated in each of the focus programs. Specifically, key informants were selected in each case to represent the overall student body in terms of age, gender, and ethnicity. Key informants are those participants who possess specialized knowledge and who are uniquely able to contribute insights to the study's findings (Goetz and Le-Compte, 1984). The authors held at least two face-to-face informal interviews with the key informants. Open-ended questioning was used to ascertain percep-tions regarding the programs' strengths and challenges, as well as participants' sense of preparedness to enter the classroom. The authors also observed all of the students, including key participants, in classes and in the field. Observation protocols used were anecdotal and intended to gather general programmatic information.

# Data Sources

A variety of data sources were used across the four distinct programs to study the phenomenon of nonconventional teacher education programs. These data were situated within the cases themselves and included faculty meetings at the university, minutes from Educational Leadership Team meetings, and interviews with the key informants from each of the four programs.

Anecdotal study data included embedded artifacts such as sample course assignments, correspondence from candidates in the programs, professional portfolios, K–12 classroom observations, and informal conversations with dis-trict administrators and course instructors. These situated artifacts were in-tended to support and enrich the information being generated through the primary data sources. Data were collected over a two-year period and jointly analyzed for the following three categories: unique program elements, program challenges, and implications or "best practices" for teacher education.

# Results

In this section, an overview is provided for each of the four non-conventional teacher education programs. Included in the case study descriptions are those elements that make the programs unique, program challenges, and suggestions related to the development of subsequent non-conventional programs. Each of the programs described is integral to a comprehensive southwest university's overall teacher education initiatives that have in large part been developed in direct response to massive regional teacher shortages. Also included in these programs are unique partnerships with regional community colleges and school districts, which are integral in attracting non-traditional and diverse teacher candidates.

Each identified program was designed on the same set of criteria. For example, the state's Professional Teaching Standards provided the support structure for all of the courses, and instructors modeled the standards' use throughout each course experience. Another commonality was the incorporation of intensive and guided practica that included observation and teaching within assigned placements at local K–12 schools.

Students in each of the programs had the opportunity to work with master practitioners and post-secondary instructors. Other key components included the use of blocked sequences of courses and student cohorts. These structural features were beneficial in that instructors were able to collaborate to create thematically driven lessons and projects, and because students had the support of a consistent set of peers. Because appropriate uses of instructional technologies were also required across the four programs, students became fluent in these critical learning tools.

While commonalities exist in the focus programs, unique elements were also imbedded into each program's design in order to accommodate targeted populations of students. In the following sections programs are described in detail addressing strengths and challenges.


## COMMUNITY COLLEGE LEARNING COMMUNITIES: CROSS-INSTITUTIONAL INNOVATION

Community colleges play a major role in attracting students of diversity and providing quality experiences in lower-division coursework. Teachers Today & Tomorrow, the first case in this reported study, provided a yearlong learning community as a freshmen experience for those interested in becoming K–12 teachers. The learning community consisted of the integration of three course themes taught over two semesters—English, education, and technology. Courses were team-taught by two instructors, and students were in their communities twice a week for four hours. Fifteen of the original 24 students continued into the second year of the community college program and 10 have subsequently been accepted into the partnering university's teacher education program.

*Unique elements.* One of the distinct advantages of partnering with community colleges is the diversity of students that these institutions attract. In the reported case, approximately half of the participants were of diverse ethnic backgrounds (predominately Hispanic and Native American). Key informants indicated that students obtained more breadth and depth about teaching because of the learning community. For example, while all students at the community college read a novel as part of their English composition classes, those in the education learning community read novels specifically about teaching and conducted research on educational topics.

Students engaged in extensive field experience early in their college career. Students were in K–12 classrooms their first semester and continued working in classrooms for every education course. Each course had a different focus and students were able to apply what they learned to real-life situations. This program had a specific emphasis on technology, which was integrated into course experiences each semester. Targeted topics related to PowerPoint, the use of the web to create professional portfolios, and a variety of lesson development tools.

*Program challenges.* Some potential challenges related directly to the team-teaching model, which was problematic when the instructors did not share a similar philosophy. In addition, the academic advisors needed to be more familiar with the learning community so that they could encourage students' participation. Because this was not occurring initially, one of the course instructors spent an inordinate amount of time recruiting students for the program. Also, it was difficult to coordinate the scheduling of content classes in other academic disciplines to work around the learning community's blocked timeframe.

*Best practices.* Successful practices in this program included involving everyone in all aspects of its implementation. Advisors, financial aid staff, recruiters, faculty, and division chairs needed to be conversant in the program's unique design and student benefits. In addition, by prescribing a program of study, students were ensured a related sequence of coursework in education, composition, and technology every semester. The prescribed program also ensured that classes were not canceled because of low enrollment. Providing release time for the lead instructor was also critical, as it ensured time for student recruitment and coordination with university faculty.

## ON-SITE TEACHER PREPARATION: COLLABORATIVE INNOVATION

Another avenue for recruiting non-traditional teacher candidates is to collaborate directly with districts to "grow their own" educators. In the site-based programs, master teachers from two districts collaborated with university faculty to develop a curriculum that reflected local standards and the districts' teacher performance measures. This particular two-year program was developed as an incentive for district employees, including office personnel and instructional aides, to complete K–8 certification coursework that would enable them to remain in their communities. The districts also gave preference for hiring students as paraprofessionals while in the program. Both undergraduate and post-baccalaureate students were encouraged to participate.

*Unique elements.* The classes in this program were scheduled in the evening and a few Saturdays so that working adults had an opportunity to earn teacher certification. Courses were held twice a week for four hours over three semesters; the fourth semester consisted entirely of student teaching. The semester schedule was based on the school districts' calendars, classes met within the school districts, and instructors were both master practitioners and university faculty. Teaching on-site offered a content-rich environment and provided districts the opportunity to observe students as future hires.

*Program challenges.* The partnership program required extensive communication between the districts and the teacher certification program. Initially, the districts focused course content so that students were exposed only to their particular programs, philosophies, and methodologies. As the student population grew to include non-district employees who were interested in future employment in other school districts, participants realized that a broader planning approach was warranted. The districts also tended to over-nurture the students. For example, district personnel were insistent on having the university handle applications and registrations rather than expecting the students to be responsible for these procedures. Curriculum control issues also arose between district- and university-based instructors. Another challenge was ensuring that the extended class meeting time afforded quality instruction. Instructors learned to adjust instruction to provide for several breaks during the four-hour session and to emphasize active involvement.

Constant collaboration was also required to avoid inconsistency between the university's regular daytime cohorts and the evening partnership programs. For example, the initial evening cohorts had the misconception that enrichment offerings, such as seminars and workshops, were reserved for traditional day students. Activities are now planned at a variety of times and days to encourage the participation of all of the unit's education students.

*Best practices.* The university and the districts have profited by the strong liaison developed during the partnership programs. This relationship led to the development of graduate-level programs targeted for district teachers and the creation of alternative field placements and practicum models. The use of practitioners to instruct pre-service teachers also provided validity to coursework because of their real-world connection and enable collaboration with university personnel to enrich course content.

The students have directly profited by the ongoing relationship with the districts. For example, one district was able to offer positions to 15 of the first class of 18 graduates. This class graduated mid-term (December) when open teaching positions are typically difficult to find. One of the graduates shared that the experience of having her principal as a program instructor boosted her performance as a first-year teacher. The teacher knew the principal's philosophies and methods, which eased the transition into the profession.

## ACCELERATING TEACHER QUALITY: INNOVATIONS ON THE FAST TRACK

Many teacher preparation units are pressured by outside competitors to develop "accelerated" certification programs. The elementary post-baccalaureate program in this study condensed the time for completion while maintaining rigorous standards through a collaborative endeavor with one of the university's partner K–8 schools. This program specifically targeted recareering adults who had background experiences in a variety of content areas. The university had grappled with the idea of an "accelerated" teacher education program for quite some time, in part to keep up with demands for teachers but also to provide an alternative to competing institutions.

*Unique elements.* Several unique characteristics were put into place in order to address initial concerns and ensure quality in the accelerated program. The decision was made to only offer this program to post-baccalaureate students. Feedback from faculty, classroom teachers, and school administrators consistently reflected that post-baccalaureate students who were seeking certification were stronger teacher candidates compared with undergraduate education students. However, because many of the post-baccalaureate students lacked classroom experience, the decision was made to develop the accelerated program as field-intensive.

The initial summer curriculum of this 11-month program included both foundation and methodology courses. The fall and spring semesters placed candidates in the classroom at a nearby community school. Students worked every day with an assigned classroom teacher and took college courses during the school day (alternating between morning and afternoon sessions). Keeping the students together as a cohort in classes and at the same school was deemed important to program success. Further, selecting faculty-practitioners to teach courses appeared to be the best avenue in getting real-life information to students in a short amount of time.

*Program challenges.* Problems and obstacles were expected in developing this new program. University-related issues included scheduling, selecting an appropriate school site, student retention, and internal cohort conflict. The compressed nature of all classes did not work well with a system designed for the traditional college semester. For example, having the existing university registration system interpret an abbreviated calendar, grade submission, and student financial aid proved to be (and remains) a challenge. Working predominantly with one school to house this program was also a challenge, as was gaining access to school classrooms with appropriate accommodations for college students. Seemingly peripheral issues, such as holidays and school closures, remained a constant distraction.

The original cohort of 14 students became 11 for various reasons, including the group's failure to get along with each other. Cohort-designed programs run the danger of the formation of sub-group "cliques." The stress on this particular cohort of students seemed to intensify the formation of an ineffectual peer group.

Students had many obstacles in completing the accelerated program. The first roadblock for students was, not surprisingly, one of time. Students were expected to be in the classroom or taking college courses all day, which did not provide them with time for planning and studying. It also did not allow adequate time for their roles outside of the classrooms, including that of spouse and/or parent. Students were advised against working while enrolled in this program. However, the resulting financial stress placed on students was a constant pressure that contributed to students' attrition.

*Best practices.* Recommendations for other programs considering a fast-track approach related to clear lines of communication, carefully selecting school sites, and a focus on career retooling. Identifying and dismissing students who did not demonstrate the disposition to be a quality teacher was also vital. Finally, creating a forum where students can learn, share, and discuss educational issues must be built into the program, so that students can regularly communicate successes, needs, and solutions to problems.

## EMERGENCY CERTIFICATION AND TEACHER ACHIEVEMENT: KEEPING "PACE" WITH INNOVATION

Despite the variety of programs being created by education units, critical shortages still require that some rural and urban districts place emergency or under-certified teachers in the classroom. The PACE program was developed to deliver the certification coursework on-site for such educators and to specifically attract recareering adults into the profession. Courses were delivered by the university at a large community college that partnered with the schools. Foundational and content coursework was provided by the community college.

*Unique elements.* Of the cases described in this study, the PACE program was the only initiative partially funded through a grant. This funding provided the students' tuition and books, as well as training and stipends for district mentors. The mentoring embedded into this program was one of its most unique and successful features. In addition to the district mentors, the university also assigned supervisors who observed the participants as they taught in the classroom. Because it was a cohort program, participants also had the informal support of peers.

This two-year program was developed for two cohorts—elementary and secondary. Secondary participants were in both middle and high school settings and focused on mathematics, science, and English. The participants were distributed across six different districts in a large rural county that primarily served students from Hispanic and Native American communities.

*Program challenges.* Several challenges were inherent to the design of this particular program, including that of distance. While a strength of this program was that it provided coursework on-site for the participants, the distance between the partnering university and the district sites was substantial and limited the pool of available and qualified university instructors. The distance also created a disconnect between the participants and university in general, which at times contributed to miscommunication and misadvisement. This problem was compounded by the absence of a focused university program coordinator to regularly ensure that lines of communication between all participants were maintained.

An additional challenge related to an incongruence between participants' perceptions of the importance of content versus the value of pedagogy. This was particularly evident with the secondary candidates, who felt very confident in their content knowledge and believed that extensive study in pedagogy was not as necessary to their success as teachers. Coupled with the state's lenient policies regarding secondary certification, these conditions led to the rapid dropout rate of the secondary candidates from the PACE program. At the conclusion of the study, only five of the original 12 secondary participants completed all of the pedagogical coursework required in the program itself. In contrast, all 14 elementary education participants successfully completed the entire two-year program.

*Best practices.* Challenges related to the program distance led to innovative practices on behalf of the course instructors in their uses of instructional technologies. Hybrid courses developed, which combined the immediate and convenient access of the Internet with periodic face-to-face meetings. Blackboard, a course support system, was also regularly used by most PACE instructors to facilitate communication with participants and to share course materials.

The structured and layered mentoring proved to be one of the key components of this initiative. Each layer provided participants with a unique kind of support. For example, the formal mentors provided participants with support that directly aligned with district expectations and policies, while the very informal peer cohort provided emotional support. Because the district mentors were often themselves classroom teachers and were not available during the school day, the university supervisors provided key feedback regarding participants' actual performance in the classroom.

The structure of this program also provided an effective model of creative partnerships in which the responsibility of developing quality teachers was jointly shared. Specifically, this program provided clear connections between a university, community college, and rural school districts. Each constituent provided specific support for the program participants and unique insight into their preparation.

# Implications for Teacher Education

Although the programs and experiences in these cases did differ, consistent components emerged as implications to be considered by other teacher education units who are developing non-conventional programs to attract non-traditional students.

### CONDITIONS FOR SUCCESS

The following section provides a brief overview of six conditions that were identified to describe successful elements in non-traditional preparation programs. These conditions are provided as guidance for other teacher education units who are developing programs to meet the unique needs of their constituents in these times of challenge and change.

*Communication.* The successes, and the challenges, of each of these programs were directly related to the level of communication among participants. This is particularly critical when forging relationships with other complex institutions, such as community colleges and districts. Face-to-face meetings with all participants, regular follow-ups, and written memos of understanding are critical in ensuring that all constituents share the same goals.

*Cohorts.* Each of the programs in this study utilized a peer cohort system. At their best, cohorts provide participants with the support that is needed to successfully complete what is often a stressful experience. However, when group dynamics are at opposition, cohorts can also have an unintended negative effect. To avoid conflict, program expectations must be made clear to participants at the onset of the program. Because the previous careers of many non-traditional candidates have a very different work culture than that of schools, seminars that directly explore schooling as a profession are highly recommended.

*Field experiences.* Varied experiences in K–12 classrooms throughout all phases of teacher preparation are critical to a program's success. It is particularly essential to ensure that teacher candidates have access to those professionals who can model best practices and have opportunities to work with students in varied contexts and of differing cultural backgrounds. Incidental experiences are much less effective than those that are directly planned and aligned with course assignments and standards.

*Partnerships.* Critical to any non-conventional program are the partnerships that are forged to support the teacher candidates. Partners bring unique expertise to the collaboration; therefore, all participants need to be involved in all phases of the program's development and share an equal stake in the outcome.

*Practical experiences.* Field experiences alone do no ensure that program participants will have the needed practical experiences to support their success as future teachers. Just as sound theory must be the foundation of a successful curriculum, direct and concrete ties to practice must also be integral and evident to participants. Using master teacher-practitioners as course instructors, for example, brings real-world experiences into coursework. Course assignments should also directly relate to the K–12 schools, to provide participants the opportunity to scaffold their own learning into successful classroom practices.

*Technology.* The use of appropriate technological tools has the potential of augmenting a successful non-conventional program. For example, technology can greatly assist in the communication between partners and can provide an alternative vehicle for instructional delivery. When used with non-traditional students, technology has the potential for accommodating the varied styles of learners while modeling effective practices for the K–12 classroom.

## CONCLUSION

As we present our findings in this longitudinal case study, we simultaneously recognize potential limitations in our study design. A specific limitation relates to the potential for researcher bias. Because we have been directly involved in and accountable for the programs' success and the progress of the students, we view the data through a very different lens than would a researcher who was outside of the study itself. We also recognize that the use of key informants does not allow us to generalize to all participants in the study. However, care was used to choose those participants who represented their peers and who had the potential for offering diverse perspectives.

The prevailing thought in current education reform focuses on collaboration, and the potential for change to occur as individuals work in cooperative ways. As noted by Miller and Stayton (1999), "collaboration and innovation in teacher education are essential ingredients for preparing teachers for increasingly diverse and challenging school populations" (p. 290). As teacher educators, we all share in the challenge and responsibility of providing a variety of routes into the K–12 classroom while encouraging candidates from diverse experiences into the profession. We also have the challenge of ensuring that these new educators are highly qualified and have the potential of making a difference with the growing diversity of K–12 students. Solutions to these challenges lie in the creativity and responsiveness of teacher education units to develop innovative non-conventional routes for the rich diversity of non-traditional teacher candidates.

# References

Berry, B. (2001). No shortcuts to preparing good teachers. *Educational Leadership, 58*(8), 32–35.

Darling-Hammond, L. (1994). Who will speak for the children? How "Teach for America" hurts urban schools and students. *Phi Delta Kappan, 76,* 21–34.

Finn, Jr., C. E., and Madigan, K. (2001). Removing the barriers for teacher candidates. *Educational Leadership, 58*(8), 29–31, 36.

Goetz, J. P., and LeCompte, M. D. (1984). *Ethnography and qualitative design in educational research.* Orlando, FL: Academic.

Imig, D. G. (1997). Professionalization or dispersal: A case study of American teacher education. *Peabody Journal of Education, 72,* 25–34.

Merriam, S. B. (1998). *Qualitative research and case study applications in education.* San Francisco: Jossey-Bass.

Miller, P. S., and Stayton, V. D. (1999). Higher education culture—A fit or misfit with reform in teacher education? *Journal of Teacher Education, 50,* 290–302.

Resta, V., Huling, L., and Rainwater, N. (2001). Preparing second-career teachers. *Educational Leadership, 58*(8), 60–63.

# Summary and Conclusions
## SUCCESSES AND CHALLENGES FOR ALTERNATIVE ROUTES TO CERTIFICATION

*Melba Spooner*
University of North Carolina at Charlotte

## Summary

The preceding chapters in this section address the task of developing and implementing alternative certification programs for non-traditional teacher education students. The four chapters explore a variety of alternative certification program models. The authors provide studies that highlight the successes and challenges as institutions of higher education respond to creating alternative pathways to certification.

Each of the four chapters in this division makes it clear that developing and implementing alternative certification programs is not a simple task. They do, however, provide an array of examples that will help us continue to examine the balance of quality and expediency in tailoring programs for teacher candidates who do not fit within the traditional model of teacher preparation.

## Focusing on Recent Immigrants and Refugees

The Newcomer Extended Teacher Education Program (ETEP) provides a framework for an alternative certification program that targets immigrants and refugees. The authors elaborate on the design of the Program and its adaptation to fit the specific needs of each individual. A key to this program is to promote the socialization process through using the theory of sociotransformative constructivism. The program is designed around several core commitments that include school and university partnerships to link practice with theory, an extended mentored internship, an embedded assessment system, and a cohort structure. The Newcomer ETEP has existed since 1999 and has evolved under the guidance of a steering committee made up of university faculty and administrators, school district teachers and administrators, and representatives from the ethnic community. Data are gathered from students in the program, mentor teachers, course instructors, and the program coordinator. The most successful aspects of the program are categorized in two ways—benefits to the K–12 classroom and benefits to graduate-level classrooms. Although there are multiple challenges and benefits, the Newcomer ETEP students bring richness to the K–12 classrooms as well as to the college classroom through their high motivation, awareness of world issues, and typically literacy in multiple languages. Even though these students bring motivation and confidence to the college and K–12 classrooms, standardized certification tests raise a barrier for them to remain in the classroom with a full and clear teaching license. The mentoring and cohort groups are seen as a socialization process and necessary for sustained successful work in the K–12 schools. At the time of this study, none of the graduates have teaching jobs in mainstream classrooms for which they were prepared. They continue in ESOL classroom and other multilingual type positions.

# A "Traditional" Approach to Alternative Certification

In chapter 2, the author investigates the New York City Teaching Fellow (NYCTF) program from "the inside out." This program was established in 2000, and literally thousands of individuals in six cohorts have entered the program. A layered approach of individual interviews, group discussions, and journal reading has been used in an attempt to understand the Fellows' development and their commitment to the program and to teaching. As researchers follow a group of Fellows through a three-year time period, they listen to how the Fellows change their thinking during their first few years of teaching in poor urban schools and how the Fellows develop a better understanding of themselves as teachers. The results are not uncommon in terms of new teacher concerns and understandings.

At the beginning, survival mode sets in and the Fellows are most concerned about lesson delivery and classroom management. As the first year progresses, they become more concerned about such issues as mandated curricula and high-stakes testing. During the second year of teaching the Fellows (who were completing their contracted two-year commitment) begin to consider whether or not they would remain in urban schools. They could either choose to leave altogether or move to the wealthier suburbs. According to these researchers, programs such as NYCTF exist to address a perceived teacher shortage, one that is in reality an issue of retention. As the Fellows continue in their second year of teaching, they have some concerns about classroom management, but the main frustration was that of lack of autonomy in teaching.

# Increasing the Number of Students from Underrepresented Minorities

Unlike the previous two chapters, chapter 3 outlines an alternative licensure program that is geared toward baccalaureate-degree-seeking students. Project Transformative Educational Achievement Model (TEAM) is designed to increase the number of underrepresented minorities who enter a teacher education program. Students recruited into this program are provided with incentives such as additional academic, social, and financial support. The program originally started on the Indiana University campus in Bloomington, and has expanded to Gary, Indianapolis, Fort Wayne, and South Bend. Since expanding to additional campuses the research questions have expanded. Project TEAM was originally started to address the shortage of teachers of color at the state and national level and to recruit students motivated to teach in urban and multicultural settings.

An important goal of Project TEAM is self-examination of ethnic identity development as well as helping ethnic minority students mediate the predominantly white campus climate. Students are in cohorts and attend Honor Seminars as ways of helping both the students and the program meet these goals.

This study was not designed to determine successes and challenges but to present discoveries about student characteristics and selected perceptions of their experiences while being in the program. The findings have implications for recruitment and support of minority students who are pursing careers in teaching. First of all, a sense of community and support is important, and second, the opportunity for openness to ethnic diversity and a sense of one's own identity is important in helping individuals mediate experiences in an unfamiliar or different climate.

# Multiple Routes to Non-traditional Teacher Certification

Chapter 4 provides yet additional models for alternative certification programs. As in the previous chapters, the impetus for developing these alternative routes is a response to the impending teaching shortage that has been looming since the 1980s. Another important factor includes tailoring each program to make teacher education available for a diverse population of students. The four case studies present multiple programs that partner with one institution of higher education. The programs involve partnerships between the university and community colleges and between the university and school districts. An elementary post-baccalaureate program was also established as a "fast track" to licensure and an emergency certification program was developed.

Each program has distinctions, yet several overarching implications for teacher education are found in each. They include:

1. **Communication**—As we all know, when working among complex organizations, frequent and clear communication is a must.
2. **Cohorts**—Consistent peer groups are cited as a very important part of each program. Sometimes opinions and experiences differ but to have an open forum with peers with whom you have built some camaraderie over time is important.
3. **Field Experiences** that provide **Practical Experiences**, as well as **Mentor Teachers**—Extended time in classrooms where students could both practice and observe master teachers model instructional and management practices is necessary.
4. **Collaborative Partnerships**—Partnerships across educational institutions (K–16) provide multiple levels of expertise and experience.
5. **Technology**—Technology opens many doors that can be helpful to students and to faculty participating in alternative certification programs. Technology may be an instructional tool or a means of communication.

# Discussion and Reflections

The authors in this division offer an array of models for alternative certification programs focused on recruiting individuals who will bring diversity and experience into the classroom. The programs are as diverse as the individuals who enter them. A recurring theme throughout each of the programs however is the value and necessity of support through peer cohort groups and the need to be engaged in substantial and extended field experiences that mirror the experiences these students will ultimately face when they enter the classroom as the sole teacher. A concern, however, is that in many alternative certification programs the students are already employed as a classroom teacher. These individuals are typically issued an emergency certificate. They "hit the ground running," so to speak and they may have content knowledge, but lack the pedagogical skills and management techniques to help them be well-rounded and effective teachers. Teachers who are certified through alternative routes lack adequate pedagogical skills which are typically taught and acquired in formal teacher preparation programs (McDiarmid and Wilson, 1991). It is therefore imperative that Colleges and Schools of Education engage in not only the debate about traditional vs. alternative teacher certification programs but also be proactive in researching and designing programs that attract quality individuals into the teaching profession and give them the experiences and coursework that will assist them in being successful teachers who want to stay in the classroom. A challenge for teacher educators and policy makers is to not only recruit but also to retain them in schools and classrooms. Programs such as the NYCTF demonstrate the ability to recruit, but are still challenged with keeping these teachers in the urban classrooms beyond their contractual commitment of two years. With that turnover, the shortage in certain geographical and in many cases, content and special education areas will continue to be a concern.

While the studies in this section add to the knowledge base about alternative certification programs, they also confirm the complexity and diversity of this issue. The external pressures for reform in teacher education and attention to diversity and highly qualified teachers will continue to mount. Projections of teacher shortages continue to sound alarms (Feistritzer, 1998). Alternative certification programs provide an avenue for experienced individuals with content expertise to enter the teaching profession, especially in critically needed areas of subject matter where shortages exist (Lutz and Hutton, 1989; Shulman, 1992).

Even though there is a large amount of research in alternative certification, the majority continues to be descriptive of programs and typically does not provide significant evaluation data (Otuya, 1992) that shows the connection between effective teachers and related student outcomes. A strong measure of program effectiveness depends on the quality of teachers as reflected in student learning outcomes. As more colleges and schools of education develop and implement alternative paths to teacher certification, the development of an evaluation system that yields data about teacher impact on student learning is an important step to include in the process.

# References

Feistritzer, C. E. (1998). *Alternative teacher certification: An overview* (The Center for Education Information). Retrieved May 11, 2004, from http://www.ncei.com/Alt-Teacher-Cert.htm

Lutz, F. W. and Hutton, J. B (1989). Alternative teacher certification: Its policy implications for classroom and personnel practice. *Educational Evaluation and Policy Analysis.* *11*(3), 237–54.

McDiarmid, G. W., and Wilson, S. M. (1991). An exploration of the subject matter knowledge of alternative route teachers: Can we assume they know their subject? *Journal of Teacher Education, 42*(2), 93–103.

Otuya, E. (1992). Alternative teacher certification—An update. *Eric Digest.* Washington, DC: ERIC Clearinghouse on Teacher Education.

Shulman, D. (1992). Alternative to certification: Are we on the right track? *Policy Briefs, 17*, 6–7.

Division 2

# ALTERNATIVE CERTIFICATION TEACHER PREPARATION PROGRAMS: EFFECTS OF PROGRAM MODELS ON TEACHER PERFORMANCE

# Overview and Framework

## ALTERNATIVE CERTIFICATION TEACHER PREPARATION PROGRAMS: EFFECTS OF PROGRAM MODELS ON TEACHER PERFORMANCE

*Judith L. Hayes*
Wichita State University

> Judith L. Hayes is an Assistant Professor of Curriculum and Instruction in the College of Education at Wichita State University, Wichita, Kansas. She is the Director of the Transition to Teaching Program and of the Raytheon Teaching Fellows Program. Her research interests include alternative certification, adult education, mentoring, and professional learning communities.

As we begin the twenty-first century, our nation's educational system is at the forefront of political platforms, parental concerns, and school reforms. In the shadow of *A Nation at Risk* and in the midst of No Child Left Behind, we grapple with the unsettling reality of low student performance, illiteracy, lack of student motivation, high teacher attrition rates, and inequities in providing equal resources for all students in all schools. In response to these concerns we develop new programs, we reallocate funding, we research effective practices and we redesign schools to maximize opportunities for the next generation to be productive, informed members in a global society. Ultimately, every educational platform, parental concern, or proposal for school reform shares the same goal, providing the most comprehensive education possible to enable all students to learn.

In the center of every classroom is a teacher, and there is wide consensus among researchers and policy makers that teacher quality is a key component of school quality and student achievement (Sanders and Horn, 1998; Sanders and Rivers, 1996; Sanders and Topping, 1999; Scheerens and Bosker, 1997; Wright, Horn and Sanders, 1997). The evidence is consistent in aligning student achievement with individual teachers (Sanders and Rivers). Therefore, the goal of all teacher education is to create effective teachers. Whether effective teachers are "made through experience" (Darling-Hammond, 1994, p. 23) or developed through the knowledge, skills and dispositions of a traditional education program, the preparation routes and standards of teacher education programs are being examined.

There is general consensus relevant to the standards expected from teacher education programs as Colleges of Education have made significant modifications to their curriculum to align with NCATE Standards, as well as the changing PK–12 Standards and Program Standards required by State Accreditation agencies. However, there are varying opinions as to the most effective preparation process employed for facilitating the development of the "highly qualified teacher" we all desire.

Add to this challenge, reports of pending teacher retirements, teacher turnover, dissatisfaction with teaching, and teacher shortages in both urban and rural schools and there is common agreement that our country faces some serious problems with respect to "how teachers are trained, licensed, recruited and hired" (Berry, 2001; Feistritzer, 2003). The National Center for Education Statistics forecasts that if the pupil–teacher ratio remains steady, at least 2.2 million new public school teachers will be needed by 2008 (Hussar, 1999).

Alternative certification is being examined as a possible solution for increasing the quantity and quality of teachers in the nation (Ingersoll, 2001). Alternative routes for certifying teachers have been available since the early 1980s. As more and more states offer alternative routes to certification the impact of teacher preparation program models relevant to teacher performance has become a common theme in educational research. In 2003, 46 states and the District of Columbia reported having some type of alternative route for certification and report that approximately 25,000 people per year have been certified to teach through alternative routes within the last five years (Feistritzer, 2003).

Since alternative teacher licensure programs are collectively defined as any route to licensure that varies from the traditional undergraduate model, this leads to multiple possibilities in program design. Typically, alternative programs allow candidates to obtain pedagogical practices in conjunction with classroom field experiences circumventing the traditional teacher education preparation process. Programs differ in their goals, selection processes and admission requirements, pre-service programs, induction support, and linkages with existing professional development programs. There are also variations with regard to cost, time, intensity, and support (Humphrey, Wechsler, Bosetti, Wayne and Adelman, 2002).

"Alternative routes to teacher certification are having a significant impact on the way all teachers are educated and brought into the profession. Few innovations in American education have spawned more controversy and debate than the alternative certification movement, and few have ultimately resulted in more positive changes" (Feistritzer, 2003).

There is substantial research available comparing traditional and alternative routes, collecting teacher perceptions and predicting potential pitfalls, but inadequately describing specific programs in relationship to student achievement (Hawk and Schmidt, 1989). The literature does, however, provide some insights into alternative certification program participants, program components, and program effectiveness (Humphrey, Wechsler, Bosetti, Wayne and Adelman, 2002). These data are useful for building a foundation for examining the characteristics of effective teachers and the influence of the teacher preparation program on the alternative teacher candidate.

The chapters in this section of the *Teacher Education Yearbook XIII* describe the effect of teacher preparation program models on teacher candidate performance and attrition. The research compares attrition patterns among teachers trained through traditional routes and alternative routes; performance assessment of alternative candidates that are mid-career changers and recent college graduates; assessment of alternative candidates in comparison with traditionally trained candidates against a performance-based model; and comparisons of teacher efficacy, effectiveness, concerns and aspirations among year 1 and year 2 alternatively trained candidates and traditionally trained first-year teachers.

## ATTRITION PATTERNS OF ALTERNATIVE CANDIDATES

Reports of teacher shortages abound. In reality, America produces enough teachers, but many of those choose not to enter the classroom and many of those that do enter leave within three years (Wise and Darling-Hammond, 1992). "The conventional wisdom is that we can't find enough good teachers. The truth is that we can't keep enough good teachers" (National Commission on Teaching and America's Future, 2003). Salaries and working conditions are recognized as factors contributing to high rates of attrition but with the recent influx of teachers entering the profession through alternative routes there is an additional factor to consider. Richard Ingersoll's data from a 2000–2001 Teacher Follow-Up Survey shows teacher preparation programs significantly reduce attrition of first year teachers. When teachers come into the classroom unprepared, attrition of first year teachers is at 25 percent. But when teachers have engaged in a coherent preparation program that assesses knowledge and teaching skill, rates of beginning teacher attrition are at 12 percent (Ingersoll, 2001).

High attrition rates are costly but seem to be an anticipated expenditure particularly in poorer urban schools and rural schools. Since many teachers prepared through alternative routes are employed in these high-needs schools, can the alternatively and traditionally prepared teachers' attrition rates be equally compared? Podgursky finds

> A simple comparison of turnover rates by years of experience of ACP (Alternative Certification Program) and traditionally trained teachers may be a misleading indicator of AC teacher's commitment to teaching. It is well established in the research literature that schools with high concentrations of minority and poor students have higher teacher turnover rates. Now suppose the propensity to quit is the same for traditional and AC teachers in similar circumstances but AC teachers are disproportionately concentrated in poorer or high poverty schools. Then we will tend to observe higher turnover rates of AC teachers, but this is a biased estimate of the true difference in turnover propensity of the two types of teachers (Podgursky, 2004).

The convergence of teacher shortages (through retirement or through attrition) and the quest for teacher quality have encouraged innovation and initiative as universities and districts partner to provide the preparation, support, and resources to place and retain *highly qualified teachers* in every classroom.

## CHARACTERISTICS OF ALTERNATIVE CANDIDATES

Individuals seeking licensure through alternative certification programs generally fall into three categories: (1) mid-career, or second-career changers; (2) recent college graduates deciding to enter teaching too late in their college program to switch majors; and (3) recent college graduates who have "partially completed" a teacher education program.

Alternative teacher education programs have changed the profile of the teacher educator by increasing the diversity and the education level of the candidates entering the profession. There's been a dramatic shift in the profile of people studying to be teachers through alternative routes. There are greater numbers of older, life-experienced people wanting to enter the teacher profession when compared with traditional preparation models. A higher percentage of these mid-career switchers are male and/or are minorities interested in teaching in high-demand areas of the country in positions generally not sought by young, white females coming out of traditional schools of education (Feistritzer, 2002).

As we look at the shift in the pool of applicants seeking to enter alternative preparation programs, selection of candidates becomes a critical factor in predicting success and in managing resources. Research has begun to look at the characteristics of successful alternative candidates as well as the selection processes employed by different teacher preparation program models.

> The success and sustainability of an alternative certification program depends on recruiting quality candidates—more so than in a traditional, college-based teaching program. A typical alternative route program accepts only a limited number of teacher candidates at any one time. The program's resources must be funneled to candidates who will be employed by participating districts, so investing resources in candidates unlikely to succeed is a lose-lose situation for programs and districts. As a result, selecting the right candidates for admission is crucial to the program's success. This is why many alternative certification programs seek a research-based, reliable, and fast assessment to use as part of the selection process (Gordon, 2004, p. 3).

The experiences and backgrounds of candidates entering an alternative program have a significant effect on their success in the classroom. Teacher preparation program models that identify characteristics of successful candidates in the selection process and individualize the student's plan of study to ensure that all program standards are met facilitate the successful transition of the alternative candidate to the classroom.

## PERFORMANCE OF ALTERNATIVE CANDIDATES

What makes a teacher good? Ultimately, the only true evidence of good teaching is the impact a teacher has on his or her students. But what is it that enables the best teachers to have the greatest impact? The Education Commission of the States (ECS) suggests:

> There is widespread agreement that strong subject-matter knowledge is a critical component of successful teaching. There is also some evidence that subject-specific pedagogical knowledge—how specifically to teach mathematics or reading or history—also is important. Beyond that, the picture becomes murky. Some experts have pointed to a positive correlation between teachers' scores on verbal ability tests and the achievement of their students, arguing that the best teachers are also intellectually the brightest. Others have insisted that the diversity of the contemporary classroom requires that successful teachers have a broad repertoire of instructional strategies. Still other experts claim that a teacher's character and attitude are strong pre-

dictors of his or her success teaching to specific kinds of students. (ECS, 2004, p. 3)

Characteristics and assessment of teachers' performance are being defined through the leading efforts of the National Board for Professional Teaching Standards and the Interstate New Teacher Assessment and Support Consortium. This research has been used to develop a set of teacher standards that can provide a framework for teacher preparation programs to use in the development of curriculum and training procedures for teacher candidates. Critics insist, however, that such efforts have no proven correlation to a teacher's ability to promote student achievement and such standards restrict the entry into teaching of talented individuals who lack such extensive—and not clearly necessary— pedagogical training. In the absence of a clear and unambiguous standard for new teachers, the job of providing adequate preparation for new teachers is difficult (ECS, 2004). Tighter regulation of teacher training programs, more stringent admission requirements to teacher education programs, and more field experience opportunities may strengthen the performance of teacher candidates but such proposals are not based on sound research or hard data but on conventional wisdom atop beliefs and ideologies (Finn and Madigan, 2001).

While policymakers around the country are concerned about the quality and supply of teachers, consensus as to how states can best ensure quality is elusive (Ruckel, 2000). Scientific evaluation of the effect of educational policies, including teacher preparation, on student achievement requires either: (1) randomized experimental study design, or (2) non-experimental longitudinal data on student achievement. Unfortunately, little research on teacher testing or licensing meets either standard and the research that does is tentative and inconclusive (Podgursky, 2004). While there have been many articles published about alternative certification programs, few meet the standards of scientific rigor that would facilitate conclusions as to teacher performance and impact on student achievement. And, just like traditional teacher preparation programs, not all alternative routes are equal in quality.

## TEACHER EFFICACY OF ALTERNATIVE CANDIDATES

Research of the past two decades has shown that the most important factor in improving student achievement is the quality of teaching, as well as the teacher's knowledge and ability to facilitate student learning (Johnson, 1999). Alternative teacher preparation routes responding to teacher shortages may place new teachers in jeopardy when they are placed in a classroom before they are properly prepared to teach (Berliner, 2000).

Reform in teacher preparation program content and pedagogy alone will not solve all the challenges in the educational reform movement. Teacher attitudes, dispositions, and own sense of efficacy seem to also impact student achievement and teacher satisfaction (Jordan and Johnson, 2001). The teacher must believe that, in general, students can learn the material and that the students can learn under his or her direction (Ashton, 1984). Alternative candidates may have difficulty believing this without the opportunity of a field-based experience or the pedagogical repertoire of strategies provided through a traditional teacher preparation program. However, alternative certification program advocates claim that successful candidates are able to transfer their knowledge from job-related practices and life experiences to the needs of their students (Finn and Madigan, 2001).

Teachers' perceptions of self-efficacy provide another lens into teacher effectiveness. Teachers' self-efficacy and confidence are important to foster early in the career, concludes Darling-Hammond (1994), because views of self-efficacy form early, are relatively difficult to change, and "have been found to be related to student achievement . . . , motivation . . . , and students' own sense of efficacy" as well as to the teachers' "feelings about teaching and their plans to stay in the profession" (p. 20). Of four studies comparing alternatively and traditionally certified teachers' sense of efficacy and confidence, two studies found the groups were similar (Guyton, Fox and Sisk, 1991; Miller, McKenna, and McKenna, 1998) while two other studies found the traditionally prepared teachers were more confident (Jelmberg, 1996; Lutz and Hutton, 1989).

The authors of the following four chapters have researched the effect of teacher preparation program models on individuals pursuing certification through alternative routes. They have identified patterns of attrition and program characteristics that can document the production of effective teachers and impact teacher training models. As Sikula (1990) states in the foreword of a 1990 ATE Publication, *Alternatives, Yes. Lower Standards, No!*, "The motivation to find more teachers prompts innovation and initiative." Research that examines innovative practices, and measures the effects of those practices on teacher performance and student achievement, provides impetus for changes in teacher preparation programs.

# References

Ashton, P. (1984). Teacher efficacy: A motivational paradigm for effective teacher education. *Journal of Teacher Education, 35*(5), 28–32.

Berliner, D. (2000, August 25). Certified teachers are better for the job. *The Arizona Republic*, p. B9.

Berry, B. (2001). No shortcuts to preparing good teachers. *Educational Leadership,* *58*(8), 32–36.

Darling-Hammond, L. (1994). Who will speak for the children? How 'Teach for America' hurts urban schools and students. *Phi Delta Kappan, 76*(1), 21–34.

Darling-Hammond, L., Chung, R., and Frelow, F. (2002). Variations in teacher preparation: How well do different pathways prepare teachers to teach? *Journal of Teacher Education, 53*(4), 286–302.

Education Commission of the States. (2004). Teacher quality. *ECS Issue Site.* Retrieved on May 28, 2004, from http://www.ecs.org/html/issue.asp?issueid = 129&subIssue ID = 63

Feistritzer, C. E. (1998). Alternative teacher certification: An overview. *National Center for Education Information.* Retrieved on May 28, 2004, from http://www.ncei.com/ Alt-Teacher-Cert.htm

Feistritzer, C. E. (2002). Alternative teacher certification: New support and new urgency. *National Council on Teacher Quality.* Retrieved on March 19, 2004, from http://www .nctq.org/press/2002_consumers_guide/feistritzer.html

Feistritzer, C. E. (2003). *Alternative routes to teacher certification: A state by state analysis.* Washington, DC: National Center for Education Information.

Finn, C. E. and Madigan, K. (2001). Removing the barriers for teacher candidates. *Educational Leadership, 58*(8), 29–36.

Gordon, G. (2004). Alternative certification and teacher insight. *Gallup Organization Education Division.* Retrieved May 28, 2004, from http://education.gallup.com/content/ default.asp?ci = 1537

Guyton, E., Fox, M., and Sisk, K. (1991). Comparison of teaching attitudes, teacher efficacy, and teacher performance of first-year teachers prepared by alternative and traditional education programs. *Actions in Teacher Education, 13*(2), 1–9.

Hawk, P. P., and Schmidt, M. W. (1989). Teacher preparation: A comparison of traditional and alternative programs. *Journal of Teacher Education, 40*(5), 53–58.

Humphrey, D., Wechsler, M., Bosetti, K., Wayne, A., and Adelman, N., (2002). *Alternative certification: Design for a national study.* SRI International, October, 2002. Menlo Park, CA: Center for Education Policy.

Hussar, W. J. (1999, August). *Predicting the need for newly hired teachers in the United States to 2008–2009.* National Center for Education Statistics (NCES 1999-026). U.S. Department Education. Retrieved May 28, 2004, from http://nces.ed.gov/ pubsearch/pubsinfo.asp?pubid = 1999026

Ingersoll, R. (2001). *Teacher turnover, teacher shortages, and the organization of schools.* *American Educational Research Journal, 38*(3), 499–534.

Jelmberg, J. (1996). College-based teacher education versus state-sponsored alternative programs. *Journal of Teacher Education, 47*(1), 60–66.

Johnson, R. (1999). Teacher licensing plan stirs opposition in Pennsylvania. *Education Week of the Web, 1.* [On-line]. Retrieved May 28, 2004, from http://www.edweek.org/ ew/1999/02pa.h19

Lutz, F. and Hutton, J. (1989). Alternative teacher certification: Its policy implications for classroom and personnel practice. *Educational Evaluation and Policy Analysis, 11,* 237–54.

Miller, J., McKenna, M. and McKenna, B. (1998). A comparison of alternatively and traditionally prepared teachers. *Journal of Teacher Education, 49*(3), 165–76.

National Commission on Teaching and America's Future. (2003). NCTAF Report. *Wide-meyer Communications*. Retrieved on May 2, 2004, from http://www.widmeyer.com/Whats_News/20030122.html

Podgursky, M. (2004). Improving Academic Performance in U.S. Public Schools: Why teacher licensing is (almost) irrelevant in R. Hess, A. Rotterham, and K. Walsh (eds.) *A Qualified Teacher in Every Classroom? Appraising Old Answers and New Ideas.* Cambridge, MA: Harvard Education Press. Retrieved May 29, 2004 from http://www.teach-now.org/frmRsr_ResearchOnATC_MPodgursky.asp

Ruckel, C. (2000). Ensuring quality teachers through alternative programs. *McRel Policy Brief.* Aurora, CO: OERI US Department of Education.

Sanders, W. L. and Horn, S. P. (1998). Research findings from the Tennessee value-added assessment system (TVAAS) database: Implications for educational evaluation and research. *Journal of Personnel Evaluation in Education, 12,* 247–56.

Sanders, W. L. and Rivers, J. (November, 1996). Cumulative and residual effects of teachers on future student academic achievement. *Research Progress Report.* Knoxville, TN: University of Tennessee Value-Added Research and Assessment Center.

Sanders, W. L. and Topping, K. J. (1999). Teacher effectiveness and computer assessment of reading: relating value added and learning information system data. Tennessee Value-Added Research and Assessment Center.

Scheerens, J. and Bosker, R. (1997). *The foundations of educational effectiveness.* New York: Pergamon.

Sikula, J. (1990). *Alternatives, Yes. Lower standards, No!* Association of Teacher Educators. Reston, VA: ATE.

Wise, A. and Darling-Hammond, L. (1992). Alternative certification as an oxymoron. *The Education Digest 57*(8), 46–48.

Wright, S. P., Horn, S. P., and Sanders, W. L. (1997). Teachers and classroom context effects on student achievement: Implications for teacher evaluation. *Journal of Personnel Evaluation in Education, 11* (1), 57–67.

CHAPTER 5

# When They Are Good . . .

## A COMPARISON OF CAREER CHANGERS AND RECENT COLLEGE GRADUATES IN AN ALTERNATIVE CERTIFICATION PROGRAM

*Maryann Dickar*
New York University

Maryann Dickar is an Assistant Professor of Teaching and Learning at New York University. Her current research is on preparing teachers for the urban context and on the impact of student culture on urban school reform.

ABSTRACT

This study compares recent college graduates to career changers participating in an Alternative Certification program to examine assumptions that inform programs like New York City's Teaching Fellows. Through a comparison of 56 Alternative Certification candidates—26 career changers and 30 recent college graduates—this study finds that career changers tended to either exceed expectations or to perform well below them while recent college graduates tended to fill out the spectrum more evenly. Career changers performing below expectations tended to lack flexibility, enter the profession casually rather than passionately and were often detached from their students. Those exceeding expectations tended to have a high commitment to teaching, have professional skills that fostered success and were able to synthesize their teacher education into their practice. Using this information Alternative Certification Programs can improve recruitment and selection of new teachers and can be tailored to more directly serve their participants. This study also raises questions about the ability of Alternative Certification programs to enable candidates to address sociocultural issues prior to entering inner-city classrooms.

Alternative Certification programs, those that allow candidates to circumvent some of the entry requirements for teaching, have been celebrated for their potential to solve teacher shortages, increase diversity and improve the quality of the teacher corps. One of the most notable programs of this kind is the New York City Teaching Fellows Program, which was initiated to tap into new sources of teachers and recruit higher-caliber candidates to teach in the city's hardest to staff schools. The program particularly targets mid-career professionals based on the assumption that these seasoned professionals can bring new perspectives to public schools and are able to draw effectively on their previous experiences bringing a culture of success to poorly functioning schools. In this chapter I explore these assumptions about career changers by comparing career-changers and recent college graduates participating in the same Alternative Certification program and teaching in the same schools.

# Description of Program

## BACKGROUND ON TEACHING FELLOWS PROGRAM

The New York City Teaching Fellows Program was created in response to a state mandate that all classrooms be staffed by certified teachers. The city was facing a severe teacher shortage and also was under fire because many of the teachers serving in the lowest performing schools were uncertified. In a bold move to improve quality and tap into new sources of teachers, then Chancellor Harold Levy established the Teaching Fellows Program on the premise that there were many talented individuals who wanted to teach but were put off by the cumbersome requirements for teacher certification. The program was designed to be highly selective and offered Fellows a free master's degree and the opportunity to begin teaching after only one summer of coursework. Though the program targets career changers, it also admits large numbers of recent college graduates and thus offers an opportunity to probe the differences between these two sources of teachers.

In order for Fellows to be considered licensed teachers they must earn the Transitional B license, New York State's alternative certification license. Candidates must pass two of the state's teacher exams, the Liberal Arts and Sciences Test (LAST), and the Content Specialty Test (CST) in their area of certification and enroll in MA programs that lead to regular certification. The Transitional B also requires that school districts provide regular on-site mentoring and that the Fellow's university also provide mentoring at least once a month. Fellows complete the program in two years during which they teach in the city schools.

## THE PROGRAM IN THIS STUDY

The Teaching Fellows Program has met with tremendous success in terms of recruiting new teachers. While admitting less than 20 percent of its applicants, the program still recruits as many as 2000 new teachers a year. In order to serve this large number of Fellows, the program has established relationships with many schools of education, both public and private. This study draws its data from one such program at Urban University (pseudonym) that served 56 Fellows in 2002-2003. In 2001 Urban University and a Community School District in the Bronx formed a partnership to prepare English, Social Studies and English Speakers of Other Languages (ESL) Teaching Fellows for the District's most troubled middle schools. In addition to the school-based mentor provided by the district, Urban University provided two full-time University Mentors called Urban Master Teachers (UMT) who work with each Fellow once a week. 56 Teaching Fellows participated in this study, 26 career changers (cc) and 30 recent college graduates (rcg).[1] Because this program is small and works with a small number of similarly performing middle schools the participants teach in very similar classroom settings.

The partnership schools for this initiative serve high poverty, overwhelmingly minority student populations. The racial composition of partnership schools varies slightly, but on average 66.5 percent are Hispanic, 26.2 percent are Black, and 7.3 percent White, Asian and Other. More than 90 percent of all students attending partnership schools receive free lunch. On average 16.4 percent of their students are meeting standards in English Language Arts, with the highest performing school having 22.4 percent on grade level in reading and 10.8 percent in the lowest performing school. Only 8.8 percent of students are meeting standards in math in these schools with the highest to lowest range being 12.1 to 4.7 percent. These schools present many challenges to teachers and more so to new teachers who did not attend similar schools and may not be as prepared as they thought to teach students who are culturally and racially different from themselves. Further, the academic struggles facing many of these

---

1. I define those Teaching Fellows who had completed college in the last five years and who had not committed to a career as Recent College Graduates. Those who had been in the workforce longer than five years were defined as career changers even though they may not have committed to a career. The majority of recent college graduates graduated in the last year and the majority of career changers are over 30 years old.

students are monumental and present new challenges for those who may have never struggled in school themselves.

# Literature Review

Though more and more research is being done about Alternative Certification (AC) Programs organized by school districts, little is known about their effectiveness (McIntyre, 2002). Studies have documented that alternative routes to teaching attract a more diverse teacher corps, particularly more men, minorities and second-career teachers (Homes, 2001; Peske, Liu, Johnson, Kaufman and Kardos, 2001; Shen, 2000). Many studies have sought to determine how Alternatively Certified teachers perform in comparison to Traditionally Certified (TC) teachers. However, none of these studies has been conclusive and about as many condemn the performance of AC candidates as praise them (Berry, 2001; Darling-Hammond, 2000; Dill and Stafford, 1992; Finn and Madigan, 2001; Wise and Darling-Hammond, 1992). Further, these studies are often flawed as Miller, McKenna and McKenna (1998) point out. Many of these studies do not use comparable samples of teachers, for example, comparing first year AC candidates to all teachers in a district or other wide sample. Other comparisons have drawn on too small a sample to assess how representative these samples are. Other researchers have pointed out that Alternative Certification has come to encompass such a broad range of programs that it is often unfair to use any one of these programs to represent the majority (Chapelle and Eubanks, 2001).

Another shortcoming in the literature is that too little of it has examined the actual experiences of AC teachers in classrooms, particularly those in programs that target failing urban schools. Also, though much debate has centered around one of the assumptions of alternative programs—that high-performing liberal arts graduates will have sufficient content knowledge to be effective teachers—we have not spent enough time probing some of the other assumptions that seem to make these programs more and more appealing to school districts (Darling-Hammond, 2000; Wise and Darling-Hammond, 1992). Particularly, one of the assumptions underlying the New York City Teaching Fellows Program is that second-career recruits will bring needed new perspectives and will be highly successful because of their previous professional successes (Goodnough, 2000). This chapter explores the different experiences of recent college graduates and career changers participating in the same Teaching Fellows program to test some of the underlying assumptions about career changers. As Alternative Certification programs proliferate and attract second-career professionals, examining the efficacy and the specific needs of this population is necessary in order to shape recruitment strategies and to hone AC programs to better meet their needs.

# Method

In order to compare the levels of success of the 56 teachers in the study, an instrument was developed by the researcher and the two UMTs, all of whom observed the participants regularly. After extensive discussion of our expectations for first-year teachers, five criteria were defined that addressed the majority of our concerns: Professional Behavior, Lesson Planning and Execution, Classroom Culture, Evidence of Growth, Problem Solving. A rubric was created using these five criteria to rate each teacher. In order to insure inter-rater reliability, a list of descriptors was generated by the raters to clarify what types of behaviors were included in each criterion.

Each Fellow was given a score of 1–4 (1 = below expectations, 2 = approaching expectations, 3 = meeting expectations, 4 = exceeding expectations) for each of the five main categories. These ratings were assigned holistically. The UMTs and the researcher rated each Fellow with whom s/he had worked, and each Fellow was rated by at least two people. Raters had access to the teaching journals, classroom teaching, course work, the school-based mentors, staff developers and supervisors of all the Fellows to inform their ratings. The ratings were then compared and discussed and a final rating was assigned. For each final rating, evidence (journals, lesson plans, conversations with supervisors) was used to support the designation. A consensus model was used for each rating.

After each Fellow had been rated on all five categories, results were entered into a database. Fellows were then sorted according to their 5 ratings into categories of those exceeding expectations, (preponderance of 4s), those meeting expectation, (mostly 3s), those struggling but progressing, (some 3's, mostly 2's) and those performing below expectations, (1's and 2's only).

Once sorted, career changers (cc) were then separated from recent college graduates (rcg). Focusing in on each sub-group, (cc performing below expectations, rcg performing below expectations, etc) patterns were identified among members of each group and profiles were created. These profiles were developed based on observations of Fellows teaching and through interviews with them, their mentors, their supervisors and staff developers, their journals (a program requirement) and the work submitted for their methods courses.

# Findings

Of the 26 career changers, 11 were exceeding expectations and 11 were below expectations. Two were meeting expectations and 2 were approaching expectations. While career changers congregated at the ends of the spectrum, recent college graduates tended to be more evenly distributed. Of 30 recent college graduates, 10 were exceeding expectations, 9 were meeting expectations, 4 were struggling but progressing and 7 were performing below expectations. Focusing in on each sub-group and drawing on our discussion of their ratings, we identified patterns amongst members of each sub-group. The differences in these patterns suggest that cc and rcg are two distinct groups that present different strengths and face different problems.

# Career-Changers

## CAREER-CHANGERS PERFORMING BELOW EXPECTATIONS

Three of the key issues that defined the first year experiences of under performing career changers were: a casual interest in teaching rather than a passionate one, alienation from students and difficulty adjusting to life in schools or rigidity.

### Casual Interest in Teaching

Many cc performing below expectations came to the program because they needed a job, not because they had a desire to teach. One Fellow admitted that he had been unemployed for more than two years and was ready to try anything when he applied to the program. Several other low-performing career changers were motivated by necessity as well. At least three others were unemployed, and another two were only employed sporadically over the last two years. One admitted that she applied to the Fellows program because it was easier than pounding the pavement. Others may also have had employment problems but simply did not disclose this information. In addition, two others were drawn to the short hours and long vacations rather than a desire to teach. For more than half of these teachers, teaching was something they came to casually or because it presented a solution to a problem rather than out of serious interest in teaching.

### Alienation from Students

Eight of the eleven cc performing below expectations exhibited discomfort with their students and were unable to connect to them. Three have been disciplined for using abusive or inappropriate language, another for not responding to student behavior at all. In some of their classes, hostility between the teacher and students is palpable. In two of their classrooms, students yelled, "I hate you!" at the teacher while an observer was present. In the classrooms of two others, students regularly cursed at the teachers. Additionally, one cc admitted she was germ phobic and didn't want her students coming near her.

The tendency not to get along well with their students was a disturbing trend among this group. Given that the Teaching Fellows Program targets the city's neediest schools where students are overwhelmingly Black and Hispanic, some of the tension may be influenced by deeply rooted negative attitudes toward minority students. No teacher made any outwardly racist remarks or behaved in a way that indicated a conscious contempt for students based on their race. However, several spoke disparagingly of their students as "animals," and "unredeemable." Some also felt that the students didn't want to learn. Of the eleven cc performing below expectations, nine (82 percent) were white and two were black. Interestingly, of the eleven cc exceeding expectations, four were of Hispanic, two were black, one was Filipino and four were white. Six of these acknowledged that they were drawn to the program because it offered an opportunity to give back or help their communities. No underperforming career changer identified such motivation. Only one member of this group indicated that working with inner-city students was part of the appeal of the program. The estrangement many felt from their students may be informed by the social context in which they work and suggests serious implications for the recruitment and preparation of all teachers working in these contexts.

It should be noted that the summer program all participants completed included a significant amount of coursework examining the impact of race, class and culture on school experiences and asked teachers to explore their own attitudes, assumptions and experiences. However, as many scholars have noted, White teachers are influenced by deeply held societal beliefs about people of color and often resist the efforts of teacher educators to divest them of these beliefs (Cochran-Smith 1995; McIntyre, 1997). The career changers in this study bear out these findings.

### Difficulty Adjusting to Life in Schools/Rigidity

Many cc performing below expectations struggled with the flexibility to meet the demands of their schools. One Social Studies teacher could not adjust to teaching a literacy class, though he was offered significant support to do so. He shut down and became very depressed instead. Many have had run-ins with administrators because they insist on doing things their way instead of the way the school expects things to be done. After being told by his principal he was not implementing the school's literacy program, one Fellow said the program was "stupid." She assigned him to professional development, but he did not attend. Several others found themselves unable to implement the District's balanced literacy program comprised of a reading and writing workshop. These teachers insisted the literacy program did not work and focused on grammar drills and aspects of teaching English that were more familiar to them.

Regardless of their discipline, many career changers had difficulty adapting to the professional cultures of their schools. Further, this group as a whole was not able to implement strategies and ideas from their teacher education courses or staff development even when they expressed a desire to do so. One teacher critiqued his own lessons noting that they did not encourage critical thinking, were overloaded with facts and did not engage students. However, he consistently used the same format because he couldn't see himself doing otherwise. These findings are consistent with those of Sokal, Smith and Mowat (2003) who found that older participants in an AC program were more rigid in their perceptions of classroom management and less open to change their attitudes. This study suggests that this same rigidity impacts instruction as well.

## CAREER CHANGERS EXCEEDING EXPECTATIONS

In sharp contrast to those performing below expectations, cc exceeding expectations consistently demonstrated a number of valuable traits that have helped them be successful. Their motivation for entering teaching was strong, and they demonstrated an ability to draw on professional behaviors developed elsewhere and an ability to synthesize new ideas into teaching practice.

### *Strong Motivation for Teaching*

Many of those cc exceeding expectations for first-year teachers had thought about being teachers for some time before applying to the Teaching Fellows and had very strong reasons for doing so. Several admitted they had wanted to be teachers when they were younger but had not had the opportunity or had been talked out of it because of the low pay and low status. Eight of the 11 teachers in this group specifically wanted to teach in underserved urban schools because of their own experiences, both positive and negative, as people of color in the public school system or as part of their commitment to social justice. Many of these participants left higher paying positions to become teachers. In general, these teachers made a decision to teach based on lifelong ambitions and passions and were drawn to the Teaching Fellows Program specifically because it targeted the populations they wanted to serve.

### Strong Professional Behaviors

All cc exceeding expectations had been successful in their previous careers and brought high levels of confidence to their work as teachers. They also brought a host of professional behaviors that served them well in their schools. They generally addressed problems quickly and directly. For example, one of these Fellows was upset that her program was changed mid-year, requiring additional planning and the loss of a class with which she was successful. She immediately spoke to her principal about her concerns and was able to negotiate a staff developer three days a week to help her with the new class and additional pay to continue working with the class slated to be taken away. Many teachers in the program faced drastic program changes and those performing above expectations generally adapted well, while those who were performing below expectations tended to be unable to recover.

In addition to good problem-solving and negotiating skills, successful cc tended to be well organized. Several of these teachers had planned their first unit ahead of time. One had already planned a field trip, and others had reading and writing folders already organized prior to the first day of class. All of these teachers had well-organized records, structured assignments clearly and followed up on student work and behavior.

Cc exceeding expectations for new teachers also drew on their professional experience in a number of idiosyncratic ways as well. Some had come from careers where they were responsible for organizing the efforts of a number of people and clearly transferred those skills to their classrooms. One was a librarian and used these skills to find rich materials for his classroom and shared a lot of information with his peers as well. Another with a theater background began a theater program in her school. These teachers tended to draw directly on their previous careers as well as on the underlying skills that had made them successful.

### Ability to Synthesize Newly Learned Theories and Skills into Practice

One of the most interesting findings of this study was that the Fellows who were doing well their first year of teaching (cc and rcg) generally had a much more positive attitude toward their teacher education programs and staff development. These teachers drew regularly on their teacher education and professional development opportunities and adapted them to the particular circumstances of their classes. More important than their openness to the strategies and activities modeled in their classes was that they were able to use them in a purposeful way, not merely to get through the next day. During one session of a methods class for English and Social Studies teachers, the instructor asked them to write about one thing they had taken from this class and used in their classrooms. Several underperforming teachers complained that they were not able to use anything they learned in their university coursework because their students wouldn't or couldn't do the kinds of activities modeled in class. Those who were doing well in the classroom read off long lists of things they had taken from their coursework and found very helpful. These teachers also were generally enthusiastic about staff development opportunities and found that these were also valuable sources of ideas for their classrooms. These high performing teachers were open to new ideas, and were able to adapt them to the specific needs of their classes.

# Recent College Graduates

Recent college graduates and career changers performing similarly shared some commonalities. Like their cc counterparts, recent graduates who were performing above expectations also possessed strong organization and interpersonal skills and synthesized their teacher education and professional development well. Further, though some rcg admitted that the ease of the application or the short hours drew them to the program, most, regardless of how they performed, were attracted to teaching as a career. However, though cc performing below expectations share some similarities with similarly performing rcg, the profiles of the two groups are actually quite different. Particularly, rcg struggle with issues of identity, authority and control, which generally did not provoke anxiety from cc. Most rcg struggle to make the transition from being students to being teachers, but those who perform below expectations are unable to do this effectively and quickly.

## RECENT COLLEGE GRADUATES PERFORMING BELOW EXPECTATIONS

### Playing at Being Teacher/Difficulties in Transitions

Many rcg were plagued by the anxiety that they were not "real" teachers. Their lack of professional experience and their youth made several of them insecure and was particularly noticeable in those who had no work experience. Many struggled to see themselves as the teacher and began altering their appearance to make themselves look more grown up shortly after school began. For example, a number of young men wore ties; a number of young women got their hair cut into more professional and shorter hairstyles. Further, several rcg expressed discomfort at being referred to by their last names.

Rcg performing below expectations were less able to transition from the role of being a student to that of being a teacher. Five of the seven performing below expectations had trouble developing a teaching identity. For example, two were more focused on the appearance of serious teaching—that the students are well behaved, that the teacher is in control—than on the actual substance of their lessons. Hence, one organized his teaching around charts he expected his students to copy. Not much thinking was going on when students were copying, but it looked like serious work. Interestingly, no cc expressed anxieties about taking on the role of teacher.

### Insecurity with Authority

For some low performing recent college graduates the difficulty in transitioning roles also created insecurity about their authority. Two of the seven responded to this insecurity by being obsessed with control in their classes. One occasionally got into physical scuffles with students over their refusal to obey him. He also constantly lectured his students about their behavior, often at the expense of actual curricular content. Two other struggling rcg sought to be loved by their students rather than feared. The teachers who wanted to be feared have images of authority that are grounded in control while those who wanted to be loved drew on images of authority that are maternal or friendship based and thus sought these kinds of relationships with their students. Those focused on control worried that students would only behave if they were sufficiently intimidated by the teacher. Those focused on emotional connections perceived that students will behave if they like their teachers. These teachers often felt personally rejected by student misbehavior. Schmidt and Knowles (1995) found similar patterns holding for unsuccessful student teachers suggesting that issues of appropriate authority in the classroom may need more exploration in teacher education. Additionally, several underperforming rcg had trouble asserting any authority in the classroom at all and were readily ignored by their students. Notably, rcg meeting and exceeding expectations are able to assert authority without drawing on either extreme.

# Conclusions

Though rcg and cc in the program shared many commonalities, differences between the two groups emerged, especially among those who were performing below expectations. Particularly, career changers did not struggle with taking on a teaching identity or with authority, but struggled with adapting to school cultures and relating to children—areas in which rcg had less trouble.

The differences amongst cc were quite striking as well. Cc tended to perform at the extremes either far below expectations or far above them. Moreover, strong indicators of who will be successful among cc emerged: strong motivation to teach and previous professional success. All of the cc performing above expectations came to teaching with a desire to serve in underserved schools, a desire to create a more just world or a great desire to be a teacher. Eight of the 11 cc performing below expectations were drawn to the program because of employment problems rather than to positive aspects of teaching.

Second, those who were successful in their previous careers were much more likely to bring that success to the classroom. However, those who were not highly effective in their previous positions were not likely to be highly effective teachers either. Cc performing above expectations generally left higher paying positions where they were quite successful. The same work ethic, professional skills and positive attitude that supported them in previous careers supports them in teaching as well.

The assumptions programs like the Teaching Fellows make about cc are somewhat supported by this study. However, the mistake these programs make is to assume that anyone changing careers was successful in their previous career and that they are changing careers because they are drawn to teaching. Cc are just as likely to lack the very skills, attitudes and desires that make them appealing as a group as they are to have them. We can further improve AC programs by being aware of the qualities of successful participants and using these profiles in the selection process. For example, AC programs targeting cc should seek concrete evidence of previous success and commitment to teaching through recommendations, portfolios, and more careful screening processes.

AC programs also need to address some of these issues through their program structure. This study demonstrates that career changers and recent college graduates face different obstacles in their first-year teaching and that more attention needs to be paid to these differences in the programs designed to serve them. Currently, both groups participate in identical programs.

The current economic outlook in cities like New York may push more unemployed people toward teaching. An article in the *Daily News* (February 9, 2003) proclaimed that "a huge factor in the program's popularity is the fact that so many New Yorkers are up a raging river job wise." The article also offered the statements from many prospective fellows emphasizing that they were there because they had lost jobs. This pool may prove to be full of talented teachers, but the data presented here suggests that the Teaching Fellows Program needs to proceed with caution. The program expects to turn away thousands of applicants this year. Tuning the selection process to be more attentive to the profiles of success outlined above may enable the program to select a stronger teacher corps.

This study also raises questions about the structure of Alternative Certification programs like the Teaching Fellows. The seven-week intensive coursework prior to teaching may not be enough time for cc to confront their rigidity and to become more interested in children. It may also not allow rcg enough time to make the transition to a professional identity. Further, all teachers, but particularly those from different cultural, racial and class backgrounds from the students they will serve, may need more time to identify and confront their own anxieties around race and class. Alienation from students, which was widely present amongst cc not meeting expectations and was not as noted in any other sub-group, may be veiled or unconscious racism. Though discussion of such issues was an important part of the summer program, there was certainly not enough to enable Fellows to confront deeply embedded assumptions they had about inner-city schools and children of color. This study indicates that those specifically drawn to teaching in the inner-city may have already done some of this exploration and are therefore better AC candidates than those who have other reasons for entering such programs.

Finally, this exploration suggests that quality teachers are entering the most poorly served schools through programs like the Teaching Fellows. Of the 56 participants in this AC program, 32 were meeting or exceeding expectations while 24 were performing below expectations in the first year. We need to do better. Drawing on the profiles of success indicated in this study, AC programs can more effectively recruit second-career professionals by putting more emphasis on motivation for teaching and previous professional success. Programs that prepare these candidates for the classroom need to be better tailored to the needs of cc and rcg. Further, teachers may need more time to overcome some of the attitudinal obstacles they face. This study raises questions about the timeframe employed by the Teaching Fellows Program (as outlined by the state's regulations for alternative certification). If these programs are to strengthen those alternative certification candidates who struggle to meet expectations their first year of teaching, they need to consider what it may take to prepare teachers to work with students quite different than themselves.

# References

Berry, B. (2001). No shortcuts to preparing good teachers. *Educational Leadership 58*(8), 32–36.

Chapelle, N. and Eubanks, S. (2001). Defining alternative certification and nontraditional routes to teaching: Similarities, differences, and standard of quality. *Teaching Change, 8*(4), 307–16.

Cochran-Smith, M. (1995). Color blindness and basket making are not the answers: Confronting the dilemmas of race, culture, and language diversity in teacher education. *American Educational Research Journal, 32(3),* 493–522.

Darling-Hammond, L. (2000). *Solving the dilemmas of teacher supply, demand, and standards: How we can ensure a competent, caring, and qualified teacher for every child.* New York: National Commission on Teaching and America's Future.

Dill, V. and Stafford, D. (1992). The Alternate route: Texas finds success. *Educational Leadership.* 50(1), 73–74.

Finn C. and Madigan, K. (2001) Removing the barriers for teacher candidates. *Educational Leadership 58*(8), 29–36.

Goodnough, A. (2000, July 2). Wanted: bored professionals who have teaching in mind. *The New York Times,* A19.

Homes, B. J. (2001). Understanding the pros and cons of alternative routes to teacher certification. *Teaching and Change 8 (4),* 317–330.

McIntyre, A. (1997). Constructing an image of a white teacher. *Teachers College Record 98*(4), 653–81.

McIntyre J. (2002). Emerging trends in teacher education. *Mid-Western Educational Researcher,* 15(1), 26–30.

Miller, J. W., McKenna, M. C., and McKenna, B. A. (1998). A Comparison of Alternatively and Traditionally Prepared Teachers. *Journal of Teacher Education.* May/June, 1998.

Peske, H., Liu, E., Johnson, S. M., Kauffman, D., and Kardos, S. M. (2001). The next generation of teachers: Changing conceptions of a career in teaching. *Phi Delta Kappan,* 83(4), 304–11.

Schmidt, M., and Knowles, G. (1995) Four women's stories of "failure" as beginning teachers. *Teaching and Teaching Education, 11*(5), 429–44.

Shen, J. (2000). The impact of the alternative certification policy: Multiple perspectives. In J. McIntyre and D. Byrd (Eds.), *Research on Effective Models for Teacher Education. Teacher Education Yearbook VIII* (pp. 235–247). Thousand Oaks, CA: Corwin.

Sokal, L., Smith, D. G., and Mowat, H. (2003) Alternative Certification teachers' attitudes toward classroom management. *The High School Journal, 86*(3), 8-16.

*Some Really Good Fellows.* (n.d.). Retrieved Sunday, February 9, 2003 from http://www.nydailynews.com.

Wise, A. and Darling-Hammond, L. (1992) Alternative certification as an oxymoron. *The Education Digest, 57*(8), 46.

# CHAPTER 6

# The Performance of Candidates in an Alternative Certification Program

*Larry Freeman*
Governors State University

*Karen Peterson*
Governors State University

*Debra Erikson*
University of Illinois–UC

Larry Freeman, PhD, is Chair (retired) of the Division of Education, Governors State University. His research interests include alternative certification and educator dispositions.

Karen Peterson, Ed.D, is a University Professor in Education, Director of the Beginning Teacher Program and Director of GSU Alternative Certification Partnership at Governors State University. Her research interests include alternative certification and mentoring.

Debra Erikson is a doctoral student at University of Illinois–UC. She is currently researching alternative certification programs.

## ABSTRACT

This chapter analyzes the assessment of candidates in an alternative certification program that has been in operation for four years. The research explores the candidates' performance from two perspectives: (1) the use of multiple measures in assessing candidates at four gateways during the preparation program and (2) comparison of principal evaluations of program completers and comparable traditionally prepared teachers working in the same setting. Assessment results show that dispositions rather than teaching skills or knowledge are the most frequent cause of less than satisfactory ratings. Analysis of the principal evaluations indicates no significant difference in the performance of alternatively and traditionally prepared teachers. These results lead to identifying issues that are briefly explored in this chapter: dispositions in teacher preparation, judging the performance of teacher education programs, and need for further development of teacher assessment technology.

# Introduction

Since its inception in 2000–2001, the Governors State University Alternative Certification Partnership has recommended 59 candidates for the Illinois initial state elementary certificate. These teachers were prepared to work in one of nine school districts serving some 20,000 students, mostly students in grades one through eight. In these districts, percentages of minority students among the districts range from 64 to 100 percent. African American students account for 76 percent of all students. In four districts, Hispanic students account for between 10 and 30 percent of the student populations. The percentage of low-income among the districts ranges from 34 to 99 percent; in the aggregate, 67 percent of all students are classified as low income.

# Purpose of Study

The purpose of this study was to examine how well the alternative certification candidates completing this program were prepared to begin teaching and how successful they are as teachers. The specific questions were: (1) how well did candidates perform when assessed against explicit performance standards by an Assessment Committee comprised of university and school personnel and (2) how does the teaching performance of alternatively and traditionally prepared teachers compare.

# Review of Research

Researchers who have examined alternative certification programs have suggested that difficulties in definitions and methodologies abound. Legler (2002) attributed these difficulties to the "fact that a variety of methodologies has been used to study A[lternative] C[ertification] programs, a variety of outcome variables has been examined, and a variety of operational definitions has been used to define variables" (p. 8). As a result of using different methodologies and assumptions, controversy tends to emerge over the meaning of research findings. Darling-Hammond (1994) and her colleagues have voiced their reservations regarding alternative certification programs and have used Teach for America, a nationwide alternative certification program, as an example of shortcomings in alternative certification programs. On the other hand, quantitative studies of Teach for America have not always supported the conclusions of its critics. In one study, Kopp (2000) examined the ratings of Teach For America (TFA) teachers by the principals who supervised them. TFA teachers were rated as "good" or "excellent" on 23 indicators of successful teaching by over 90 percent of the principals surveyed. Another study examined the effectiveness of TFA teachers in the Houston school system on student achievement as compared to other teachers. The results of this research suggested that students of TFA teachers achieved at slightly higher (although not statistically significantly higher) levels than the students of other teachers (Raymond, Fletcher and Luque, 2001).

Legler (2002) concluded that "those who have lost faith in the ability of higher education programs to adequately prepare teacher candidates (such as Haberman, 1991) look for evidence that supports alternative certification, while those with an interest in maintaining the traditional (but strengthened) model of teacher education [such as Darling-Hammond, Wise, and Klein, 1999] look for deficits in the alternative model" (22). Frederick Hess' (2002) response to a study of the impact of Teach For America and other non-traditionally certificated teachers by Laczko-Kerr, and Berliner (2002) illustrates Legler's observation. Hess describes the Laczko study as "the kind of methodologically problematic research that gives so much education scholarship a bad name" (p. 1) and concludes with these stinging criticisms: "It appears that the scholars in this case either did not recognize major analytic concerns or chose to ignore them. In either case, one would normally expect that the referees at a scholarly journal would catch points of such obvious concern and address them" (p. 2).

Zeichner and Shulte (2001) detail concerns and flaws in studies of alternative certification. They observe that:

> the issue of alternative teacher certification programs has been one of the most controversial and confusing topics in the discourse about U.S. teacher education during the past 20 years. [The confusion arises from the] problematic nature of the research that has been conducted on alternative programs . . . [and] . . . from the lack of clarity over the definition of an alternative program. (p. 266)

As a result of their review of 21 studies of 13 alternative certification programs, the authors conclude that "the peer-reviewed research examined in this article tells us some things about the efficacy of alternative certification programs" (p. 278). They conclude, for instance, that the research regarding the teaching competence of alternatively certified teachers based on classroom observations is "very weak." At best, they say "it shows that alternatively certified teachers are as competent as traditionally certified teachers under some conditions" (p. 277).

Perhaps the most rigorous research comparing alternatively and traditionally prepared teachers is the study conducted by Miller, McKenna, and McKenna (1998). In this study, the researchers matched each of 41 graduates of Georgia Southern's alternative certification program with a traditionally trained teacher working in the same middle schools. All 82 subjects had three years' experience. When evaluations of their teaching and student test scores for both cohorts were compared, there were no significant differences.

# Description of the Governors State University Program

The Governors State University Alternative Certification Partnership sponsors a program leading to the Illinois initial elementary certificate. It has an urban focus and was developed in response to state requirements stipulating that candidates have a minimum of a bachelor's degree and five years of work experience. The selection process results in roughly one in three applicants being admitted into the program. In addition to submitting documents such as transcripts and letters verifying work experience, candidates take several tests, and complete the Star Teacher Selection Interview (Haberman, 1995). To be accepted into the program, candidates must present an employment contract with a participating district. Candidates begin classes in March and complete sixteen credit hours of professional education coursework before beginning their internship in August. Mentors support candidates throughout their internship. In-district mentors, trained by the University, spend at least one half day per week co-teaching and co-planning with candidates. University mentors supplement the work of district mentors. For instance, if a candidate does not remediate difficulties within a couple of weeks, University mentors work directly with that candidate to resolve the problem. Candidates complete the program in 16 months, which includes coursework prior to, during and after full-time teaching during an academic year. The coursework and required experiences address all of the objectives outlined in the University's traditional elementary preparation program, including those for general education.

The program's Assessment Committee, comprised of representatives from the University and participating districts, assesses and evaluates candidates using a performance-based model. In making its assessments, the Committee reviews multiple measures, including university supervisor and principal evaluations, grades, portfolios, and faculty assessments of knowledge, skills, and dispositions to assess whether candidates have met performance standards at each of four gateways throughout the program. The first assessment occurs after the candidate has completed five required courses comprising Cores I and II of the program. The second and third assessments occur at the end of each semester during the candidate's first year of teaching. While teaching, candidates complete a required Reflective Teaching seminar course each semester. The final assessment occurs after a summer session in which the candidate completes a required seminar course and any other coursework that the Assessment Committee may have determined a candidate needed to address weaknesses in teaching performance. The fourth and final assessment is summative and assesses the candidate's performance throughout the program.

At each of the four gateways, the Committee has made one of three determinations regarding the performance of each candidate: satisfactory, satisfactory with concern, or unsatisfactory. To be recommended for certification, the candidate must be rated "satisfactory." For an example of items reviewed at a particular gateway, see Appendix A.

# Methodology

To respond to the first question of how well candidates perform when assessed against explicit performance standards by the Assessment Committee, the ratings and decisions made by the Assessment Committee were reviewed and analyzed. In three successive years, there have been three cohorts totaling 64 candidates. The information used in responding to the second question of how the teaching performance of alternatively prepared teachers (APTs) compares with the teaching performance of traditionally prepared teachers (TPTs) was drawn from principal evaluations of candidates in their second or third year of teaching and principal evaluations of similarly situated teachers who completed traditional teacher education programs. There were 43 APTs in their second or third year of teaching. The superintendent of each of the participating districts provided evaluations of both kinds of teachers following the directions outlined in Appendix B. These directions detailed how the TPT was to be identified and provided that in problematic cases, the superintendent and the program director were to confer about how to determine appropriate TPTs. For instance, if an APT was teaching at the kindergarten level and there was no comparable TPT with the same or even similar teaching experience teaching kindergarten in that building, an appropriate TPT teaching at the primary level might be identified. In 13 cases, no comparable TPTs could be identified.

Each of the districts used a different instrument to guide and record evaluations. Because of these differences, there was no attempt to compare candidates and teachers across districts. The number of categories in any one instrument ranged from four to nine and the number of items under categories varied significantly from one instrument to another. A summary of the categories found in each of the evaluation instruments is presented in table 6.1. While it was tempting to collapse the various categories used on the instruments into generalized categories, each instrument had several items under each category. Examination of these items indicated that there was no way to cleanly separate the categories into generalized categories without distorting the ratings. As a result, no effort was made to generalize findings to the district or partnership level.

Each of the evaluation instruments used by the districts in this comparison used a three-point rating system: excellent, satisfactory, and unsatisfactory. These ratings were recorded as 2, 1, and 0, respectively, in order to permit calculation of averages. In some cases the principal provided an overall rating for each

**Table 6.1    Categories Used in District Evaluation Instruments**

| Evaluation Category | District[1] | | | | | |
|---|---|---|---|---|---|---|
| Use of Preparation Time | | | | D | | |
| Planning & Organization | | B | C | D | E | F |
| Instruction | A | B | | D | E | F |
| Assessment | | | C | | E | |
| Knowledge of Content | | | C | D | E | |
| Student Involvement | | | | D | | |
| Record Keeping | | | | D | | |
| Knowledge of Student Development | | | C | | | |
| Social development | | | C | | | |
| Student Relationships | A | B | | | | |
| Classroom Management | A | B | C | D | E | F |
| Classroom Climate | | B | C | | E | |
| Classroom Control | | | | D | | |
| Personal | | | | | | F |
| Non-instruction | | | | | E | |
| Cooperating With Colleagues | | B | C | | | |
| Professional | A | B | C | | | |
| Parent Relationships | A | B | | | | |
| Number of Categories | 5 | 8 | 9 | 8 | 7 | 4 |

[1]District identifiers are the same as in table 6.4.

category; if not, an average rating for each category was derived by calculating the mean average of the ratings for the items within that category. An overall mean average for each teacher was then calculated from these category averages.

# Results

Table 6.2 summarizes the actions of the Assessment Committee following its determinations regarding the extent to which candidates were meeting program standards. Since each of 64 candidates was rated four times, there were a total of 256 ratings. Approximately 22 percent of all ratings were "satisfactory with concerns" or "unsatisfactory" at some time during the assessment process. The highest percentages of these ratings were given in the first two ratings, 25 percent after completion of initial coursework and 34 percent after the first semester of teaching. Even after the second semester, the percentage of unsatisfactory ratings was about 8 percent. Summative ratings of unsatisfactory accounted for more than 6 percent of the ratings.

Table 6.3 provides an analysis of the reasons for the Assessment Committee's actions. These data were developed by reviewing the minutes of the Assessment Committee, which describe the Committee's actions and, if not the exact reason for the action, the kind of remediation required. These data indicate that when candidates were rated less than satisfactory, the cause in 60 percent of the cases was not undeveloped skills or knowledge, but candidates' dispositions. Of the four candidates who completed all components of the program and were given a summative rating of unsatisfactory, three received the ratings solely because of dispositional problems and the other exhibited problems related to both skills and dispositions. Data used to assess dispositions are provided by faculty and supervisors who review such areas as professional behavior, appreciation of human diversity, commitment to collaboration with colleagues and parents,

**Table 6.2   Assessment Committee's Assessment of Candidates**

| Cohort | n | 1st Assmt | | | 2nd Assmnt | | | 3rd Assmnt | | | 4th Assmnt | | | Total | | |
|---|---|---|---|---|---|---|---|---|---|---|---|---|---|---|---|---|
| | | $S^1$ | SC | U | S | SC | U | S | SC | U | S | SC | U | S | SC | U |
| 1 | 25 | 21 | 3 | 1 | 17 | 2 | 6 | 19 | 4 | 2 | 23 | 0 | 2 | 80 | 9 | 11 |
| 2 | 18 | 16 | 2 | 0 | 11 | 6 | 1 | 15 | 1 | 2 | 16 | 0 | 2 | 58 | 9 | 5 |
| 3 | 21 | 11 | 10 | 0 | 14 | 7 | 0 | 16 | 4 | 1 | 21 | 0 | 0 | 62 | 21 | 1 |
| Total | 64 | 48 | 15 | 1 | 42 | 15 | 7 | 50 | 9 | 5 | 60 | 0 | 4 | 200 | 39 | 17 |
| % | | 75 | 23 | 2 | 66 | 23 | 11 | 78 | 14 | 8 | 94 | 0 | 6 | 78 | 15 | 7 |

$^1$S = Satisfactory; SC = Satisfactory with concerns; U = Unsatisfactory.

**Table 6.3  Summary of Assessment Committee's Reasons for Satisfactory with Concerns or Unsatisfactory Ratings[1]**

| Cohort | Total Candidates | No. Rated Below Satisfactory | Percentage Rated Below Satisfactory | Percentage of Reasons for Ratings Below Satisfactory | |
|---|---|---|---|---|---|
| | | | | Academic | Disposition |
| 1 | 25 | 10 | 40% | 40% | 60% |
| 2 | 18 | 7 | 39% | 29% | 71% |
| 3 | 21 | 14 | 66% | 36% | 64% |
| Total | 64 | 31 | 48% | 37% | 63% |

[1]The number of ratings below satisfactory includes all candidates who were rated as less than satisfactory at any of the gateways. To be recommended for certification a candidate must be rated satisfactory at Gateway 4.

commitment to ethical behavior, and commitment to life-long learning. Other areas reviewed by the committee include attendance and punctuality, payment of fees, and response to program requests. Candidates with recurrent disposition issues may be required to take a workshop, the Professional Educator, during the second summer of the program during which dispositional issues are addressed.

Table 6.4 presents the results of comparing the principal evaluations of the 30 pairs of APTs and TPTs described above. The table lists the average score for each type of teacher in the pair and shows the difference in the average scores by subtracting the TPT average score from the average score for the APT teacher. In 13 pairs, the TPTs have a higher score. There is no difference in scores for six pairs. In 12 pairs, the APTs received a higher rating than the traditionally prepared teacher. Among the pairs in which the TPT were rated higher than the APT, the average difference in average scores was 0.31. Among pairs in which APTs were rated higher, the average difference was 0.44.

There are variations in the ratings among and within districts. For instance, in District A, of the eight pairs, seven of the TPTs have higher averages than APTs. But in District C, in five of the eight pairs, APTs have higher ratings. In District B, in five out of seven cases, there is no difference in ratings. And in District E all alternatively prepared teachers have higher ratings. Explanations for these patterns are not readily apparent and suggest the need for further analysis.

# Implications for Teachers and Teacher Educators

The assessment of teacher candidates in standards-driven, performance-based teacher education programs is likely to focus increased attention on dispositions,

**Table 6.4  Comparison of Performance of Alternatively and Traditionally Prepared Candidates**

| District | Average Ratings on Annual Evaluation | | Difference |
| | Alternatively Prepared | Traditionally Prepared | |
|---|---|---|---|
| A | 1.3 | 1.9 | -0.6 |
| A | 1.3 | 1.7 | -0.4 |
| A | 1.0 | 1.4 | -0.4 |
| A | 1.4 | 1.6 | -0.2 |
| A | 1.4 | 1.5 | -0.1 |
| A | 1.1 | 1.2 | -0.1 |
| A | 1.8 | 1.7 | 0.1 |
| B | 1.8 | 2.0 | -0.2 |
| B | 1.9 | 2.0 | -0.1 |
| B | 2.0 | 2.0 | 0.0 |
| B | 1.8 | 1.8 | 0.0 |
| B | 2.0 | 2.0 | 0.0 |
| B | 2.0 | 2.0 | 0.0 |
| B | 2.0 | 2.0 | 0.0 |
| C | 1.4 | 2.0 | -0.6 |
| C | 1.4 | 1.9 | -0.5 |
| C | 1.3 | 1.7 | -0.4 |
| C | 2.0 | 1.9 | 0.1 |
| C | 2.0 | 1.8 | 0.2 |
| C | 2.0 | 1.8 | 0.2 |
| C | 1.1 | 0.7 | 0.4 |
| C | 1.2 | 0.6 | 0.6 |
| D | 2.0 | 1.3 | 0.7 |
| E | 1.1 | 1.1 | 0.0 |
| E | 1.3 | 1.1 | 0.2 |
| E | 1.7 | 1.3 | 0.4 |
| E | 2.0 | 1.1 | 0.9 |
| E | 2.0 | 1.0 | 1.0 |
| F | 0.9 | 1.2 | -0.3 |
| F | 1.9 | 2.0 | -0.1 |
| Total | 1.6 | 1.6 | 0.0 |

perhaps giving equal weight to assessment of dispositions along with the knowledge and skills that have traditionally been the focus of candidate assessment. Moreover, this study like several others, suggests that continued attempts to show either alternative or traditional programs as superior should be largely abandoned and energy should be devoted to determining what specific characteristics of both program types are related to preparing successful teachers. Finally, the technology for assessing teaching performance, both formative and summative, is very much in formative development and requires continued refinement.

## THE MATTER OF DISPOSITIONS

The concept of dispositions in teacher preparation and assessment has considerable potential as a means for capturing, analyzing, and changing patterns of behavior engaged in by teacher candidates. Of particular concern are those patterns that actively retard or promote student learning. However the rudimentary character of our understanding of dispositions becomes obvious when confronted with actual cases of problems in teaching performance. Rather than viewing dispositions as a series of statements about desired ways of behaving that may or may not be responsive to particular situations, the focus needs to be moved to assisting the teacher to adopt different dispositions in the classroom in an attempt to create the most effective fit between and among the teacher and students. The same may be true for working with colleagues or superiors. It appears that development of such an understanding of dispositions might best be evolved by using theories of human development that consider cognitive and personal development together. One such model was developed by David E. Hunt (1974). He and his colleagues describe this approach as one in which "persons are characterized on the CL [Conceptual Level] dimension that ranges from a very concrete level at which the person is unsocialized and capable of only very simple information processing to a complex stage where the person is self-responsible and capable of processing and organizing information in a complex fashion" (p. 221). Oja (1990) provides additional direction for this inquiry: "The work in developmental theory has powerful implications for teacher education and staff development. Teachers at higher, more complex stages of human development appear as more effective in classrooms than their peers at lower stages" (p. 3). In her work she has addressed the question: "If there was strong support for the idea that teachers at higher developmental levels are more effective in managing classrooms and meeting individual needs of students, then can we create an educational program designed to promote such development?" (p. 3).

The GSU program is beginning its work in this area by using the Hunt conceptual development test with its current cohort of students. In addition, the GSU program is beginning to examine the work of Parker Palmer (1998) who raises the question "How can the teacher's selfhood become a legitimate topic in education and in our public dialogues on educational reform?" (p. 3). More specifically, the question is whether personal identity and integrity, as articulated by Palmer, are among the sources of dispositions. From a more practical point of view, it appears that teacher educators must move from the current, rough-and-ready understandings of dispositions to more sophisticated conceptions which support analysis of what patterns of teacher behavior frustrate or promote student learning in a specific classroom and demonstration of how best to assist the teacher to adopt the desired patterns of behavior.

## JUDGING TEACHER PREPARATION PROGRAMS

Two principles appear necessary to move toward deeper understanding of how to judge the merits of teacher preparation programs: (1) emphasis on progress, not perfection, and (2) an acceptance of diversity among teacher education programs. When non-traditional approaches of teacher education are proposed and implemented, historically the profession's response has often been one of suspicion and often an uninformed conclusion that the non-traditional approach cannot be as good as or better than the traditional approach. Underlying this characteristic response is an assumption that one kind of program, in this case traditional programs, are the ultimate model of preparation. The case, however, appears to be that both traditional and alternative programs are attempting to focus on continuous improvement and this is where the emphasis should be.

The program from which the data for this study was derived is specifically focused on preparing teachers for a group of districts that share many features of urban schools. Other teacher education programs sponsored by the same University do not have such a specific focus; these programs attempt to prepare teachers for not only these same districts but also for some wealthier and non-minority communities in the Chicago metropolitan area. Evidence about the performance of these more traditional programs (e.g., NCATE accreditation) appears to suggest they would be judged by most raters as doing a good to excellent job. Attempting to demonstrate that one kind of program is superior to another in this context appears to serve no one. There is likely a wide range of quality in both traditional and alternative programs, and perhaps alternative programs offer specific advantages such as responding directly to regional needs.

## TECHNOLOGY OF TEACHER ASSESSMENT

Major questions about the adequacy of assessment of pre- and in-service teachers have been in the foreground as this study was conducted. While the Assessment Committee used multiple measures in its holistic assessments, their predictive validity has not yet been significantly tested over several years. Moreover, because they represent virtually the only source of information about in-service teacher performance, principal evaluations were used as a primary source of evidence. Theories of teaching and assessment underlying the instruments and their use may be inadequate and there was likely considerable variation in the sophistication of the principals' skills in conducting the assessments. Significant progress in preparing teachers, whether alternatively or traditionally, will likely require moving beyond conventional reliance on numerical ratings which attempt to reduce the complex, multidimensional character of a particular individual's performance to a single symbol. This is particularly true with respect to assessing dispositions of teachers.

Ulhlenbeck, Verloop, and Beijaard (2002) provide concrete direction in addressing the issues raised by the current state of affairs in assessing teachers, beginning or experienced. They consider the relationship between what is known about teaching and what is known about assessment. This consideration results in the identification of what they term "implications" of research about teaching and assessment; they present fifteen such implications along with the issues related to each implication. For instance, one of the implications of research about teaching is that "the diversity of what teachers know and can do should be captured by the assessment and result in a differentiated profile" (p. 262).

The issue raised by this implication of research is "how to reach an overall decision: Are decisions based on compensation rules [i.e., consideration of the context in which the teacher works] or on minimum competence standards?" (p. 262). Finally Uhlenbeck and her colleagues outline a process for developing an assessment procedure that is responsive to the implications of research on teaching and assessment. This process, they suggest, is not only "a complex technical process but also, and perhaps even more so, a social process" (p. 268) that may require the development of new dispositions on the part of teacher educators.

# Conclusion

After four years of experience pursuing performance-based assessment—using multiple measures, focusing on standards, and engaging in focused discussion and analysis of candidates' performance—the GSU program has demonstrated that performance assessment is complex. The program's experience is that recommending or not recommending candidates based on performance rather than input contributes to better teachers in classrooms. Continued exploration of varied models of preparation and varied models of assessment to meet needs in diverse contexts will contribute to further understanding of this complex endeavor.

# References

Darling-Hammond, L. (1994). Who speaks for the children? How Teach for America hurts urban schools and students. *Phi Delta Kappan, 76*(1), 21–34.

Darling-Hammond, L., Wise, A., and Klein, S. (1999). *A license to teach: Raising standards for teaching.* San Francisco: Jossey-Bass.

Haberman, M. (1991, November 6). Catching up with reform in teacher education. *Education Week, 11*(10), 29–36.

Haberman, M. (1995) *Star teachers of children in poverty.* West Lafayette, IN: Kappa Delta Pi.

Hess, F. M. (2002). Advocacy in the guise of research: The Laczko-Kerr-Berliner study on teacher certification. In new teacher quality studies: Putting lipstick on a pig. *21st Century Schools Project Bulletin, 2*(18). Washington, D.C.: Progressive Policy Institute. Retrieved 5 October 2003, from http://www.ppionline.org/ppi_ci.cfm?knlgAreaID =110&subsecid=900001&cont e ntid=250847

Hunt, D. E. and Sullivan, E. V. (1974). *Between psychology and education.* Hinsdale, IL: Dryden Press.

Kopp, W. (2000). Ten years of Teach for America. *Education Week, 19*(41), 48–53.

Laczko-Kerr, I., and Berliner, D. C. (2002). The effectiveness of "Teach for America" and other under-certified teachers on student academic achievement: A case of harmful public policy, *Education Policy Analysis Archives, 10*(37). Retrieved 5 May 2003, from http://epaa.asu.edu/epaa/v10n37/.

Legler, R. (2002). *Alternative certification: A review of theory and research.* NCREL. Retrieved 10 October 2003, from http://www.ncrel.org/policy/pubs/html/altcert/ intro.htm.

Miller, J., McKenna, M., and McKenna, B. (1998). A comparison of alternately and traditionally prepared teachers. *Journal of Teacher Education, 49*(3), 165–76.

Oja, S. N. (1990, April). Developmental theories and the professional development of teachers. Paper presented at the Annual Meeting of the American Educational Research Association, Boston, MA.

Palmer, P. (1998). *The courage to teach.* San Francisco: Jossey-Bass, Inc.

Raymond, M., Fletcher, S., and Luque, J. (2001). *Teach for America: An evaluation of teacher differences and student outcomes in Houston, Texas.* Stanford, CA: CREDO

Uhlenbeck, A. M., Verloop, N., and Beijaard, D. (2002). Requirements for an assessment procedure for beginning teachers: Implications from recent theories on teaching and assessment. *Teachers College Record, 104*(2), 242–72.

Zeichner, K. M. and Schulte, A. K. (2001). What we don't know from peer reviewed research about alternative teacher certification programs. *Journal of Teacher Education, 52*(4), 266–82.

## APPENDIX A

# Governors State University
# ALTERNATIVE CERTIFICATION PARTNERSHIP
## Assessment Committee Record

# GATEWAY # 3 (following the winter semester)

Candidate _____ District _____ School _____

\_\_\_\_District Administrator evaluations

\_\_\_\_University Supervisor formative (2) and summative
evaluations

\_\_\_\_Evaluation of knowledge and skills by faculty

\_\_\_\_Evaluation of dispositions by faculty/staff

\_\_\_\_Evaluation of lesson plans

\_\_\_\_Evaluation of grade recording procedures

\_\_\_\_Portfolio entries

\_\_\_\_Course grade

\_\_\_\_Attendance record

\_\_\_\_Administrative issues:

    \_\_\_\_Financial obligations

    \_\_\_\_Registration

    \_\_\_\_Other:

**SCORING GUIDE**

$\checkmark$ = Good
$\checkmark$- = Fair
— = Poor

**Assessment Committee recommendation upon completion of Winter
semester of Core 3:**

\_\_\_\_Satisfactory Progress

\_\_\_\_Satisfactory Progress with some concerns

\_\_\_\_Unsatisfactory

    \_\_\_\_Workshop recommendations:

    \_\_\_\_Professional Educator

____Planning

____Classroom Management

____Technology


Conference Date: _____

Conference Date: _____
Remediation Plan Developed _____

## APPENDIX B

# Excerpts from
# Proposal for Evaluation of Performance of Alternatively Certificated Teachers Prepared by Governors State University Alternative Certification Partnership

Proposed procedural assumptions:

1. The identity of all teachers whose evaluations are included in this study and of all schools will be confidential. Results will be reported in such a way that identities cannot be inferred.
2. School principals will provide the research team with copies of the relevant evaluations. The research team will return copies given them to the school so they may be destroyed by the principal.
3. Because of differences in evaluation procedures, comparisons will be made only at the school level. There will be no attempt to generalize to a district or partnership level.
4. The Partnership participants will be compared against other teachers teaching in the same building, at the same grade level, and who have the same number of years' teaching experience.
5. In cases where there are no teachers meet the criteria listed in (4) above, the research team will consult with the Director of the Partnership, the principal, and the superintendent to determine if there are other teachers in the building or district who would serve as appropriate comparisons.

Here are proposed steps for carrying out this study:

1. Determining the schools in which participants in the Alternative Certification Partnership are teaching and/or have taught. Participants who may be teaching in non-partnership districts will be included in this study only for those years that they taught in partnership districts.
2. Identifying the teachers in those schools with whom Partnership participants are to be compared.
3. Examining and recording relevant information from evaluation forms for both Partnership participants and other teachers identified.
4. Aggregating data, both quantitative and qualitative. For the quantitative

data, the following procedure will be used. A quantitative score will be determined for each evaluation. For each dyad, the score for the comparison teacher will be subtracted from the score for the Partnership teacher. These differences will then be aggregated at the school, district, and partnership levels.

# CHAPTER 7

# Teach For America and Regularly Certified Teachers: Teacher Efficacy, Teaching Concerns, Career Aspirations, and Teaching Effectiveness

*Lorene C. Pilcher and Donald C. Steele*
Georgia State University

> Lorene C. Pilcher is Professor Emeritus, Department of Early Childhood Education, Georgia State University. She continues to conduct research in the areas of teacher development and program evaluation.

> Donald C. Steele is a research and statistical specialist in the Department of Early Childhood Education, Georgia State University. His research interests include teacher education and program evaluation.

## ABSTRACT

To assess the effects of training and experience on teachers, regularly certified first-year teachers (regular), Teach For America first-year teachers (TFA1), and Teach for America second-year teachers (TFA2) were compared on general and personal teacher efficacy, teaching concerns, and student achievement. Regular and TFA1 teachers were also compared on principals' ratings and career plans. Regular teachers were higher than TFA1 and TFA2 teachers on general teacher efficacy, and higher than TFA1, but not TFA2, teachers on personal teacher efficacy. Groups did not differ on self, task, and impact concerns. The regular teachers were higher than TFA1 teachers on achievement test classroom averages in reading, English/language arts, and mathematics. TFA2 teachers did not differ significantly from either regular or TFA1 teachers, and the TFA2 classroom averages fell between those of regular and TFA1 teachers. Regular and TFA1 teachers did not differ on principals' ratings or career plans.

# Objectives

One objective of this research is to ascertain whether teacher education and teaching experience affect teachers' feelings and their effectiveness in educating children. Three groups of teachers that teach in the same schools and differ on training and experience are compared on teacher efficacy, teaching concerns, and student achievement. Since this study compares first- and second-year Teach for America (TFA) teachers and first-year teachers from accredited teacher education programs, an additional objective is to provide a better understanding of the influence of the TFA model on teachers. An evaluation of TFA teachers not only provides insight into TFA's effectiveness but also yields information to university and school-based mentors for guiding the professional development of these teachers.

# Perspectives

Teach for America (TFA) is a national service corps of recent college graduates who commit to teaching for two years in low-income communities. Corps members, recruited from prestigious colleges, have majored in all academic areas, but few have had any teacher education. Recognizing that these recruits need training, TFA provided an intensive summer program for the entire group of recruits prior to dispersing them to school districts with which it has hiring agreements. TFA continues to support training for these teachers by securing help from teacher education programs in the locations in which they teach, and this training enables many recruits to complete state credentialing programs during their two years of service. TFA teachers have been the subject of numerous articles but few empirical studies. Arguments both for and against TFA have been so prolific that they have made their way into the popular press (e.g., Wilce, 2002).

# Teachers' Background Characteristics

## ACADEMIC POTENTIAL

Although no empirical comparison was found, TFA teachers are rumored to be superior in academic ability to teacher education graduates. Wendy Koop, founder of TFA, surmises that these bright young people could not be recruited into the classroom if they had to take much time to get prepared (cited in Darling-Hammond, 1994). She suggests that their superior intelligence and advanced knowledge of academic content provide them an advantage as teachers. However, the relationship between teachers' academic ability and the achievement of children in their classrooms is open to question. Goldhaber and Anthony (2003) presented data suggesting that college students majoring in areas other than education have greater academic potential than teacher education majors. However, they concluded from an extensive review that the few studies showing a relationship between teachers' academic proficiency and children's achievement are confounded by "measurement issues and issues of causality" (p. 18). Thus, even if TFA teachers are actually brighter than teachers from teacher education programs, this characteristic may not mean that they will be better teachers.

## TEACHER TRAINING AND CERTIFICATION

Goldhaber and Brewer (2000) stated that their data provided little evidence for requiring all teachers to have standard certification. However, Darling-Hammond, Berry, and Thoreson (2001) took issue with Goldhaber and Brewer's interpretation. They clearly believe that teacher education programs leading to standard certification give teachers an advantage. Darling-Hammond and Youngs (2002) provide a detailed account of the arguments against the teacher education requirement for teacher certification and present their responses to each one. Stoddart and Floden (1996) proposed that alternative and traditional routes to certification would produce teachers with different kinds of expertise, since the two paths place different amounts of emphasis on subject matter, pedagogy, and the role of personal experience.

According to Feistritzer and Chester (2002), TFA teachers should not be categorized as alternatively certified teachers. They state, "Teach for America is not an alternative teacher certification program" (p. 12) and point out that TFA teachers differ from participants in other alternative teacher preparation programs in numerous ways. They object to generalizing TFA data to alternatively certified teachers, indicating that this use of data is inappropriate, "since the program is not an alternate route program, and its participants only make a two-year commitment" (p. 12). However, even though the attrition rate has been shown to be high (Darling-Hammond, 1994), many TFA teachers do eventually become certified and remain in teaching or a related field in education (Wilce, 2002). Although arguments about whether teacher education enhances teacher performance are prolific (Goldhaber and Brewer, 2000; Darling-Hammond, Berry, and Thoreson, 2001; Tell, 2001), the few empirical studies of untrained teachers in general and TFA teachers in particular yield inconsistent results (Laczko-Kerr and Berliner, 2002; Raymond, Fletcher, and Luque, 2001).

## TEACHING EXPERIENCE

Koop states that "we really believe teachers are made through experience" (quoted in Darling-Hammond, 1994, p. 23). There is some evidence that teachers' experience does have a small effect on children's achievement. Rivkin, Hanushek, and Kain (2000) report that the effect of teacher experience on elementary school mathematics achievement is small but significant and that gains in teaching effectiveness tend to occur over the first few career years. After reviewing a large number of contradictory studies, Goldhaber and Anthony (2003, p. 16) concluded that the results "tilt in the direction of suggesting that experience actually is a predictor of teacher quality." They also concluded that the benefits of experience tend to occur in the first few years of teaching. These studies do not directly address TFA teachers. Whether teachers in general profit from experience is unclear, and whether TFA teachers in particular benefit from experience has not been studied. The TFA requirement that teachers remain in the same school district for 2 years affords the opportunity to evaluate the effects of early teaching experience on teachers' feelings and effectiveness.

# Teacher Outcome Characteristics

## EMOTIONAL QUALITIES

Schutz and Lanehart (2002) stated, "emotions are intimately involved in virtually every aspect of the teaching and learning process . . ." (p. 67). Teachers' emotions involve their feelings and perceptions about themselves, including feelings of efficacy (Taschannen-Moran, Hoy, and Hoy, 1998), concerns about various components of teaching, (Rogan, Borich, and Taylor, 1992), and moti-vational goals and intentions (Schutz and Lanehart, 2002). Although these par-ticular emotional qualities have not been compared for TFA teachers and their counterparts from teacher education programs, Darling-Hammond, Chung, and Frelow (2002) compared several groups of teachers in their first year of employment in New York City on their feelings of preparedness. They found that the teachers who graduated from teacher education programs felt better prepared to teach than TFA teachers. Teacher education graduates might also be expected to feel more efficacious and less concerned about their performance than TFA teachers, since they obtain classroom experience during training that provides them an opportunity to work out many problems well before they are employed as independent teachers. In contrast, TFA teachers begin teaching with little or no classroom experience and limited familiarity with the inner-city culture into which they are initiated.

*Teacher Efficacy.* Hoy and Woolfolk (1993) define teacher efficacy as the extent to which teachers believe they have the capacity to affect student perform-ance. Many studies have shown that teacher efficacy is related to numerous teacher behaviors as well as to student achievement (Goddard, Hoy, and Hoy, 2000). Self-doubt and concerns about one's adequacy are common for begin-ning teachers (Taschannen-Moran, Hoy, and Hoy, 1998) and may be especially acute for teachers who have had no training and are unfamiliar with low-income classrooms. Darling-Hammond, et al. (2002), found a correlation between feel-ings of preparedness and teacher efficacy. Although they also found that TFA teachers felt less prepared than the others, they did not report a comparison of TFA and the other teachers on teacher efficacy. Teachers' feelings of efficacy have been shown to increase as they gain experience (Taschannen-Moran, et al. 1998), but the effects of experience on untrained teachers' feelings are not known.

*Teacher Development: Concerns.* Fuller's construct of teaching concerns em-phasizes the importance of teachers' feelings to their development (Fuller, 1969; Fuller and Bown, 1975; Rogan, Borich, and Taylor, 1992). Based on studies of pre-service and in-service teachers, Fuller and her colleagues presented a model that defines teacher development as a progression through different concern clusters that predominate at various levels of training and experience. The model specifies that teachers are preoccupied first with *self* concerns, including worries about their adequacy and others' perceptions of their competence. Next, con-cerns about the *task* of teaching, including resources, duties, curriculum, and time, are predominant. Ultimately, teachers develop concerns about their *impact* on children's social, emotional, and cognitive development. Fuller's model would predict that first-year teachers would be preoccupied with *self* concerns. Contrary to Fuller's model, Kagan (1992) concluded that *impact* concerns are high throughout teachers' careers and are initially higher than *self* concerns. Turley and Wood (2002) also found that *impact* concerns were higher than the other 3 types of concerns for first-year teachers. They proposed that this contradiction of Fuller's model reflects changes in teacher education. The results of other recent studies (Pigge and Marso, 1997; Watkins and Quay, 2000) indicate that impact concerns are the highest of the 3 concerns categories even at the preservice level. Thus, current entrants into the teaching profession, whether through a regular teacher education program or an alternative route, may be different from those of Fuller's time. TFA teachers' concerns have not been studied.

*Motivational Goals and Intentions: Career Plans.* Darling-Hammond (1994) reported that TFA teachers in 1990 had an attrition rate that was nearly twice that of other new teachers. No recent data were found to indicate whether that attrition rate has changed over the last decade. Darling-Hammond, et al. (2002) found an association between feelings of preparedness and plans to stay in teaching and also found that TFA teachers felt less prepared than graduates of teacher education programs. However, they did not report a comparison of TFA teachers and their cohorts from teacher education programs on their plans to stay in teaching. Because TFA teachers only make a 2-year commitment to teaching, they would be expected to have the intention of leaving the field earlier than regular teachers.

# Teacher Effectiveness

*Student Achievement.* Only 2 studies of TFA teachers' classroom achievement were found. Laczko-Kerr and Berliner (2002) and Raymond, Fletcher, and Luque (2001), comparing TFA teachers' classroom achievement with that of other teacher groups, obtained opposing results. While Laczko-Kerr and Berliner suggested that TFA was a way for the teachers "to make some money" and that they were "hurting our young, vulnerable, inner-city students," Raymond, et al. stated, "On average, the impact of having a TFA teacher was always positive" (p. xii). In both studies, many of the reported differences were small and not statistically significant. In the Laczko-Kerr and Berliner study, a portion of the comparison group taught in higher socioeconomic level schools than the TFA group; in the Raymond, et al. study, the comparison group included teachers with other forms of alternative, as well as regular, certification.

*Principal's Ratings.* Assessing teacher effectiveness through principals' ratings, Kane, Parsons, and Associates (1999) reported that the majority of TFA teachers obtained principals' ratings of "good" or "excellent." The TFA teachers were not compared to other teachers.

# Method

*Participants.* The participants in this study were 3 groups of teachers. The first group consisted of 18 TFA teachers (TFA2) who had minimal teacher education and were in their second year of teaching. This was the first TFA group to begin teaching in low-income elementary schools in Atlanta, Georgia. During their first year of teaching, they had no organized on-going training. At the beginning of their second year they entered a teacher education program. An additional group of 21 TFA teachers (TFA1) had minimal training and experience. They began teaching in the same elementary schools in which TFA2 teachers were working one year after the TFA2 teachers began. A comparison group consisted of 21 first-year, fully trained and certified teachers (regular) who had graduated from an accredited teacher education program but had minimal experience as independent teachers, in that they were in their first year of teaching. These comparison teachers were located in the same schools as the TFA1 and TFA2 teachers. The 3 groups were matched as closely as possible on the grade level taught. A $\chi^2$ indicated that the grade levels did not differ for the 3 groups.

*Procedure.* At the same time that TFA2 teachers started their second year of teaching and TFA1 teachers began their first year of teaching, both TFA1 and TFA2 teachers entered the same teacher education program, which was negotiated between TFA and Georgia State University. The program was designed especially for the TFA teachers and required 2 evening classes a week plus some Saturday classes. It also included mentoring by a college instructor who visited the teachers' classrooms approximately once every 2 weeks. A detailed description of the program is presented elsewhere (Urban Alternative Preparation Program Manual, 2003).

The regular first-year teachers were not participating in a teacher education program. One of the teachers in the this group did begin taking one course toward a master's degree in education.

*Measures.* In April of the year the TFA teachers began their training program, classroom achievement tests were administered by the schools and data were obtained on the 3 groups of teachers. The measures used are described below.

*The Teacher Efficacy Scale.* Prior to this study, Pilcher and Steele (2002) revised the Hoy and Woolfolk Teacher Efficacy Scale (1993). They added 8 items to Hoy and Woolfolk's 10-item scale and factor-analyzed 208 teachers' responses to the 18 items. Their factor analysis confirmed Hoy and Woolfolk's two factors (subscales) measuring *General* teacher efficacy (*GTE*) and *Personal* teacher efficacy *(PTE)*. GTE refers to teachers' beliefs about the power of external factors versus the influence of teachers. This belief extends beyond the individual capabilities of the particular teacher to teachers in general. An item example is "the amount a student can learn is primarily related to family background." *PTE* refers to teachers' confidence in their ability to overcome obstacles to student learning. This is a statement about the efficacy of one's own teaching or self-perception of competence. An item example is "if I really try hard, I can get through to the most difficult or unmotivated students." The Teacher Efficacy Scale, with its factor loadings, is presented in table 7.1. The

**Table 7.1   Factor Loadings for the Teacher Efficacy Questionnaire**

| Item | Personal | General |
|------|:--------:|:-------:|
| 1. The amount a student can learn is primarily related to family background. | | .67 |
| 2. When it comes right down to it, a teacher really can't do much because most of a student's motivation and performance depends on his or her home environment. | | .72 |
| 3. When I really try, I can get through to most difficult students. | .43 | |
| 4. I think I am very good at teaching writing. | .65 | |
| 5. If parents would do more for their children, I could do more. | | .46 |
| 6. I think I am very good at teaching mathematics. | .65 | |
| 7. If a student did not remember information I gave in a previous lesson, I would know how to increase his/her retention in the next lesson. | .60 | |
| 8. I have good writing skills. | .57 | |
| 9. If one of my students couldn't do a class assignment, I would be able to accurately assess whether the assignment was at the correct level of difficulty. | .61 | |
| 10. I consider myself very good at learning science. | .48 | |
| 11. A teacher is very limited in what he/she can achieve because a student's home environment is a large influence on his/her achievement. | | .80 |
| 12. I think I am very good at teaching science. | .59 | |
| 13. If a student in my class becomes disruptive and noisy, I feel assured that I know some techniques to redirect him/her quickly. | .50 | |
| 14. I think I am very good at teaching reading. | .58 | |
| 15. If students are not disciplined at home, they are not likely to accept any discipline. | | .68 |
| 16. I am very good at learning mathematics. | .50 | |
| 17. If I really try hard, I can get through to even the most difficult or unmotivated students. | .52 | |
| 18. I consider myself to be a good reader. | .52 | |

table indicates that the test is comprised of 2 factors, *PTE* and *GTE*, and that the loadings are high for each factor.

*The Revised Teacher Concerns Checklist.* This instrument is a 40 item Likert Scale based on Fuller's model of teacher development. This questionnaire has progressed through several versions, starting with the one by Fuller and Borich (Borich, 1988). The instrument used here is Steele and Pilcher's (2002) revision of the Rogan, et al. (1992) version. Steele and Pilcher reduced the scale to 40 items by eliminating the 5 items that Rogan, et al. found to be ambiguous. Using data from 468 teachers, they replicated the earlier factor structure, the amount of the variance accounted for by the factors, and the reliability of the factors. The revised scale, like the earlier one, yields 3 factors (subscales) measuring concerns about *Self, Task,* and *Impact. Self* concerns involve uncertainty about one's adequacy and apprehension about others' perceptions. *Task* concerns are worries about the methodology and logistics of teaching, including resources, duties, curriculum, and time. *Impact* concerns focus on children's social, emotional, and cognitive needs. The scale and the factor loadings are presented in table 7.2.

*Career Plans Questionnaire.* The teachers in the regular and TFA1 groups provided written answers to the question, "What are your career plans after you have taught for two years?" TFA2 teachers were not available when this questionnaire was administered.

*The Criterion-Referenced Competency Tests (CRCT).* These criterion-referenced tests were professionally constructed for the Georgia State Department of Education to measure the acquisition of skills and knowledge described in the state's Quality Core Curriculum in the areas of reading, English/language arts, and mathematics. Predominantly multiple-choice, the electronically scored tests were administered in every grade except kindergarten, so kindergarten teachers could not be included in the analysis of this measure. These tests were administered in April.

*Principals' Rating Scale.* This measure was used for the regular and TFA1 teachers. Principals rated each teacher as poor, fair, very good, or excellent on each item of the 20-item Likert scale developed by Kane, Parsons, and Associates (1999). Table 7.3 presents this scale.

# Results

*Teacher Efficacy and Teaching Concerns.* Because the teaching concerns and teacher efficacy subscales consisted of different numbers of items, raw scores were converted to scale scores by dividing each person's score by the number of items in the subscale. Table 7.4 presents the scale score means and standard

**Table 7.2   Factor Loadings of the Revised Teacher Concerns Checklist**

| | Factor Loadings | | |
|---|---|---|---|
| Item | Impact | Task | Self |
| Understanding what factors motivate students to study. | .73 | | |
| Increasing students' feelings of accomplishment. | .83 | | |
| Meeting the needs of different kinds of students. | .68 | | |
| Recognizing the social and emotional needs of students. | .79 | | |
| Understanding the psychological and cultural differences that underlie the diverse backgrounds of students in my class. | .74 | | |
| Diagnosing student learning problems. | .31 | | |
| Seeking alternative ways to ensure that students learn subject matter. | .74 | | |
| Challenging unmotivated students. | .82 | | |
| Helping students to value learning. | .81 | | |
| Whether each student is reaching his or her maximum potential. | .77 | | |
| Adapting myself to the needs of different students. | .76 | | |
| Whether students can apply what they learn. | .74 | | |
| Wide range of student achievement in my class. | .64 | | |
| Understanding ways in which student health and nutritional problems can effect learning. | .56 | | |
| Guiding students toward intellectual and emotional growth. | .82 | | |
| Understanding why certain students make slow progress. | .73 | | |
| Having too little control over the curriculum. | | .51 | |
| Insufficient clerical help for teachers. | | .64 | |
| Too many non-instructional duties. | | .69 | |
| Inadequate assistance from specialized teachers. | | .53 | |
| Lack of public support for schools resulting in inadequate resources. | | .49 | |
| Too many standards and regulations set for teachers. | | .67 | |
| The rigid instructional routine. | | .55 | |
| The inflexibility of the curriculum. | | .67 | |
| Lack of opportunity for professional growth. | | .56 | |
| Working with too many students each day. | | .38 | |
| My ability to maintain the appropriate degree of class control. | | | .40 |
| Doing well when a supervisor is present. | | | .52 |
| My ability to work with disruptive students. | | | .43 |
| Getting students to behave. | | | .46 |
| Obtaining a favorable evaluation of my teaching. | | | .55 |
| Not being able to cope with troublemakers. | | | .53 |

**Table 7.2    (Continued)**

| Item | Factor Loadings | | |
|------|--------|------|------|
| | *Impact* | *Task* | *Self* |
| Whether the students respect me. | | | .51 |
| The principal may think there is too much noise in my classroom. | | | .60 |
| My peers may think I am not doing an adequate job. | | | .76 |
| Having an embarrassing incident occur in my classroom for which I might be seen as responsible. | | | .76 |
| Having my inadequacies become known to other teachers. | | | .75 |
| Losing the respect of my peers. | | | .64 |
| My ability to prepare adequate lesson plans. | | | .40 |
| Managing my time efficiently. | | | .16 |

**Table 7.3    Means and Standard Deviations (in parentheses) for Principals' Rating Scale**

| Characteristics | Regular Teachers | TFA 1 Teachers |
|-----------------|------------------|----------------|
| 1. Achievement orientation and drive to succeed | 3.27 (0.59) | 3.30 (0.87) |
| 2. Assuming responsibility and following through on it | 3.13 (0.52) | 3.20 (0.89) |
| 3. Openness to feedback and willingness to learn | 3.07 (0.59) | 3.05 (0.89) |
| 4. Having a positive and optimistic attitude | 3.20 (0.56) | 3.20 (0.89) |
| 5. Having a realistic perspective | 3.00 (0.38) | 2.90 (0.72) |
| 6. Managing time efficiently in class and in other activities | 3.00 (0.66) | 2.85 (0.86) |
| 7. Acting with sensitivity to others | 3.00 (0.38) | 3.05 (0.83) |
| 8. Knowledge of the subject matter | 3.13 (0.52) | 3.15 (0.75) |
| 9. Motivation and dedication to teaching | 3.20 (0.56) | 3.50 (0.69) |
| 10. Setting clear academic goals | 3.00 (0.38) | 3.10 (0.72) |
| 11. Curricular planning | 2.87 (0.52) | 3.00 (0.80) |
| 12. Having high expectations for students | 3.07 (0.46) | 3.40 (0.69) |
| 13. Motivating students | 3.00 (0.54) | 3.20 (0.89) |
| 14. Involving parents and/or guardians in the education of their children | 2.80 (0.56) | 3.25 (0.85) |
| 15. Creating a classroom environment that is conducive to learning | 2.93 (0.59) | 3.10 (0.91) |
| 16. Working with other faculty and administrators | 3.00 (0.38) | 3.40 (0.68) |
| 17. Identifying with the needs of the community | 2.80 (0.41) | 2.80 (0.89) |
| 18. Maintaining classroom control | 2.93 (0.59) | 2.85 (0.93) |
| 19. Having concern for children's well-being | 3.07 (0.46) | 3.40 (0.68) |
| 20. Working with disruptive students | 3.07 (0.46) | 2.75 (0.85) |

**Table 7.4    Scale Score Means and Standard Deviations (in parentheses) for Teacher Efficacy and Teaching Concerns**

| Variable | Regular Teachers Mean (SD) (n = 21) | TFA1 Teachers Mean (SD) (n = 19) | TFA2 Teachers Mean (SD) (n = 18) |
|---|---|---|---|
| Personal Efficacy[a] | 4.81 (0.67) | 3.95 (0.63) | 4.29 (0.63) |
| General Efficacy[a] | 3.32 (1.08) | 3.01 (0.98) | 2.92 (0.82) |
| Impact[b] | 3.53 (1.01) | 3.63 (0.65) | 3.85 (0.64) |
| Task[b] | 3.30 (0.86) | 3.01 (0.60) | 3.06 (0.61) |
| Self[b] | 2.86 (0.88) | 2.60 (0.54) | 2.56 (0.56) |

Note: For scale comparability, scale scores were obtained by dividing raw scores by the number of items in a particular subscale.
[a]A higher score indicates greater efficacy.
[b]A higher score indicates greater concerns.

deviations for *personal* and *general* teacher efficacy and *impact, task, and self* teaching concerns. To determine whether the 3 groups differed on these feelings a one-way MANOVA was computed, with group being the independent variable and the 2 efficacy and 3 concerns scores being the dependent variables. The MANOVA was significant, $F (10, 108) = 3.81$, $p < .01$. The consequent ANOVAs indicated a difference on *personal* teacher efficacy, $F (2, 57) = 9.59$, $p < .01$, and on *general* teacher efficacy, $F (2, 57) = 7.10$, $p < .01$. Sheffe tests showed that on *personal* teacher efficacy regular teachers were higher than TFA1, but not TFA2 teachers. The two TFA groups did not differ significantly from each other, and TFA2 scores were between those of the regular and TFA1 teachers. On *general* teacher efficacy, regular teachers were higher than both TFA1 and TFA2 teachers.

The ANOVAs for the *impact, task, and self* concerns indicated that the groups did not differ on any of the 3 concerns categories. Contradictory to the Fuller model, all groups were higher on *impact* than on *self*, indicating that they had more mature concerns than Fuller's model would predict.

*Career Plans.* Responses about career plans were categorized into 5 categories. No difference occurred between the regular and the TFA1 teachers in their plans to remain in education, $\chi^2 (1) = 1.60$. The majority of both groups planned to either teach or prepare for some other school position. Table 7.5 shows the number of teachers in each category of career plans.

*Teacher Effectiveness.* Table 7.6 presents the means and standard deviations of the classroom averages of the children's scores on the subscales of the CRCT for the 3 groups of teachers. The test was constructed in such a way that a score of 300 represented achievement at grade level for each grade. That is, if a child had a score of 300, that child's achievement was exactly at grade level. To deter-

Table 7.5   Percentage of Unsuccessful (below Grade Level) and Successful (at or above Grade Level) Students on the Criterion Referenced Curriculum Test (CRCT)

| | | Group | | |
| Area | Achievement Level | Regular Teachers | TFA1 Teachers | TFA2 Teachers |
|---|---|---|---|---|
| Reading | Unsuccessful | 22.7% | 47.2% | 29.1% |
| | Successful | 77.3% | 52.8% | 70.9% |
| English/Language Arts | Unsuccessful | 17.8% | 41.4% | 32.6% |
| | Successful | 82.2% | 58.6% | 67.4% |
| Mathematics | Unsuccessful | 34.1% | 54.7% | 39.6% |
| | Successful | 65.9% | 45.3% | 60.4% |

mine whether student achievement differed for the 3 groups, a one-way MANOVA was computed. The independent variable was group. The dependent variables were the 3 areas of achievement measured by the *CRCT*: *reading, English/language arts,* and *mathematics*. The MANOVA was significant, $F(6, 96) = 2.75$, $p < .05$. ANOVAs indicated that the groups differed on all 3 achievement areas: *reading, F (2, 49) = 8.91, p < .01; English/language arts, F (2, 49) = 8.39. p < .01;* and *mathematics, F (2,49) = 4.52, p < .05.* In all achievement areas, Sheffe tests indicated that regular teachers had significantly higher classroom averages than TFA1, but not TFA2, teachers. The differences between TFA1 and TFA2 teachers' classroom averages were not statistically significant. For every achievement area, classroom averages of TFA2 teachers fell between those of regular and TFA1 teachers. For all 3 groups of teachers these averages were above 300, the score representing grade level.

Table 7.5 presents the percentage of successful (at or above grade level) and unsuccessful (below grade level) students in the classrooms of the 3 groups of teachers. To determine whether the 3 groups differed on successful and unsuccessful students, an initial $\chi^2$ was computed using a 3 (groups) x 2 (success

Table 7.6   Means and Standard Deviations (in parentheses) of Classroom Averages for the Criterion Referenced Curriculum Test (CRCT)

| Achievement Area | Regular Teachers Mean (SD) | TFA1 Teachers Mean (SD) | TFA2 Teachers Mean (SD) |
|---|---|---|---|
| Reading | 325.31 (17.24) | 306.67 (16.66) | 314.25 (14.27) |
| English/Language Arts | 323.87 (17.71) | 307.00 (13.05) | 315.06 (13.71) |
| Mathematics | 317.59 (23.03) | 302.44 (13.25) | 309.13 (11.28) |

level) contingency table for each achievement area. The $\chi^2$'s were significant for *reading*, $\chi^2$ (2) $=$ 42.06, $p <$ .001; *English/language arts*, $\chi^2$ (2) $=$ 37.63, $p <$ .001; and *mathematics*, $\chi^2$ (2) $=$ 25.33, $p <$ .001. To compare each group with every other group, the contingency tables were partitioned, and follow-up $\chi^2$'s, adjusted for repeated analyses, were computed. For *reading*, regular teachers had a greater proportion of successful students than TFA1 teachers, $\chi^2$ (1) $=$ 28.05, $p <$ .001, but did not differ from TFA2 teachers. Also, TFA2 teachers had a greater proportion of successful students than TFA1 teachers, $\chi^2$ (1) $=$ 14.89, $p <$ .001. For *English/language arts*, regular teachers had a greater proportion of successful students than TFA1 teachers, $\chi^2$ (1) $=$ 34.47, $p <$ .001, and TFA2 teachers, $\chi^2$ (1) $=$ 10.25, $p <$ .01. TFA1 and TFA2 teachers did not differ from each other. For *mathematics* regular teachers had a greater proportion of successful students than TFA1 teachers, $\chi^2$ (1) $=$ 15.46, $p <$ .001, but did not differ from TFA2 teachers. TFA1 and TFA2 teachers did not differ.

*Principals' Ratings.* A MANOVA, with the independent variable being group and the dependent variables being the 20 items on the *Principals' Rating Scale*, was not significant. Table 7.3 presents the means and standard deviations for each item on the *Principals' Rating Scale*. All ratings for both the TFA1 and the regular teachers were above the theoretical mean of 2.5. Thus, principals had positive opinions of both groups. An inspection of the standard deviations indicates that there was a greater spread from poor to excellent for the TFA1 teachers than for the regular teachers.

# Implications for Teacher Educators

Although the results of this study indicate that both training and experience have some influence on teachers' feelings and effectiveness, training is the more powerful source for imparting *general* teacher efficacy. First-year teachers who had been through a teacher education program were superior to both groups of TFA teachers on this characteristic. Thus, compared with the other teachers, those who participated in a teacher education program believe that teachers have the ability to overcome external factors that shape children. This finding suggests that the regular teachers' extensive training informed them that external forces are not immutable and that teachers can change even those children from the most problematic situations.

*Personal* teacher efficacy refers to teachers' perceptions of themselves as individuals who can affect children's learning. For the development of this type of efficacy, training is important as indicated by the regular teachers' superiority over the TFA1 teachers. Experience also has an influence as the TFA2 teachers' beliefs were positioned between those of the other two groups, and they did not differ significantly from either of the groups. Thus, teachers may learn through both training and experience that they personally can have an effect on children, but training seems to be necessary to provide confidence that the teaching profession can be an agent of change.

Neither training nor experience influenced concerns as conceptualized by Fuller (Fuller, 1969; Fuller and Bown, 1975). *Impact* concerns were the highest of the 3 concerns categories for all groups, suggesting that these teachers were more focused on children than on themselves, others' opinions of them, or time and resource limitations. The concerns of both regular and TFA teachers are contradictory to the Fuller model, which specifies that teachers progress consecutively through *self, task,* and *impact* concerns. Turley and Wood (2002), finding first-year teachers to be higher in *impact* than in *self* or *task* concerns, attributed the inconsistency of their findings with Fuller's model to changes in teacher education over the years. Whereas earlier teachers may have chosen teaching because it was one of the few careers open to them, present-day individuals who choose teaching over more lucrative careers may do so because they are motivated to help children learn or to influence social change.

The lack of difference between the first-year regular and TFA teachers on career plans suggests that current TFA teachers have different attitudes about remaining in teaching than the TFA teachers of 1994 when Darling-Hammond reported TFA teacher attrition to be very high. On the other hand, actual attrition could not be measured here, and the measure of remaining in education was obtained through self-report. The fact that this report was anonymous may have increased its validity.

Both training and experience influenced classroom averages in all 3 of the achievement areas measured by the CRCT: *reading, English/language arts,* and *mathematics.* The differences between the regular and TFA1 teachers were statistically significant for all areas. The differences between the regular and the TFA2 teachers were not statistically significant, but neither were the differences between the TFA1 and TFA2 teachers. In all areas, the TFA2 teachers' classroom averages fell between those of the regular and the TFA1 teachers. These findings indicate that teachers' effectiveness can be enhanced by experience, even in the face of a lack of prior participation in a teacher education program.

The findings for the proportion of successful (at or above grade level) and unsuccessful (below grade level) children in the classrooms indicate that training is the most salient influence on the proportion of successful children in *English/language arts.* In that area, the regular teachers had more successful and fewer unsuccessful students than either group of TFA teachers. The findings for the other 2 achievement areas were similar to those for classroom achievement. Regular teachers had more successful students than TFA1, but not TFA2, teachers.

A more precise evaluation of the teachers' influence on children's achievement would entail comparing the 3 groups of teachers on their children's gains from the beginning to the end of the school year. For such an evaluation, one of 2 procedures could be used. One procedure would be to use the previous year's achievement test scores as covariates; the other would be to compare the 3 groups of teachers on differences between each child's previous and present achievement scores. However, these analyses could not be done because the school system did not administer achievement tests to all grade levels in the previous year, and it changed the tests it administered from one year to the next.

The averages of the principals' ratings did not favor one group over the other. Their ratings of both the regular and the TFA first-year teachers were high. Informally, 2 different principals stated that a particular teacher was the best first-year teacher they had ever seen. One of these teachers was a regular teacher, and the other was a TFA1 teacher. Inspection of the data as well as the standard deviations showed that the TFA teachers had a wider range of ratings from poor to excellent than the regular teachers. Almost all regular teachers were rated good and excellent. No regular teacher received a rating of poor, whereas several TFA teachers received that rating. However, the percentage of TFA teachers rated excellent was higher than that of the regular teachers.

Training appears to be the most salient influence on teacher performance, as suggested by the findings that all achievement differences that did occur favored the regular teachers. Although experience does not seem to be as powerful as training, the finding that TFA2 teachers produced classroom averages that were lower, but not significantly lower, than those of the regular teachers suggests that experience can compensate to some extent for a lower level of training. While these findings support the value of teacher preparation prior to beginning teaching, no group had below-grade-level classroom averages, and principals' mean ratings did not differ for TFA and regular teachers.

The results of this study should be interpreted with the caveat that comparisons were not between completely untrained teachers and fully trained teachers, but between *minimally* trained and fully trained teachers. When the data were collected, the TFA teachers had completed only one semester of an abbreviated program. Their training was not as concentrated and intensive as the training for regular teacher education majors in the same department. The TFA courses did not include as many clock hours, and the assignments had to be shortened. The faculty discerned that these teachers could not always complete the work assigned because of competing demands on their time. Managing their classrooms, planning lessons, and participating in their school activities resulted in exhaustion and preoccupation with the problems of their day. Their first priority was their teaching, and they seemed to be determined to make it work. They generally felt positive about the training, but many seemed to have the attitude that coming to class was an intrusion on the minimal amount of private time available for preparing for their children. Although it is possible for untrained beginning teachers to accommodate training while struggling to keep up with the demands of teaching, a more tolerable and effective strategy would be to prepare them before they begin independent teaching.

The TFA teachers were placed in schools in the most poverty-stricken neighborhoods in the city, and this type of placement seems to be typical in all the districts in which they teach. A very positive advantage of this study over most other studies comparing regular and TFA teachers is that the comparison group of regular teachers and the TFA teachers came from the same schools. Comparison groups in most other TFA research have consisted of very large samples from a wide range of schools. However, caution is necessary in interpreting the results of this study. The sample is small, and the sample size could not be the same for all variables. A different sample may yield entirely different results. School researchers know the practical limitations of conducting research in public schools. As in the case of many other school research projects, the conditions under which this research was conducted were not faultless, but they were the best that were obtainable in the situation.

# References

Darling-Hammond, L. (1994). Who will speak for the children? How "Teach for America' hurts urban schools and students. *Phi Delta Kappan, 76*, 21–34.

Darling-Hammond, L, Berry, B., and Thoreson, A. (2001). Does teacher certification matter? Evaluating the evidence. *Educational Evaluation and Policy Analysis, 23*, 57–77.

Darling-Hammond, L., Chung, R., and Frelow, F. (2002). Variation in teacher preparation: How well do different pathways prepare teachers to teach? *Journal of Teacher Education, 53*, 286–302.

Darling-Hammond, L., and Youngs, P. (2002). Defining "highly qualified teachers": What does "scientifically-based research" actually tell us? *Educational Researcher, 31*, 13–25.

Feistritzer, C. E., and Chester, D. T. (2002). Alternative teacher certification: A state-by-state analysis 2002. (National Center for Education Information Report). Washington, DC.

Fetler, M. (1999). High school staff characteristics and mathematics test results. *Education Policy Analysis Archives, 7(9)*. Retrieved August 2003 from http://epaa.asu.edu/epaa/v7n9.html.

Fuller, F. F. (1969). Concepts of teachers: A developmental conceptualization. *American Educational Research Journal, 6*, 207–26.

Fuller, F. F., and Borich, G. D. (1992). *Teacher concerns checklist*. Austin: University of Texas, Research and Development Center for Teacher Education.

Fuller, F. F., and Bown, O. H. (1975). Becoming a teacher. 25–52. In *Teacher Education: The seventy-fourth yearbook of the National Society for the Study of Education, Part II*, ed. K. Ryan. Chicago: The University of Chicago Press.

Goddard, R. D., Hoy, W. K., and Hoy, A. W. (2000). Collective teacher efficacy: Its meaning, measure, and impact on student achievement. *American Educational Research Journal, 37*, 479–507.

Goldhaber, D., and Anthony, E. (2003). *Teacher Quality and Student Achievement* (Report No. 115). New York: Educational Resources Information Center Clearinghouse on Urban Education.

Goldhaber, D. and Brewer, D. J. (2000) Does teacher certification matter? High school teacher certification status and student achievement. *Educational Evaluation and Policy Analysis, 22*, 129–45.

Hawkins, E. F., Stancavage, F. B., and Dorsey, J. A. (1998). *School policies affecting instruction in mathematics.* Washington, DC: National Center for Education Statistics.

Hoy, W. K., and Woolfolk, A. E. (1993). Teachers' sense of efficacy and the organizational health of schools. *The Elementary School Journal, 93*, 356–72.

Kagan, D. M. (1992). Professional growth among preservice and inservice teachers. *Review of Educational Research, 62*, 129–69.

Kane, Parsons, and Associates, Inc. (1999). A Survey of principals in schools with Teach For America corps members. (Teach For America Report). New York.

Laczko-Kerr, I, and Berliner, D. C. (2002). The effectiveness of "Teach for America" and other under-certified teachers on student academic achievement: A case of harmful public policy," *Education Policy Analysis Archives, 10*. Retrieved July 8, 2003, from http://epaa,asy,edu/epaa/v10n37/.

Laczko-Kerr, I, and Berliner, D. C. (2003). In harm's way: How under-certified teachers hurt their students. *Educational Leadership, 60*, 34–39.

Olson, L., and Jerald, C. D. (1998). The challenges. *Education Week* [On-line]. http://www.edweek.org/qc98/challenges/teach/te-n.htm.

Pigge, F. L., and Marso, R. N. (1997, March). A longitudinal study of relationships between candidates' abilities, development of teaching concerns, and success in entering teaching. Paper presented at the meeting of the American Educational Research Association, Chicago.

Pilcher, L. C., and Steele, D. C. (2002). [Factor Analysis of the Teacher Efficacy Scale]. Unpublished raw data.

Raymond, M., Fletcher, S. H., and Luque, J. (2001). *Teach for America: An evaluation of teacher differences and student outcomes in Houston, Texas.* CREDO, Thomas B. Fordham Foundation, Washington, DC.

Rivkin, S. G., Hanushek, E. A., and Kain, J. F. (2000). *Teachers, schools and academic achievement.* Working Paper. Retrieved August 10, 2004, from http://www.utdallas.edu/research/greenctr/Papers.htm.

Rogan, J. M., Borich, G. D., and Taylor, H. P. (1992). Validation of the stages of concern questionnaire. *Action in Teacher Education, 14*, 43–49.

Schutz, P. A., and Lanehart, S. L. (2002). Introduction: Emotions in education. *Educational Psychologist, 37*, 67–68.

Steele, D. C. and Pilcher, L. C. (2002, October). *The Teachers' Concerns Checklist: A replication.* Paper presented at the meeting of the Georgia Educational Research Association, Savannah, GA.

Stoddart, T. and Floden, R. (1996). Traditional and alternate routes to teacher certification: issues, assumptions, and misconceptions. 80–106. In *Currents of reform in preservice teacher education*, ed. K. M. Zeichner, S. L. Melnick, and M. L. Gomez. New York: Teachers College Press.

Taschannen-Moran, M., Hoy, A., and Hoy, W. K. (1998). Teacher Efficacy: Its meaning and measure. *Review of Educational Research, 68*, 202–48.

Tell, C. (2001). Making room for alternative routes. *Educational Leadership, 58*, 38–41.

Turley, S., and Wood, A. L. (2002, April). *A longitudinal study of new teacher concerns: Induction in a district consortium.* Paper presented at the meeting of the American Educational Research Association, New Orleans, LA.

Urban Alternative Preparation Program. (2003). (Available from Early Childhood Education, College of Education, Georgia State University, Atlanta, GA 30303).

Watkins, L. L., and Quay, L. C. (2000, April). *Concerns and Personal Teacher Efficacy of alternative and traditional education students and first- and second-year teachers.* Paper presented at the meeting of the American Educational Research Association, New Orleans.

Wilce, H. (2002, Jan. 25). Just for Starters. *Times Educational Supplement, The New York Times*, 12.

# CHAPTER 8

# Attrition Patterns of Inadequately Prepared Teachers

*Jianping Shen and Louann Bierlein Palmer*
Western Michigan University

Dr. Jianping Shen is a professor of educational leadership in the Department of Teaching, Learning, and Leadership, Western Michigan University. His specializations include leadership theories, policy analysis, and research methods. He has about 50 refereed articles in English.

Dr. Louann Bierlein Palmer is an assistant professor of educational leadership in the Department of Teaching, Learning, and Leadership, Western Michigan University. Her research focuses on the impact of broader K–12 and higher education reform policies, and she has presented and published broadly for both policy and academic audiences.

## ABSTRACT

This study inquired into teacher attrition by conducting survival analyses on national data drawn from the Baccalaureate and Beyond Longitudinal Study 1993–1997 (B&B:93/97). By analyzing this national sample of college graduates, we took a longitudinal perspective on teacher attrition, determining the survival pattern of all new teachers. In addition, we examined the connection between attrition and various ways of entry into teaching. The sample size of the study was 1,702 (weighted $N = 181,313$). The study found that about 34 percent of those who entered teaching left by the end of the fifth year. In addition, those entering teaching without being fully prepared to teach (i.e., those who did not complete student teaching, receive certification, and participate in a teacher induction program), were more likely to leave. The findings raise policy questions about non-traditional routes to teaching that may not include all aspects of adequate preparation for such teachers.

# Introduction

The retention of elementary and secondary teachers has been an issue of continuing concern in education. In addition to the issue of quality, high rates of teacher attrition disrupt program continuity and planning, hinder student learning, and increase school districts' expenditures on recruiting and hiring. In this study we inquire into one segment of the new teacher population, those who enter the classroom without adequate preparation and/or those without full certification. This survival analysis used data collected during the Baccalaureate and Beyond Longitudinal Study 1993–1997 (i.e., B&B:93/97), which is a national longitudinal survey of recent college graduates.

The number of states allowing some type of alternative certification program increased from 8 in 1983, to 18 in 1986, to 46 plus the District of Columbia in 2003 (Feistritzer and Chester, 2003). Empirical studies indicate that the impact of such alternative certification policies has been mixed. This study examines the attrition patterns of those who begin teaching without participating in all aspects of what some deem adequate preparation (i.e., student teaching, and an induction program) and full certification, compared with those following the more traditional preparation and certification routes.

We begin by reviewing the literature on various kinds of entries into teaching and teacher attrition. We then discuss the methodology of the study, including data source, sample, and data analysis method. Finally, we present the results and discuss the implications of the findings.

# Literature Review

## ALTERNATIVE PREPARATION PROGRAMS

Recent years have witnessed the continuing debate on alternative teacher certification programs and their impact on the teaching force (Wright, 2001). The arguments for alternative certification are multifaceted. One argument, as summarized by Stoddart and Floden (1995), is that there has been a shortage of qualified teachers in urban schools and in subject areas such as math and science, and therefore, alternative certification should be employed to alleviate such shortages. Second, it has been argued that good teaching is based primarily on subject matter knowledge and an enthusiasm for teaching (e.g., Kearns, 1990; Kramer, 1991). Hence, opportunities should be provided to people who are competent in subject matter knowledge but who would not otherwise have the opportunity to go into teaching. A third argument is that alternatively certified teachers are older, more likely to come from minority groups, and more likely to have worked in other jobs than the traditional teacher education population. Therefore, the teaching force can be diversified through alternative certification (Cornett, 1990; Stoddart, 1990), which is particularly true for urban schools (Natriello and Zumwalt, 1993; Stoddart, 1993). Finally, it has been argued that university-based teacher education has monopolized preparation of teachers, and alternative certification introduces competition into this area (Bliss, 1990; Cornett, 1990).

The arguments against alternative certification are also multifaceted. It has been argued that alternative certification lowers the cost of entering teaching and degrades the professional status of teaching (Kirby, Darling-Hammond, and Hudson, 1989). A second argument claims that students—particularly those disadvantaged students in inner-city schools where teacher shortages occur more frequently—are hurt by this policy (Darling-Hammond, 1994). Third, the assumption that teachers certified alternatively know the subject matter and can learn to teach by working on the job has been questioned (Feiman-Nemser and Buchman, 1987; Kennedy, 1991). Some research suggests that pedagogical content knowledge plays a very important role in teaching and that teachers without teacher education or certified by alternative routes have more difficulties learning to teach than do those certified traditionally (Grossman, 1989a, b; McDiarmid and Wilson, 1991). Finally, it has been argued that alternative certification fails to fulfill the promise that it will recruit those who have higher academic qualifications (Natriello, Hansen, Frisch, and Zumwalt, 1990).

Recent empirical studies indicate that teachers' certification or licensing status is related to students' learning. Goldhaber and Brewer (2000) found that except for mathematics and science teachers with emergency certificates, fully certified teachers have a statistically significant positive impact on student test scores relative to teachers who are not certified in their subject area. Using the same data source, Darling-Hammond, Berry, and Thoreson (2001) argued that even for math and science, those teachers who have more teacher education training appear to do better in producing student achievement. Furthermore, as cited by Darling-Hammond (2000), Fuller's study (1999) indicated that when school districts have higher percentages of licensed teachers, their pass rates on the Texas state achievement tests are significantly higher, after holding constant some characteristics related to student family background, school, and teacher. Fetler's research (1999) also found that when the percentage of teachers on emergency certificates is higher, average student score is significantly lower, after controlling for student poverty. Furthermore, Grossman's (1989a, b) in-depth qualitative studies of first-year English teachers described the difficulties experienced by those who entered teaching without teacher education. Finally, using national data collected in 1993–1994 and 1994–1995, researchers found that alternative certification policies have not fulfilled all their promises (e.g., Shen, 1997, 1998, 2000).

## TEACHER ATTRITION

Teacher attrition is a key factor that impacts the characteristics of the teaching force. National surveys conducted by the U.S. Department of Education indicated that about 20 percent of new teachers leave teaching within the first three years of entering teaching (Whitener et al., 1997). Overall, the teacher attrition pattern follows a U-shaped curve over a life cycle. Attrition rate is high for young teachers during the early stage of their professional lives, low for middle-aged teachers and high again for senior teachers as they approach retirement (Grissmer and Kirby, 1987; Murnane, Singer, and Willett, 1989; Singer, 1993).

Darling-Hammond (2003) notes there is mounting evidence that links inadequate teacher preparation and higher attrition rates. She cited several state-based studies depicting higher attrition rates among teachers coming from alternative certification programs (e.g., Raymond, Fletcher and Luque, 2001).

From a national perspective, work by Henke, Chen and Geis (2000) found attrition rates to be significantly lower among those teachers who received more adequate preparation. These researchers analyzed data from the Baccalaureate and Beyond Longitudinal Study 1993–1997 (B&B: 93/97), and found that 15 percent of those who had participated in a student teaching experience prior to entering the classroom left the profession within five years, compared to 29 percent of those who had not completed student teaching. Of those involved in a first-year teacher induction program, 15 percent left, compared to 26 percent of those who had not participated in a teacher induction program. And 14 percent of those with certification left, compared to 49 percent of those without certification. These national data, along with a growing number of state-specific research studies, all point to a strong linkage between adequate teacher preparation and lower attrition rates.

# Conceptualization and Research Question

So why are analysis derived from the B&B: 93/97 national data set (such as the one reported in this article, and that done by Henke, et al., 2000) of such value, and what more can be learned from this data set?

The longitudinal national data available through the B&B: 93/97 gives such studies methodological rigor. Many previous studies on teacher attrition are based on retrospective data. One of the shortcomings associated with retrospective data is that there is a time gap, and thus there is a possible reconstruction process based on the experience after leaving teaching or continuing to teach for a period of time. Another shortcoming with other national data sets is that researchers must investigate the phenomenon of teacher attrition using a short time span. For example, studies have been conducted to inquire into teacher attrition by analyzing the data from Schools and Staffing Survey (SASS) 1990–1991 and Teacher Follow-up Survey (TFS) 1991–1992 (e.g., Shen, 1997a, 1997b), and SASS 1993–1994 and TFS 1994–1995 (e.g., Boe, Bobbitt, Cook, and Barkanic, 1998; Boe, Bobbitt, Cook, Barkanic, and Maislin, 1998). For both data sets, the time gap is only one year between the main survey and the subsequent follow-up survey. The study reported here (using B&B: 93/97) has month-to-month data on new teachers' employment status during a five-year period.

Using longitudinal data over a longer period of time is the analysis approach that this current study takes. As will be discussed in detail in the methodological section, this study uses survival analysis methods to fully utilize the information in the data. Previous studies on teacher attrition often divide teachers into two groups: those who leave and those who continue. This dichotomized variable loses a lot of information because it does not indicate when a teacher leaves. The outcome measure of this reported study—months of teaching before attrition happens or does not happen—is much richer than just a dichotomous variable.

# Method

## THE DATA SOURCE

The data of the study are extracted from the Baccalaureate and Beyond Longitudinal Study 1993–1997 (i.e., B&B:93/97). B&B:93/97 was designed to examine the post-baccalaureate experiences of 1992–1993 bachelor's degree recipients. Following a sample of approximately 11,200 men and women who received bachelor's degrees between July 1992 and June 1993, the available data on this cohort include interviews conducted as part of the 1993 National Postsecondary Student Aid Study (NPSAS:93) when the students were seniors in college, the Baccalaureate and Beyond First Follow-up conducted in 1994 (B&B:93/94), and the Second Follow-up in 1997 (B&B:93/97). Transcript data from the NPSAS institutions are also available for most of the cohort. Therefore, the data allow researchers to study the connections between college graduates' careers as undergraduates and their post-baccalaureate experiences as students and employees. Among others, the B&B:93/97 study provides data to address issues related to patterns of preparation for, and engagement in, teaching.

## THE SAMPLE

The B&B cohort was comprised of 11,192 individuals who were determined eligible for follow-up in 1997. A full 83 percent of the sample responded to all three rounds; these 9,274 respondents (weighted $N = 1,181,376$) are classified as the B&B panel. Among the B&B panel, 1,702 respondents (weighted $N = 181,313$) went into teaching and they constituted the sample of the study.

## DATA ANALYSIS APPROACH

A Cox regression model is used to examine teacher attrition in the B&B:93/97 subsample specified previously. This data analysis approach is a form of survival or event history method. Survival analysis enables researchers to use various factors—for example, gender—to predict teacher attrition over a period of time. Methodologically, survival analysis is an excellent approach to modeling the length of time it takes for an event to take place, even when some of those in the sample have not experienced the event. We can model when an event is likely to occur by using survival analysis methods.

Studies on teacher attrition usually dichotomize the event, that is, they create a dichotomous variable that divides the teachers into two categories—those teachers who leave or continue. The dichotomous variable is then used as an outcome measure to be predicted by various variables such as gender and race/ethnicity. The problem with the approach to dichotomizing the outcome measure is that a large amount of information is lost. For example, if a researcher chooses to use the dichotomous approach to study teacher attrition over a period of ten years, through the dichotomy those who left teaching during the first year are classified the same as those who left during the tenth year. Since we have data on teachers' month-to-month employment status, we are able to use the Cox model, one designed to be used with continuous data.

# Results

## OVERALL ATTRITION PATTERN

Figure 8.1 shows the cumulative survival pattern of new teachers. Among 1,702 college graduates who entered teaching at different points of time after gradua-

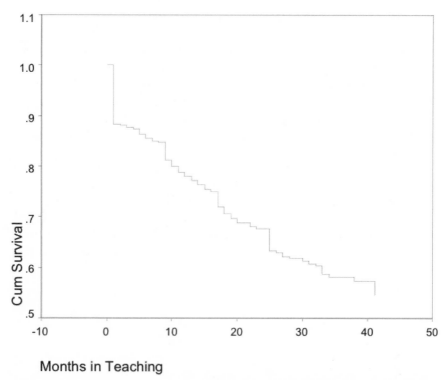

Months in Teaching

**Figure 8.1.  Estimated Survival Function for College Graduates Who Entered Teaching (cumulative survival rate over 40-month period)**

tion, 579 left teaching within the 40-month (five-academic-year) period of graduation from college, with an attrition rate of 34.0 percent. Based on the panel sampling weights, the attrition rate is slightly higher at 34.2 percent. The attrition occurred steadily over the time with a noticeable precipitation during the first month and at the end of each academic year, a pattern that is consistent with the usual attrition rate at the end of an academic year. The cumulative survival rates, as estimated in the life table, are 81.1 percent at the end of the first academic year, 72.0 at the end of the second, 63.3 at the end of the third, 58.7 at the end of the fourth, and 54.6 percent at the end of the fifth academic year. The estimated attrition rates in this study are higher than another national study based on the Teacher Follow-up Survey 1993–1994, that found about 20 percent of the new teachers leave teaching within the first three years of entering teaching (Whitener et al., 1997). The data analysis approach of the current study, taking into account different time points for entry as well as the current study's sampling frame, might be a factor in leading to a different estimate.

## VARIOUS TYPES OF ENTRY INTO TEACHING

In addition to examining the overall attrition pattern for new teachers, this study examines attrition rates as they relate to "various kinds of entry into teaching" as viewed from five perspectives on the teacher: (1) how a teacher first entered teaching; (2) extent of teacher preparation; (3) whether teacher was certified to teach when the follow-up surveys were conducted in 1994 and 1997; (4) whether teacher was certified when the 1997 follow-up survey was conducted; and (5) highest certification in 1994 or 1997.

*How a teacher first entered teaching.* There is a statistically significant difference in hazard rates between those identified as "prepared, taught," and those who "taught, no training" when they first entered teaching (figure 8.2) (Wald = 117.1, $df = 1$, $p < .001$). From the "taught, no training" group to the "prepared, taught" group, there is a statistically significant 355 percent increase in hazard rates. The data unequivocally demonstrate that those who "prepared,

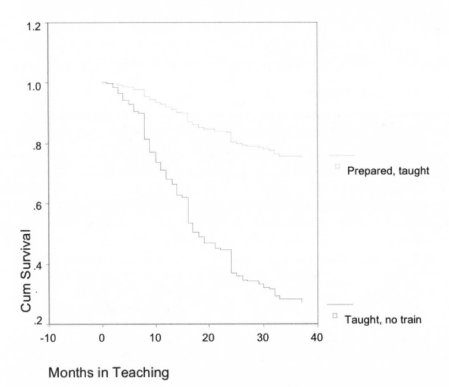

Figure 8.2.    Estimated Survival Functions for Two Groups That Entered Teaching Differently

taught" are much more likely to stay in teaching than those who "taught, no training."

*Fully prepared to teach.* Figure 8.3 shows the survival pattern of two groups of teachers who are or are not fully prepared to teach. According to the definition used by the National Center for Education Statistics for the B&B: 93/97 data set, "fully prepared to teach" includes "the completion of all the following: student teaching, getting certified and participating in a teacher induction program." The hazard rate for those teachers who are not fully prepared is 111 percent more than that for those who are fully prepared to teach. Statistically, those who are fully prepared are significantly more likely to stay in teaching (Wald = 26.6, $df = 1$, $p < .001$).

*Ever certified to teach.* The data in figure 8.4 indicate that those ever certified to teach are much more likely to stay in teaching than those not ever certified. The hazard rate for those ever certified was only about 17 percent of that for

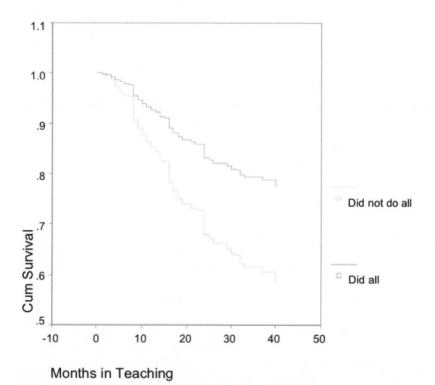

Figure 8.3.   Estimated Survival Functions for Two Groups of Teachers with Different Levels of Teacher Preparation

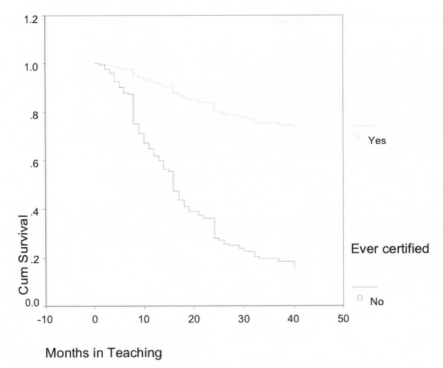

Figure 8.4. Estimated Survival Functions for Two Groups of Teachers Who Were or Were Not Ever Certified to Teach

those not ever certified, a difference that is statistically significant (Wald = 208.3, $df$ = 1, $p$ < .001).

*Current certification status in 1997.* Using data from "whether currently certified to teach" when the 1997 survey was conducted, we compare the survival pattern of those who were or were not currently certified to teach in 1997. The hazard rate for those who were certified to teach was only about 33 percent of those who were not certified, and the difference is statistically significant (figure 8.5) (Wald = 46.7, $df$ = 1, $p$ < .001).

*Highest certification in 1994 or 1997.* The data in this paragraph provide a perspective on, among those who are certified, how the type of certification is related to teacher attrition. The data in figure 8.6 suggest that there is a statistically significant difference in attrition patterns among those who have various types of certification (Wald = 9.7, $df$ = 1, $p$ < .05). In comparison to the group with the most complete level of certification (labeled "advanced" within this national data set), the hazard rates for those with "emergency and other" or "probationary" certification increase by 213 and 111 percent, respectively; and

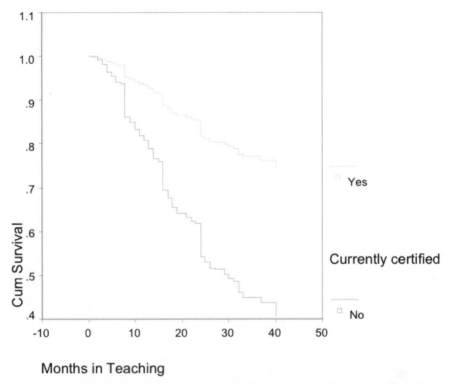

Figure 8.5.   Estimated Survival Functions for Two Groups of Teachers Who Were or Were Not Currently Certified to Teach in 1997

the increases are statistically significant or marginally significant (Wald = 5.3, $df = 1, p = .021$; Wald = 3.6, $df = 1, p = .057$, respectively). In comparison with the "advanced" certification group, the hazard rates for attrition increase by 18 percent for the "regular" certificate group and 28 percent for the "temporary" certification group, but the increases are not statistically significant.

# Summary and Discussion

The results described reveal a relationship between teacher attrition, on the one hand, and adequate preparation and full certification on the other. Using this national sample, the evidence is unequivocally clear that: (1) those who enter teaching fully prepared are more likely to stay in teaching than those who are not; (2) those who are certified are more likely to stay in teaching than those

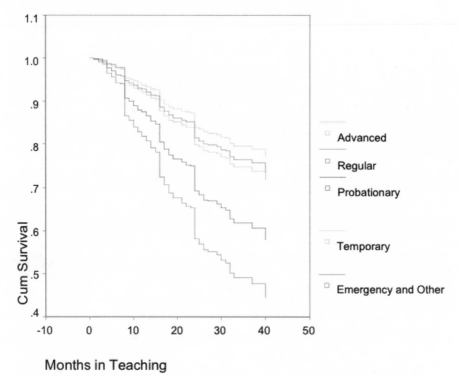

Months in Teaching

**Figure 8.6.    Estimated Survival Function for Teachers with Different Levels of Highest Certification in 1994 and/or 1997**

who are not; and (3) those who have "emergency and other" certificates are more likely to leave teaching than those who have advanced and regular certification. Ideally, if we had a time-varying variable on certification status, we would arrive at a definitive relationship between certification and attrition. However, when we operationalized entry into teaching in five different perspectives and the results all point to the same direction—those who enter teaching without full preparation, uncertified, or with "emergency and other" certificates are much more likely to leave teaching. The results clearly indicate that it is more difficult to survive in the teaching profession for those who enter teaching without adequate preparation and certification.

The findings of the study spotlight several policy concerns. First, the overall attrition rate for new teachers is higher than previously found from other national studies. Data indicate that about 34 percent of those who enter teaching at some points in the 5-year period after obtaining a bachelor's degree leave teaching by the end of the fifth academic year. The estimated cumulative survival rates are 81.1 percent by the end of the first academic year, 63.3 percent by the end of the third academic years, and 54.6 percent by the end of the fifth academic year. Even among those who enter teaching fully prepared, which is defined as completing student teaching, getting certified, and participating in a teacher induction program, the attrition rate is still as high as 26.4 percent by the end of the 5-year period. Teacher attrition disrupts program continuity and planning, hinders student learning, and increases school districts' expenditures on recruiting and hiring. As Ingersoll (2001, 2002) argues, teacher attrition is one of the most important factors contributing to teacher shortages.

The other key policy issue focuses on those entering teaching through various alternative routes that may not include all aspects of being fully prepared. The findings support what other studies are finding (e.g., Darling-Hammond; 2003; Grossman, 1989a, 1989b, 1990, 1994), that those more fully prepared and with full certification (usually aspects of traditional preparation program and high-quality alternative certification programs) are more likely to stay in teaching. Generally speaking, those who enter teaching via emergency certificates or those with less stringent kinds of alternative certification, do not continue to teach as long as those who enter teaching via the traditional route of teacher education.

Given the increasing teacher shortage and the proliferation of non-traditional entries in teaching, these findings have serious implications for the professional community as well as society to reflect upon how to attract and retain quality teachers for our nation's children. The revolving door for teachers is simply not constructive for student learning and the professionalization of our teaching force.

# Note

The research reported in this chapter was extracted from a larger project made possible by a grant from the Small Grants Program, Spencer Foundation. The data presented, the statements made, and the views expressed are solely the responsibility of the authors.

# References

Bliss, T. (1990). Alternate certification in Connecticut: Reshaping the profession. *Peabody Journal of Education, 67*(3), 35–54.

Boe, E., Bobbitt, S. A., Cook, L, H., Barkanic, G., and Maislin, G., (1998). *Teacher turnover in eight cognate areas: National trends and predictors.* Philadelphia: University of Pennsylvania.

Boe, E., Bobbitt, S. A., Cook, L. H., and Barkanic, G. (1998). *National trends in teacher supply and turnover for special and general education.* Philadelphia: University of Pennsylvania.

Cornett, L. M. (1990). Alternate certification: State policies in the SREB states. *Peabody Journal of Education, 67*(3), 55–83.

Darling-Hammond, L. (1994). Who will speak for the children? *Phi Delta Kappan, 76*(1), 21–34

Darling-Hammond, L. (2000). Teacher quality and student achievement: A review of state policy evidence. *Education Policy Analysis Archives, 8*(1). Retrieved February 23, 2001, from http://epaa.asu.edu/epaa/v8n1/

Darling-Hammond, L. (2003, May). Keeping good teachers: What leaders can do. *Educational Leadership, 60*(8), 6–13.

Darling-Hammond, L., Berry, B., and Thoreson, A. (2001). Does teacher certification matter? Evaluating the evidence. *Educational Evaluation and Policy Analysis, 23*(1), 57–77.

Feiman-Nemser, S., and Buchman, M. (1987). When is student teaching teacher education? *Teaching and Teacher Education, 3*(4), 255–73.

Feistritzer, C. E., and Chester, D. T. (2003). *Alternative teacher certification: A state-by-state analysis 2003.* Washington, DC: National Center for Education Information.

Fetler, M. (1999). High school staff characteristics and mathematics test results. *Education Policy Analysis Archives, 7*(9) [Entire issue]. Retrieved November 9, 1999, from http://epaa.asu.edu/epaa/v7n9.html

Fuller, E. J. (1999). *Does teacher certification matter? A comparison of TAAS performance in 1997 between schools with low and high percentages of certified teachers.* Austin: Charles A. Dana Center, University of Texas at Austin.

Goldhaber, M., and Brewer, D. (2000). Does teacher certification matter? High school certification status and student achievement. *Educational Evaluation and Policy Analysis, 22*(2), 129–45.

Grissmer, D. W., and Kirby, S. N. (1987). *Teacher attrition: The uphill climb to staff the nation's schools.* Santa Monica, CA: Rand Corporation.

Grossman, P. L. (1989a). Learning to teach without teacher education. *Teachers College Record, 91*, 191–208.

Grossman, P. L. (1989b). A study in contrast: Sources of pedagogical content knowledge for secondary English. *Journal of Teacher Education, 40*(5), 24–31.

Grossman, P. L. (1990). *The making of a teacher: Teacher knowledge and teacher education.* New York: Teachers College Press.

Grossman, P. L. (1994). *Preparing teachers of substance: Prospects for joint work.* Seattle: Occasional Paper No. 20, Center for Educational Renewal, College of Education, University of Washington.

Henke, R. Chen X., and Greis, S. (2000). *Progress through the teacher pipeline: 1992–1993 college graduates and elementary/secondary school teaching as of 1997.* Washington DC: National Center for Education Statistics, U.S. Department of Education.

Ingersoll, R. M. (2001). Teacher turnover and teacher shortages: An organizational analysis. *American Educational Research Journal, 38*(3), 499–534

Ingersoll, R. M. (2002). The teacher shortage: A case of wrong diagnosis and wrong prescription. *NASSP Bulletin, 86*(631), 16–32.

Kearns, D. (1990, February 28). Do teachers really need licenses? *Wall Street Journal,* p. 14.

Kennedy, M. M. (1991). Some surprising findings on how teachers learn to teach. *Educational Leadership, 49*(3), 14–17.

Kirby, S. N., Darling-Hammond, L., and Hudson, L. (1989). Nontraditional recruits to mathematics and science teaching. *Educational Evaluation and Policy Analysis, 11*(3), 301–23.

Kramer, R. (1991). *Ed school follies: The miseducation of America's teachers.* New York: The Free Press.

McDiarmid, G. W., and Wilson, S. M. (1991). An exploration of the subject matter knowledge of alternate route teachers: Can we assume they know their subjects. *Journal of Teacher Education, 42*(2), 93–103.

Murnane, R. J., Singer, J. D., and Willett, J. B. (1989). The influences of salaries and "opportunity costs" on teachers' career choices: Evidence from North Carolina. *Harvard Educational Review, 59*, 325–46.

Natriello, G., Hansen, A., Frisch, A., and Zumwalt, K. (1990). *Characteristics of entering teachers in New Jersey.* Unpublished manuscript. Teachers College, Columbia University, New York.

Natriello, G., and Zumwalt, K. (1993). New teachers for urban schools? *Education and Urban Society, 26*(1), 49–62.

Raymond, M., Fletcher, S., and Luque, J., (2001). *Teach for America: An evaluation of teacher differences and student outcomes in Houston, Texas.* Stanford, CA: Center for Research on Educational Outcomes, The Hoover Institution, Stanford University.

Shen, J. (1997a). Has the alternative certification policy materialized its promise? A comparison between traditionally and alternatively certified teachers in public schools. *Educational Evaluation and Policy Analysis, 19*(3), 276–83.

Shen, J. (1997b). Teacher retention and attrition in public schools: Evidence from SASS91. *Journal of Educational Research, 91*(2), 81–88.

Shen, J. (1998). The impact of the alternative certification policy on the elementary and secondary teaching force in public schools. *Journal of Research and Development in Education, 32*, 9–16.

Shen, J. (2000). The impact of the alternative certification policy: Multiple perspectives. 235–47. In *Research on effective models for teacher education: Teacher education year book VIII,* ed. J. D. McIntyre and D. M. Byrd. Thousand Oaks, CA: Corwin.

Singer, J. D. (1993). Are special educators' career paths special? Results from a 13-year longitudinal study. *Exceptional Children, 59*, 262–79.

Stoddart, T. (1990). Los Angeles Unified School District Intern Program: Recruiting and preparing teachers for the urban context. *Peabody Journal of Education, 67*(3), 84–122.

Stoddart, T. (1993). Who is prepared to teach in urban schools? *Education and Urban Society, 26*(1), 29–48.

Stoddart, T., and Floden, R. E. (1995). *Traditional and alternative routes to teacher certification: Issues, assumptions, and misconceptions.* East Lansing, MI: National Center for Research on Teacher Learning.

Whitener, S. D., Gruber, K. J., Lynch, H., Tingos, K., Perona, M., and Fondelier, S. (1997). *Characteristics of stayers, movers, and leavers: Results from the teacher follow-up survey: 1994–1995.* Washington, DC: U.S. Department of Education.

Wright, S. (2001). The alternative route to certification. *Techniques, 76*(5), 24–27.

# Summary and Conclusions

## ALTERNATIVE CERTIFICATION TEACHER PREPARATION PROGRAMS: EFFECTS OF PROGRAM MODELS ON TEACHER PERFORMANCE

*Judith L. Hayes*
Wichita State University

## Summary and Conclusions

Across the country, and even within a single state, alternative teacher licensure programs—like traditional programs—cannot all be viewed as equal in terms of content, duration, rigor, and support for learning how to teach (Berry, 2001). Alternative certification is defined using broad terms and includes so many different program designs that it is inaccurate to collectively make inferences based on all alternative program models, or to selectively draw conclusions based on a single alternative program model.

The chapters in this division describe the effect of alternative teacher preparation program models on teacher candidate performance and attrition. The goal of any teacher education program, alternative or traditional, is to create an effective teacher. Each of these studies indicates that the training given to prospective teachers impacts their performance in the classroom.

The first chapter in this division, the NYU program study, investigates the performance of teacher candidates dividing them into two groups—career-changers and recent college graduates. The research findings conclude that the two groups presented distinct patterns. Career changers are split between those exceeding expectations and those performing below expectations with a few candidates in the middle areas. Recent college graduates are more evenly spread across the continuum with almost equal numbers exceeding expectations, performing below expectations and meeting expectations.

The second chapter, on the Governors University, researches the performance of alternative candidates (career changers) measured against a set of program standards and in comparison with teachers that completed a traditional teacher education program. The data show no difference in performance of traditional and alternative candidates based on principal's evaluations of the two groups in this study. The findings from the performance assessment, given by the University Assessment Committee to alternative candidates, indicates that candidates that failed to meet program standards lacked professional dispositions necessary to make a successful transition to teaching.

The third chapter examines research from the Teach For America Program comparing year 1 and year 2 teachers in the alternative program with first-year teachers from accredited traditional education programs to investigate personal feelings of efficacy in relationship to teacher performance and student achievement. According to Pilcher and Steele, training is the most significant influence on teacher performance as suggested by the findings that all achievement differences that did occur favored traditionally trained teachers. Traditionally trained teachers score in the middle ranges; TFA teachers have a wider range of ratings from poor to excellent.

The final chapter in this division by J. Shen and L. Bierlein-Palmer compares attrition patterns of teachers educated through traditional teacher preparation programs with those entering through alternative certification programs. Their study includes all candidates entering the teaching profession. In a nationwide study, their research findings indicate a relationship between teacher attrition and the teacher preparation model. Teachers entering the profession through traditional teacher preparation programs are compared with teachers entering the profession through other routes. Teachers emerging from other routes include entry from all alternative preparation programs, as well as those with emergency, restricted, and probationary certification. The findings indicate that those who enter teaching fully prepared are more likely to stay in teaching, and those who enter through abbreviated routes are more likely to leave teaching. According to Shen and Palmer, teacher training can reduce high rates of attrition and positively impact impending teacher shortages.

Based on the findings in the first three chapters of this division, six common factors are suggested as influencing the production of effective teachers through alternative preparation programs. Those factors are (1) program admission criteria; (2) candidate dispositions considered in the selection and preparation process; (3) program development and support to candidates; (4) program duration—extending over a longer period of time (6 weeks compared to 2 years); (5) program instruction differentiated based on candidates' strengths and weaknesses—variation of needs among diverse pool of candidates; and (6) programs that are standards based with alignment of curriculum content performance assessments.

The teacher candidates identified in the first three chapters fall into three categories: recent college graduates, mid-career-changers, and Teach For America teachers. Recent college graduates could include candidates that made a decision too late in their college program to teach, or individuals that began a teacher education program, did not complete it, and are now returning. Mid-career-changers are those individuals who make a decision to pursue teaching later in life, following experiences that were gained through other careers. Teach For America teachers are basically recent college graduates who commit to teaching in low-income urban or rural schools for a period of two years. Although there are shared characteristics as recent college graduates, these candidates enter the profession with short-term expectations and a different set of motivational factors.

The six recurring themes found in the research from the chapters in this division are discussed below.


## PROGRAM ADMISSION CRITERIA

Alternative teacher licensure programs generally are designed to entice persons from various educational, occupational and life experiences to become teachers, thereby increasing the quantity and diversity of applicants to the profession (Feistritzer, 1998; Wise and Darling-Hammond, 1992). Each of the alternative programs represented in this research are comprised of participants from diverse backgrounds with varied ages and life experiences. Selection of alternative candidates against an established set of criteria is a common characteristic in the NYU's alternative program (admitting only 20 percent of its applicants), and in the Governors State University partnership (selecting one out of three applicants). In the Teach for America program, candidates enter the program with a 2-year commitment to teach in high-needs schools. The primary discussion of TFA candidates in this research targets the period of time after candidates were selected and during their 2-year teaching experience.

The NYU study suggests there are early indicators among career changers of candidates who will be successful in the teaching profession evidenced through individual factors that motivate entry into teaching and previous professional success. According to Dickar, refining the selection process to identify the profiles for success may enable a program to select a stronger corps of teacher candidates.

## CANDIDATE DISPOSITIONS

Dispositions of teacher candidates are receiving increased attention in standards driven, performance-based teacher education programs. Research from Governors University (see chapter 6 by Freeman, Peterson, and Erikson) supports the rationale for examining teacher dispositions. They suggest that

> Considering teacher dispositions has potential as a means for capturing, analyzing, and changing patterns of behavior engaged in by teacher candidates, particularly when patterns retard or interfere with student learning. Rather than viewing dispositions as a series of statements about desired ways of behaving that may or may not be responsive to particular situations, the focus needs to be moved to assisting the teacher candidate and the teacher to adopt different dispositions in the classroom in an attempt to create the most effective fit between and among teacher and students.

The research from NYU notes differences in career changers who enter alternative teacher preparation programs based on a desire to teach as compared with those career changers entering motivated by necessity—they need a job. Their findings reveal that the students assessed as underperforming never indicated an intrinsic desire to give back or help their communities as a motivational factor for entering teaching. Career changers who were successful in their previous careers are much more likely to bring that success to the classroom.

Some candidates in alternative programs may possess the necessary skills and knowledge to teach but are unable to successfully transition into the teacher profession as a result of behaviors or attitudes that are demonstrated through their dispositions. Career changers in the NYU study who exceed expectations in performance assessments shared common traits that contributed to their success. They also are able to synthesize new ideas and skills and implement them into their teaching repertoire.

At Governors University the faculty assesses candidates' dispositions, reviews professional behaviors, and discerns commitments to life-long learning. Additional coursework may be required if recurrent dispositional issues are evident.

Emotions and feelings of efficacy are involved in the teaching and learning process. To what degree a teacher believes they have the capacity to affect student performance impacts student achievement and teacher satisfaction. Training and experience seem to influence teachers' feelings and achievement. Teach for America teachers, compared with regular teachers, indicate lower feelings of efficacy. Training increases teachers' perceptions of efficacy. Darling-Hammond, Chung and Frelow (2002) find a correlation between feelings of preparedness and teacher efficacy which is supported in the research from Teach for America, NYU, and the Governors State University.

## PROGRAM DEVELOPMENT

The evolution of a program, beginning with a small cohort of teachers and expanding to accommodate increased numbers of candidates, influences the development of teacher preparation models and impacts candidates in the preparation process. There is a strong mentoring component in all three program models, NYU, Governors University, and Teach for America, providing ongoing assistance to teacher candidates.

NYU provides Urban Master Teachers from the university to mentor the new teachers and provide ongoing support throughout the program. Governors University works in partnership with the participating districts to provide mentors to co-teach and co-plan with new teachers as well as providing university program mentors to give supplemental assistance while regularly monitoring candidates' progress and needs. Teach for America requires weekly classes of their candidates to provide support and also includes mentoring by a college instructor that visits the teachers' classrooms on a regular basis. Ongoing mentor support, university–district partnerships, and collaboration and interactions within a cohort of new teacher candidates provide a foundation within a teacher preparation model to facilitate the growth and development of the novice teacher.

## PROGRAM DURATION

The three program models discussed in this research suggest that the duration of a teacher preparation program influences teacher performance and attrition. Each of these programs provides training prior to entering the field experience and continues support over a period of time facilitating the candidates' transition into the profession.

NYU research on two groups of candidates entering the program, recent college graduates and career changers, concludes that the coursework prior to teaching may not be a long enough time for individuals to confront personal biases and to change attitudes necessary for professional identity (see chapter 5 by Dickar). The Governors University program continues over a 16-month period of time. The coursework is aligned with the objectives of the traditional teacher preparation program, including the general education requirements. A number of professional education courses (16 hours) must be completed before candidates are placed in a classroom. Teach for America candidates participate in an intensive summer program before placement in teaching positions. Support training continues from ongoing teacher education programs adjacent to place-ment locations. Many recruits are able to complete state credentialing require-ments during their two years of service.

## PROGRAM INSTRUCTION DIFFERENTIATED BY CANDIDATE NEEDS

The first chapter in this division examines the differences in the characteristics of students in an alternative program in New York. M. Dickar compares new teachers that are career changers with recent college graduates entering the pro-fession through an alternative preparation model. The differences in the strengths and weaknesses of candidates in the two groups suggest possibilities for delineating program instruction to accommodate individual needs. This re-search suggests that programs that prepare candidates for the classroom need to be better tailored to the needs of the individual candidates.

The candidates discussed in the first three chapters of this division (chapters 5, 6, and 7) include recent college graduates, career changers, and Teach for America teachers. Each group of candidates possesses a unique set of characteris-tics. Teacher preparation program models that differentiate instruction with an understanding of those characteristics and of individual needs can provide rele-vant, meaningful instruction and support as needed.

## PROGRAM STANDARDS

All three of the teacher preparation program models represented through the research in the first three chapters of this division include a set of program standards and assessments as a component of the teaching model. Candidates entering in NYU's program must pass two state teacher exams, the Liberal Arts and Sciences Test (LAST) and the Content Specialty Test (CST), in their area of certification to meet requirements for the state alternative license. Governors State University evaluates their candidates on a performance-based model in alignment with specific standards. Multiple measures of assessment are em-ployed focusing on the candidates' output rather than input. Teach For America assesses students' attitudes and feelings of efficacy in relationship to their per-formance as measured by the university and by the school principal.

Analysis of candidates' performance even when aligned with standards driven program models is complex. When given the diverse context of alternative programs the complexity of assessment is magnified. However, both traditional and alternative teacher preparation programs need to focus on *progress not perfection* (see chapter 6 by Freeman, Peterson, and Erikson).

Strong alternative teacher preparation programs have models that have been designed in response to community needs. They have established criteria for selection of candidates determined by skills and dispositions and have designed programs in alignment with standards and tailored to individual needs. Ongoing support is provided throughout the duration of the program as well as assessment of candidates' skills and attitudes at multiple points throughout the program.

In summary, each of these studies contributes data to facilitate understanding of alternative teacher preparation programs and identifies the characteristics of those programs that are positively impacting the training of effective teachers. As profiles of success are identified, alternative programs can utilize the research to recruit teacher candidates, provide effective teacher training and support, reduce patterns of attrition, and guide professional development.

# References

Berry, B. (2001). No shortcuts to preparing good teachers. *Educational Leadership, 58*(8), 32–36.

Darling-Hammond, L., Chung, R., and Frelow, F. (2002). Variations in teacher preparation: How well do different pathways prepare teachers to teach? *Journal of Teacher Education, 53*(4), 286–302.

Feistritzer, C. E. (1998). Alternative teacher certification: An overview. *National Center for Education Information.* Retrieved on May 28, 2004 from http://www.ncei.com/Alt-Teacher-Cert.htm

Wise, A. and Darling-Hammond, L. (1992). Alternative certification as an oxymoron. *The Education Digest 57*(8), 46–48.

Division 3

# NON-TRADITIONAL MODELS OF PROFESSIONAL DEVELOPMENT

# Overview and Framework

## NON-TRADITIONAL MODELS OF PROFESSIONAL DEVELOPMENT

*Christy L. Faison*
Rowan University

> Christy L. Faison is the Associate Provost for Academic Affairs and Professor of Education at Rowan University. Her areas of responsibility include academic policies, curriculum, and accreditation. Her research interests include collaborative teaching and the integration of technology in teacher education.

According to Judy Salpeter (2003), "Never before has pressure been so high to find ways to support teaching and learning through effective professional development" (p. 34). The No Child Left Behind Act's requirement for highly qualified teachers in every classroom by 2005–2006 means that current classroom teachers need access to high-level professional development. Traditionally, professional development has taken the form of inservice workshops and guest presentations of minimal duration and intensity, limited interaction, and with little or no follow-up. These types of professional development activities often lack direct connection to district goals and provide no observable effect on education (Kelleher, 2003). According to Gaudelli (2001), professional development is frequently done to teachers, rather than in collaboration with them, and assumes that teachers are deficient. In recent years, however, researchers have attempted to delineate factors that contribute to effective professional development. Research suggests that something more than the traditional methods of professional development are needed. Models are needed that take into account the context of learning and the background, experiences, expectations, and motivations of the teachers (Gaudelli, 2001). The National Staff Development Council (NSDC) in its revised standards for staff development (2001) categorizes its standards for effective professional development into three broad categories: context (culture in which learning takes place), process (how learning will be delivered), and content (knowledge and skills). These standards guide districts in the planning and implementation of professional development experiences that promote outcomes designed to result in better student learning. Further, the NSDC has added the goal that all teachers in all schools will experience high-quality professional learning as part of their daily work by 2007.

Factors that contribute to effective professional development include opportunities to acquire new knowledge and skills, sufficient time to participate in and reflect on learning experiences, teacher collaboration and teamwork, administrative support, and a focus on improving student learning (Crowther and Cannon, 2002; Guskey, 2003). However, the investigations of these factors have mostly been limited to teachers' perceptions of their effectiveness and their satisfaction with the learning experience as opposed to the impact those experiences have on student learning (Guskey, 2003).

The investigations in this division study alternative strategies for providing professional development and report the results of the use of those strategies with current classroom teachers. The three chapters that follow—chapters 9, 10, and 11—provide examples of non-traditional models of professional development that include peer coaching and the use of technology. Two of the chapters examine the delivery of professional development through online instruction and support. Salpeter states that "experts are recognizing that one component of the most successful new models of professional development is technology that supports 'anytime, anywhere' learning communities where educators can converse, collaborate, and share best practices" (2003, p. 35). The January 2003 report of the National Commission on Teaching and America's Future states that "Technology is perhaps the most important—and most under-utilized— tool for providing teachers access to the targeted professional development they need, when and how they need it" (p. 28).

Online professional development helps districts overcome obstacles of time, space, and the need to serve large numbers of teachers with multiple needs. It also expands resources available to districts with limited funding. Further, online professional development promotes sustained learning opportunities with the use of online learning communities. Most online professional development opportunities are also supplemented with face-to-face meetings, consultations, or mentoring. The two chapters included here investigate the delivery of an online teacher education program for ESOL training (English for Speakers of Other Languages) in rural and suburban areas, and the use of an online professional development environment to support urban teachers using specific curriculum materials in their classrooms.

The third chapter studies the effectiveness of coaching on teacher practice.

Coaching supports effective professional development factors such as collaboration and reflection and "dissolves the walls of isolation . . . that exists in teachers' classrooms . . ." (McLymont and da Costa, 1998, p. 3). Further, the intent of coaching is to bring about positive changes in the practices of classroom teachers that support student learning through providing peer models who are knowledgeable resources. This study looks specifically at elementary and secondary teachers in a large urban district involved in peer coaching, and examines the effectiveness of coaching on mathematics instruction, and as a tool to improve teaching and learning in general.

All of the studies in this division diverge from the use of the traditional forms of professional development that are still prominent in many districts throughout the United States. These studies, instead, present research-based models that attempt to provide teachers and districts with alternative methods for the delivery of professional development opportunities.

# References

Crowther, D. T. and Cannon, J. R. (2002). Professional development models: A comparison of duration and effect. *Proceedings of the Annual International Conference of the Association for the Education of Teachers in Science.* (ERIC Document Reproduction Service No. ED465639)

Gaudelli, W. (2001, November). *Professional development, global pedagogy, and potential: Examining an alternative approach to the episodic workshop.* Paper presented at the annual meeting of the National Council for the Social Studies, Washington, DC.

Guskey, T. R. (2003). What makes professional development effective? *Phi Delta Kappan, 84,* 748–50.

Kelleher, J. (2003). A model for assessment-driven professional development. *Phi Delta Kappan, 84,* 751–56.

McLymont, E. F. and da Costa, J. L. (1998, April). *Cognitive coaching the vehicle for professional development and teacher collaboration.* Paper presented at the annual meeting of the American Educational Research Association, San Diego, CA.

National Commission on Teaching and America's Future. (2003). *No dream denied: A pledge to America's children. Summary report.* Retrieved June 3, 2004, from http://documents.nctaf.achieve3000.com/summary_report.pdf

National Staff Development Council. (2001). *Standards for professional development (revised).* Retrieved June 1, 2004, from http://www.nsdc.org/standards/index.cfm

Salpeter, J. (2003). Professional development: Twenty-first century models. *Technology and Learning, 24,* 34–50.

# CHAPTER 9

# Facing the Challenge of Online ESOL Teacher Education in an Era of Accountability: A Collaborative Model

*Abdelilah Sehlaoui*
Emporia State University

*Cynthia Anast Seguin*
Emporia State University

*Kimberley Kreicker*
Emporia State University

Dr. Abdelilah Salim Sehlaoui is Assistant Professor at Emporia State University, Department of Foreign Languages. Sehlaoui has extensive K–12 teaching experience. He published in cross-cultural communicative competence in ESOL teachers, second/foreign language reading, and the sociocultural dynamics of computers in ESOL. He co-authored four federal grants in professional development training in TESOL.

Dr. Cynthia Anast Seguin is Associate Professor at Emporia State University, Department of School Leadership and Middle/Secondary Teacher Education. Seguin co-authored four federal grants providing training for preservice/inservice teachers in multicultural education and English Language Acquisition. Dr. Seguin has extensive K–12 teaching experience. Research/publication interests include multicultural education assessment and online learning.

Dr. Kimberley Kreicker is an ESOL Resource Specialist at Emporia State University, Department of Foreign Languages, for Project Best, a Title III professional development grant to Emporia State University on behalf of the Shawnee Mission (Kansas) District. Kreicker has worked extensively in K–12 ESOL education, with an emphasis on high-impact rural contexts.

## ABSTRACT

The number of English language learners in America's public schools continues to grow at an ever-accelerating rate. This creates tremendous challenges for educators and students alike. School districts often struggle to provide teachers with the professional development they need to meet the academic and personal needs of their ELL students. This challenge is frequently amplified in rural areas, where resources may be limited due to geographic isolation, inadequate funding, and other factors. To meet these challenges, Emporia State University created a collaborative teacher education model to provide English for Speakers of Other Languages training and support to teachers in several heavily impacted school districts across the state. This report provides data regarding a non-traditional model for delivery of ESOL teacher education. Information is shared from six perspectives: objectives of the model, theoretical framework and related research, methods of instructional delivery, data collected, results/conclusions, and implications for teachers and teacher educators.

# Introduction

The number of English language learners (ELL) in America's public schools continues to grow. This creates tremendous challenges for educators and students alike. School districts often struggle to provide teachers with the professional development they need to meet both the academic and personal needs of their ELL students. This challenge is frequently amplified in rural areas, where resources may be limited due to geographic isolation, inadequate funding, and other factors.

Kansas demographics have shifted dramatically in the past ten to fifteen years with an influx of immigrants from Mexico, Central America, and Asia. Typically, non-English-speaking families moved into Kansas communities to work in agriculture and other labor-intensive industries (Harrison, 1998; Wood, 1988). New industrial plants and agribusinesses (such as meat processing) have resulted in a sudden increase of ELL students in rural Kansas schools, most of which were homogeneous prior to 1989 (Judd and Kreicker, 1998). Schools in these communities are often ill-prepared to face the challenges of educating their newest students.

To meet these challenges, Emporia State University (ESU) created a collaborative teacher education model to provide English for Speakers of Other Languages (ESOL) training and support to several heavily impacted school districts across the state. This chapter provides data on this non-traditional model for delivery of ESOL teacher education. Information is shared from six perspectives: (1) Objectives of the model; (2) Theoretical framework and related research; (3) Methods of instructional delivery; (4) Data collected; (5) Results/conclusions; and (6) Implications for teachers and teacher educators.

# Objectives of the Model

Emporia State University created a consortium of faculty from the College of Liberal Arts and Sciences, the Teachers College, two regional educational services centers, the Kansas State Department of Education, and educators in high-impact rural and suburban school districts from across the state. Urban areas were not included, as the major urban areas in Kansas already have long-standing ESOL programs, with a number of well-trained teachers in place. A consortium-wide needs assessment was conducted, which identified the districts' most compelling needs. These needs included:

1. an inadequate number of ESOL-certified P–12 teachers;
2. insufficient access to ESOL professional development opportunities;
3. inadequate instructional services for ELL students, with low numbers of ELL students meeting state standards and/or demonstrating mastery of English;
4. a lack of appropriate monitoring and assessment procedures for ELL students;
5. a lack of ESOL instructional materials, technical support, and resources; and
6. a need to develop awareness of, and respect for, other cultures.

The consortium then designed three Title III Professional Development grant proposals, with collaboration as their foundation. The ultimate goal was for ESU to create an innovative, online, teacher education program—designed to provide effective ESOL teacher education in rural and suburban areas—which would ultimately enhance the academic achievement of P–12 ELL students in the consortium districts. This program would train existing classroom teachers in the consortium districts, and would lead them to Kansas certification in ESOL. Courses would include cultural awareness, teaching methodology,

ESOL assessment and evaluation, linguistics, and a practicum. Licensed P–12 teachers, paraprofessionals, and other school staff were to be included in the training. The ESOL teacher training model that emerged has five main objectives:

1. to develop and implement a professional development instructional program resulting in improved teaching efficacy;
2. to develop appropriate, research-based instructional and assessment strategies, resources, and curricula specific to ELL students;
3. to establish an ongoing professional development model for all school staff to sustain these essential skills;
4. to collect and analyze data for program improvement; and
5. to develop and implement a comprehensive evaluation plan utilizing data collection and feedback from project participants, as a way to regularly evaluate and refine the program.

# Theoretical Framework and Related Research

Creating effective learning environments for ELL students is the responsibility of all members of the school community (Milk, Mercado, and Sapiens, 1992, p. 15). This is especially true since ELL students typically spend most of their school day in the mainstream classroom, and ". . . responsibility for instructing ELL students in both content and language falls increasingly upon teachers in mainstream classrooms" (Cornell, 1995, p. 15). The academic success or failure of ELL students, then, depends greatly upon the quality of instruction they receive from their mainstream classroom teachers. Yet recent studies report that as many as 60 percent of the teachers working with ELL students in monolingual English classroom settings are teaching without certification or formal training in that area (Menken and Antunez 2001; National Clearing House for English Language Acquisition, 2002; Pelavin Associates, 1999), and as many as 80 percent of teachers surveyed feel unprepared to teach a diverse student population (Holloway, 2003, p. 90). As Anstrom (1998) states, "perhaps the most important link in effective mainstream instruction of ELL students is the classroom teacher. Since both research and logic suggest that teachers who receive appropriate training are more likely to create supportive instructional environments than those without such preparation, defining and implementing appropriate training are critical to ELL achievement" (p. 20).

Therefore, Emporia State University's program is designed to train teachers who are already in the classroom. This helps to ensure a relatively stable teaching force of individuals who are more likely to be committed to their hometowns—the communities and regions that had been experiencing this new and rapid influx of ELL students (Kreicker, 2003), and would also ensure having ESOL-trained staff in districts where hiring a separate ESOL teacher is neither practical nor affordable.

Training existing classroom teachers is further supported by the research of Collier and Thomas (1999), Lim and Watson (1993), Genessee (1999), and others, showing that it is possible—even desirable—to teach ESOL through content-based instruction, provided specific elements (such as active, hands-on methods) are present. These findings support the idea that classroom teachers can utilize strategies in which the English language is naturally and functionally learned through interaction with classroom content. As Lim and Watson state, ". . . combining authentic and natural language experiences with content-centered classroom practices leads to optimal language learning and optimal subject matter learning." (p. 387)

Research-based instructional strategies and professional development practices are the basis for the ESU model. These include content-based strategies developed by the Center for Applied Linguistics (CAL), as well as needs assessments, knowledge of target content, and institutional experiences that would establish creative learning environments for effective professional development. These are based on the research of Cummins (1981), Krashen (1981, 1983), O'Malley and Chamot (1986, 1990), O'Malley and Valdez-Pierce (1996), and others.

In order to reach the far-flung members of the consortium, courses are designed to be conducted almost entirely online, via WebCT. Teacher participants are provided with high-quality texts and ESOL resource materials, which they read, incorporate into their teaching, and reflect upon both individually and as a group. The project coursework is aligned to state standards, and is rich in links to online sites for serving ELL students. The project also provides a wide variety of ESOL teaching resources which can be borrowed for both individual use and for the training of consortium staff beyond the projects' participating teachers. In-service and preservice educators all across the state can use the Internet to access detailed information about the available resources and can request to have the desired materials delivered to their door via regular mail.

Since meaningful change in teaching practice rarely takes hold over the long term unless support systems for change are created within the context of an entire school setting (Leithwood, 1990), the online learning communities used in the ESU model help to bring isolated practitioners together for collaboration and sharing beyond the length of the training program. Grant faculty are available both online and in person to provide support to the participating teachers and schools throughout the life of the grant, and ESU staff will be available well into the future. Regular face-to-face visits with the participant teachers and their schools makes it possible for ESU to assist in addressing specific classroom and district needs, and therefore the needs of individual ELL students.

In addition to the research base, ESU's theoretical framework also is shaped by national and state standards, identified needs of the consortium districts, and the conceptual framework of the ESU Teachers College, which utilizes research on effective practices and professional development to bridge the gap between teachers' proficiencies and ESOL standards for teaching. Since the challenge for ESOL professional development lays in moving teachers from their current teaching approach toward creating optimal learning environments for ELL students, professional development programs must focus on how ELL students learn. Given the often atypical experiences and needs of second language learners, the native languages and cultures of ELL students play an important role in learning, even in settings where English is the primary language of instruction (Sehlaoui, 1999). Integrating students' linguistic and cultural background is empowering for both learners and teachers (Sehlaoui, 2001), an additional fact that the ESU project sought to address. The Collaborative Model for Online ESOL Teacher Education is illustrated in Figure 9.1.

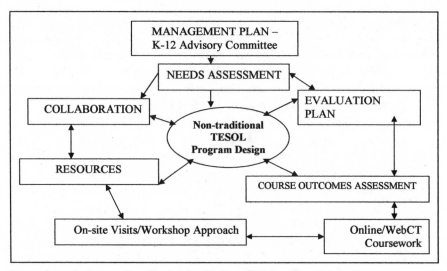

Figure 9.1   Collaborative Model for Online ESOL Teacher Education

# Methods of Instructional Delivery

## TECHNIQUES AND METHODS OF DELIVERY

The director of the ESOL Teacher Education program at ESU developed online coursework leading to Kansas ESOL certification in the year 2000. The Multicultural Specialist in the Teachers College also designed an online course in diversity education, which is a required part of Kansas ESOL certification. Each class was then launched and pilot-tested. This online method of delivery became the basis of the Title III Professional Development grant proposals. In 2001, the collaborative efforts of these two ESU departments (the Department of Foreign Languages, in the College of Liberal Arts and Science, and the Department of School Leadership and Middle/Secondary Teacher Education, in the Teachers College) and the consortium participants yielded $4 million in grants to implement this new program. The grants provided four new faculty members, who became key partners in working with teachers in the participating districts.

## RESOURCES AND MATERIALS

New ESOL resources were purchased through grant funds and housed at the university, regional service centers, and districts for use of teachers in the grant project as well as university in-service and advanced candidates. A professional development plan for participating districts was implemented, to help all staff address the needs of ELL students to meet state standards. Project faculty also provided ongoing staff development within the districts on an as-needed basis, in addition to the training provided to selected teachers through the ESOL certification portion of the project.

## PARTICIPANT SELECTION

Teacher participants were selected through a formal application process according to criteria established by the Professional Development Leadership Team, which included representatives from the university, P–12 district administrators, staff from regional service centers, and the State Department of Education. Participants were expected to have: (1) a commitment (disposition) to continue professional growth and service to the profession; (2) strong pedagogical skills;

(3) a demonstrated willingness to address the needs of diverse learners; (4) a principal's letter of recommendation addressing excellence criteria; and (5) a willingness to adhere to a learning contract which outlines duties and responsibilities of project participants. Study participants included online cohort groups of 20 teachers for each 15 credit hour program required for ESOL certification, in addition to traditional on-campus students, for a total of 362 participants.

## ASSESSMENT AND EVALUATION

The teacher education program had a strong foundation in assessment of multicultural/diversity outcomes (Seguin, Ambrosio, and Hogan, 2000; Seguin and Ambrosio, 2002). Additionally, the university had participated in an innovative 'Teacher Work Sample" (TWS) project to assess preservice candidate's ability to:

1. Plan and deliver effective instructional units;
2. Employ meaningful classroom assessments; and
3. Analyze and reflect on their experiences.

The TWS assessment model provided both candidate and overall program evaluation data. Because of the successful TWS implementation for undergraduates, the grant consortium included the TWS in the ESOL teacher certification process, further strengthening teacher accountability. Through the use of multiple measures, including the TWS, evaluation evidence was analyzed to determine progress toward meeting ESOL course goals and objectives. These measures included:

1. focus groups and exit interviews;
2. pre- and post-tests;
3. classroom observations and videotaped self-assessments;
4. teacher online reflection logs/discussion boards;
5. midterm and final course evaluations;
6. external evaluator reports;
7. monthly reports from project faculty;
8. Teacher Work Sample assessment;
9. state-mandated PRAXIS test results; and
10. Classroom observations (Sheltered Instruction Observation Protocol).

Assessment measures included in this chapter are pre- and post-tests, midterm and final course evaluations, the TWS, and classroom observations. The evaluation plan provides a comprehensive evaluative look at project effectiveness through a team approach. Furthermore, the evaluation plan uses theme-based qualitative methods and descriptive statistical analyses that focus on systemic reform and student outcomes. Table 9.1 illustrates the range of program evaluation and accountability.

# Findings

## QUANTITATIVE DATA

Candidate content knowledge is assessed through the TWS as a summative assessment during the ESOL Practicum. Candidates demonstrate their ability to

**Table 9.1   Summary of Project Evaluation Instruments and Purposes**

| Data Collection Technique | Description of Data Collected | Data Source | Collection Personnel | Completion Date |
|---|---|---|---|---|
| Participant Profile Form | Baseline data about participants | Project participants | Project Personnel | September |
| Focus Group/ Individual Interviews | Project activities and impact | Project participants | Project Personnel | May |
| Survey Instruments | Satisfaction with activities; impact on teaching/learning | Project participants | Project Personnel | December, May |
| Anecdotal Data Collection | Advocacy impact of training on students' learning | Project Participants | Project Personnel | December, May |
| Observation instruments | Instructional effectiveness | Project participants | Project Personnel | December, May |
| Teacher online discussions | Evaluation data | Project participants | Project Personnel | December, May |
| Teacher portfolio TWS | Evaluation data; impact of teacher's training on learning | Project Participants | Project Personnel | Last Semester of coursework |

plan, deliver, and assess content based on state and national standards; to analyze and reflect upon student learning; and to identify professional development opportunities for improving their knowledge and skills.

Since the TWS is relatively new, ESU has not yet established baseline scores. This will be completed in fall, 2004. Because the percentages of 90, 80, and 70 are frequently used in courses as criteria for the grades "A," "B," and "C" respectively, comparable percentages and grades are used as points of reference for the TWS in this report (that is, 90 percent or higher is exceptional, 80–89 percent is very good, and 70–79 percent is acceptable).

For Factor 2 of the TWS (Unit Learning Goals), candidates must demonstrate content knowledge by preparing age-appropriate objectives that measure high- and low-level knowledge/skills. As shown in table 9.2, candidate mean scores on Factor 2 far exceed the acceptable score level (12.6) and approach the exceptional score level (16.2). Except for a 0.3 score decrease for secondary candidates in Spring 2003, they show a steady increase. Of the 362 completing the TWS, 91 percent (329) score higher than 12.6 (70 percent). Additional TWS data are provided in later sections. Table 9.2 provides mean scores for TWS Factor 2.

Follow-up surveys of program graduates and their employers provide information regarding candidates' content knowledge. Table 9.3 lists items and mean ratings from the most recent graduate and employer follow-up studies that relate to content knowledge. Eighty percent or more of both graduates and employers indicate "Very Well Prepared" or "Well Prepared" on content knowledge items, providing strong evidence that candidates possess the necessary content knowledge.

Since Kansas has just begun to require the PRAXIS content area exam for teaching licensure, ESOL PRAXIS test data are not available. The 2003–2004 PRAXIS data will first be available in fall of 2004. The program candidates' growth in content knowledge is demonstrated, however, through pre- and post-tests. Table 9.4 shows an increase in candidates' post-test score in terms of content knowledge, from 56–80 percent with an average of 59 percent.

The university's English for Speakers of Other Languages (ESOL) licensure program has been reviewed and approved by the Kansas State Department of

**Table 9.2   Mean Scores for Teacher Work Sample Factor 2 (Unit Learning Goals)**

|  | Spring 2002 | Fall 2002 | Spring 2003 |
|---|---|---|---|
| All Candidates (18 points possible) | 15.83 | 16.05 | 16.25 |
| Elementary (18 points possible) | 16.04 | 16.15 | 16.52 |
| Secondary (18 points possible) | 15.51 | 15.94 | 15.64 |

**Table 9.3    Mean Ratings of Content Knowledge Items of Initial Candidates from 1998 to 2000 Graduate and Employer Follow-up Studies**

| Survey Type Item Number and Topic | PK–12 | PK–5 | 6-8 | 9-12 | ALL | Very Well Prepared or Well Prepared | Needs Help or Was Not Prepared |
|---|---|---|---|---|---|---|---|
| **Graduate Survey** | | | | | | | |
| Integration of Knowledge | 4.07 | 4.04 | 4.13 | 4.13 | 4.06 | 80.8% | 2.3% |
| Content Knowledge | 4.11 | 4.11 | 4.24 | 3.96 | 4.12 | 80.0% | 3.8% |
| **Employer Survey** | | | | | | | |
| Subject-Matter Competency | 4.17 | 4.21 | 3.95 | 4.33 | 4.15 | 84.1% | 0.7% |

**Table 9.4    Candidates' Post-Test Content Knowledge Scores**

| Pre-Test Scores | | Post-Test Scores | | Improvement | |
|---|---|---|---|---|---|
| Number Correct | Percent Correct | Number Correct | Percent Correct | Number | Percent |
| 14 | 56% | 15 | 60% | 1 | 4% |
| 15 | 60% | 18 | 72% | 3 | 12% |
| 17 | 68% | 20 | 80% | 3 | 12% |
| 9 | 36% | 14 | 56% | 5 | 20% |
| 12 | 48% | 20 | 80% | 8 | 32% |
| 15 | 60% | 19 | 76% | 4 | 16% |
| 17 | 68% | 19 | 76% | 2 | 8% |
| 17 | 68% | 19 | 76% | 2 | 8% |
| 13 | 52% | 17 | 68% | 4 | 16% |
| 16 | 64% | 18 | 72% | 2 | 8% |
| 18 | 72% | 20 | 80% | 2 | 8% |
| 15 | 60% | 17 | 68% | 2 | 8% |
| 16 | 64% | 19 | 76% | 3 | 12% |
| 11 | 44% | 15 | 60% | 4 | 16% |
| 14 | 56% | 17 | 68% | 3 | 12% |
| 18 | 72% | 20 | 80% | 2 | 8% |
| 17 | 68% | 17 | 68% | 0 | 0% |
| 12 | 48% | 18 | 72% | 6 | 24% |
| MEANS: **14.78 (59%)** | | | | | |

Education (KSDE), and with no areas cited for improvement. Since assessment of content knowledge is one of the functions of the KSDE review, program content knowledge has been externally judged to meet state and national standards.

All program candidates are required to complete an advanced field experience activity, in the form of a practicum. Table 9.5 illustrates information collected from the post-practicum follow-up survey from 362 candidates (the data includes our on-campus and non-grant online courses compiled together). Table 9.6 shows 89 percent exceeding and meeting expectations. Table 9.7 illustrates course final evaluation results.

## QUALITATIVE DATA

Teacher comments after completing the project were collected. A theme-based analysis of data from focus groups, midterm and final online course evaluations, observations, and self-assessments revealed patterns in candidates' responses:

1. *Feelings of preparedness:*
    All participants reported feelings of preparedness, such as: "I feel very prepared." "I had little or no experience in theories behind ESOL prior to class. Thanks for your help!" "My philosophy of education is changing with all I'm learning." "Striving for student success is my ultimate goal and with the knowledge I have gained I feel ready."

2. *Feedback on improvements made:*
    The majority of participants (89 percent) reported improvements, such as: "I work with people now who are in the program and they seem comfortable with the changes." "My teaching styles have changed to better fit the needs of ESL students; my assessments and activities are more accessible to them." "I redesigned assessments." "I am more aware of the needs that my ESL students have and more aware of how to meet those needs."

3. *Benefiting from the project in terms of resources, strategies, and networking:*
    All participants reported benefits, such as: ". . . useful rubrics, logs, response sheets, etc., that can be copied and used in classroom." "This past year's experience has been an amazing learning experience, in which I have absorbed a lot of valuable information to integrate into my classroom and enhance my instruction/ELL learning."

**Table 9.5     Sample Response Data to Post-Practicum Survey Questions**

| Questions | Student Responses | | | | | |
|---|---|---|---|---|---|---|
| | Yes | % | No | % | None | % |
| 1. Would you recommend the program to a colleague? | 356 | 98.34 | 3 | 0.82 | 3 | 0.82 |
| 2. Did you benefit from the program? | 361 | 99.72 | 0 | 0.00 | 1 | 0.27 |
| 3. Did you benefit in terms of: | | | | | | |
|    A. Instructional Strategies | 352 | 97.23 | 8 | 2.20 | 2 | 0.55 |
|    B. Resources | 350 | 96.68 | 5 | 1.38 | 2 | 1.93 |
|    C. Networking, Collaboration | 350 | 96.68 | 8 | 2.20 | 2 | 0.55 |
|    D. Assessment Strategies | 360 | 99.44 | 1 | 0.27 | 1 | 0.27 |
|    E. Cross-Cultural Communication | 360 | 99.44 | 0 | 0.00 | 2 | 0.55 |
|    F. Cultural Awareness | 361 | 99.72 | 0 | 0.00 | 1 | 0.27 |
| 4. Have you used new strategies? | 354 | 97.79 | 4 | 1.10 | 4 | 1.10 |
| 5. Which have you used most? | | | | | | |
|    A. TPR | 360 | 99.44 | 2 | 0.55 | 0 | 0.00 |
|    B. Communicative Approach | 350 | 96.68 | 12 | 3.39 | 0 | 0.00 |
|    C. Audio-Lingual Method | 360 | 99.44 | 2 | 0.55 | 0 | 0.00 |
|    D. Direct Instruction | 340 | 93.92 | 22 | 6.07 | 0 | 0.00 |
|    E. Phonic Method | 360 | 99.44 | 2 | 0.55 | 0 | 0.00 |
|    F. Modifying Curriculum | 300 | 82.87 | 62 | 17.12 | 0 | 0.00 |
|    G. Linguistic Analysis | 310 | 85.63 | 52 | 14.36 | 0 | 0.00 |
|    H. Authentic Assessment | 320 | 88.39 | 42 | 11.60 | 0 | 0.00 |
|    I. Cross-Cultural Communication | 181 | 50.00 | 181 | 50.00 | 0 | 0.00 |
|    J. Cultural Awareness | 300 | 82.87 | 62 | 17.12 | 0 | 0.00 |
|    K. Sheltered Instruction | 361 | 99.72 | 1 | 0.27 | 0 | 0.00 |
|    L. Natural Approach | 181 | 50.00 | 181 | 50.00 | 0 | 0.00 |
| 6. Has this program positively affected your students' learning? | 362 | 100 | 0 | 0.00 | 0 | 0.00 |
| 7. Which did you learn . . . ? | | | | | | |
|    A. TPR | 280 | 77.34 | 82 | 22.65 | 0 | 0.00 |
|    B. Communicative Approach | 280 | 77.34 | 82 | 22.65 | 0 | 0.00 |
|    C. Audio-Lingual Method | 262 | 72.37 | 100 | 27.62 | 0 | 0.00 |
|    D. Direct Instruction | 360 | 99.44 | 2 | 0.55 | 0 | 0.00 |
|    E. Phonic Method | 360 | 99.44 | 2 | 0.55 | 0 | 0.00 |
|    F. Modifying Curriculum | 280 | 77.34 | 82 | 22.65 | 0 | 0.00 |
|    G. Linguistic Analysis | 280 | 77.34 | 82 | 22.65 | 0 | 0.00 |
|    H. Authentic Assessment | 350 | 96.68 | 12 | 3.39 | 0 | 0.00 |
|    I. Cross-Cultural Communication | 282 | 77.90 | 80 | 22.09 | 0 | 0.00 |
|    J. Cultural Awareness | 282 | 77.90 | 80 | 22.09 | 0 | 0.00 |
|    K. Sheltered Instruction | 361 | 99.72 | 1 | 0.27 | 0 | 0.00 |
|    L. Natural Approach | 310 | 85.63 | 52 | 14.36 | 0 | 0.00 |

**Table 9.6   Sheltered Instruction Observation Protocol Results, Fall 2003**

| Number of SIOPs Administered | Exceeding Expectation* | | Meeting Expectation* | | Approaching Expectation* | | Below Expectation* | |
|---|---|---|---|---|---|---|---|---|
| | # | % | # | % | # | % | # | % |
| 362 | 195 | 54% | 125 | 35% | 42 | 11% | 0 | 0% |

PERCENTAGE EXCEEEDING OR MEETING EXPECTATION: 89%

**\*Scale for Expectation Categories:**
Exceeding Expectation Score of 90–100%
Meeting Expectation Score of 80–89%
Approaching Expectation Score of 70–79%
Below Expectation Score of 0–69%

# Implications for Teachers and Teacher Educators

With the wide variety of school settings in Kansas—and the diversity of the state's ELL student population—it is essential to ensure that every Kansas teacher is prepared to teach all students. Many of the needs that were identified by the ESU consortium in Kansas are common to isolated rural (as well as suburban) districts throughout the nation (Dale, 2000). In general, a scarcity of resources coupled with lack of access to opportunities for professional development means that ELL students are often taught by teachers who lack ESOL training and experience; are often misplaced in instructional programs; perform poorly on standardized assessments; receive limited academic support from home; are likely to be misunderstood by their community at large; and are at greater risk of being placed in special education and/or leaving school before graduation (Dale).

The findings reported herein are undoubtedly limited by the preliminary nature of the data. However, the ESU online teacher training program is showing exceptional promise as a highly effective model, especially for teachers in rural and suburban areas. Evidence of its effectiveness will continue to be refined as part of the inherent mechanisms for program improvement.

As a final note, professional development may be extended outside the official scope of the project, as participants will be able to sharpen their technology skills and apply their earned fifteen hours of graduate credit (ESOL Certification) toward a Masters degree, which further improves their professional development. Several former program participants are already taking advantage of this opportunity.

**Table 9.7  Course Final Evaluation Results**

| Evaluation Items<br>Rating Scale:<br>5=Very High, 4=High, 3=Medium, 2=Low, 1=Very Low | Item<br>Rating | Category<br>Rating |
|---|---|---|
| COURSE LOGOSTICS | | 3.6 |
| 1. Grading procedure was fair and relevant to goals | 3.1 | |
| 2. Practicums were targeted to course objectives | 4.1 | |
| 3. Technical help was always available when necessary | 3.6 | |
| 4. Materials were useful & aligned for achieving the objectives of the course | 4.0 | |
| 5. Your personal expectations were met | 3.4 | |
| | | |
| SELF-RATING | | 4.0 |
| 1. My effort to take advantage of the course content was | 4.1 | |
| 2. The amount of information I feel I learned in this course was | 3.4 | |
| 3. My ``comfort zone'' with technology and learning improved as a result of this course is | 4.1 | |
| 4. My interest in continuing to improve via distance learning is | 4.6 | |
| **Overall Rating** | | **3.8** |

# References

Anstrom, Kris. December 1998. Preparing Secondary Education Teachers to Work with English Language Learners: Science. *NCBE Resource Collection Series No. 11.* Retrieved October 2, 2003, from http://www.ncela.gwu.edu/ncbepubs/resource/ells/science.htm

Collier, V. P., and Thomas, W. P. (1999, August/September). Making U.S. schools effective for English language learners, part 1. *TESOL Matters,* 9 (4), 1–6. Alexandria, VA: Teachers of English to Speakers of Other Languages, Inc.

Cornell, C. (1995, Winter). Reducing failure of ELL students in the mainstream classroom and why it is important. *The Journal of Educational Issue of Language Minority Students,* 15. Boise, ID: Boise State University.

Cummins, Jim. (1981). The role of primary language development promoting educational success for ELL students. 3–49. In *Schooling and ELL students: A Theoretical Framework.* California State Department of Education, Office of Bilingual Bicultural Education. Los Angeles, California State University, Evaluation, Dissemination and Assessment Center.

Dale, K. (2000). *Internal Market Report,* Southwest Plains Regional Service Center.

Genessee, F., (Ed.). (1999). *Program alternatives for linguistically diverse students* (Educational Practice Report, No. 1). Santa Cruz, CA: Center for Research on Education.

Harrison, M. M. (1998). Homegrown solutions: A resourceful Kansas town adapts to changing demographics. *Teaching Tolerance, 7* (1), 20–25.

Holloway, J. H. (2003). Research link: Managing culturally diverse classrooms. *Educational Leadership, 61* (1), 90–91.

Judd, J., and Kreicker, K. (1998). When the ideal isn't possible. *NABE News.* Washington, DC: National Association for Bilingual Education.

Krashen, S. D. (1981). *Second language acquisition and second language learning.* Oxford: Pergamon Press.

Krashen, S. D. and Terrell, D. 1983. *The natural approach: Language acquisition in the classroom.* Hayward, CA: Alemany Press.

Kreicker, K. (2003). Kansas teachers' perceptions of the English for Speakers of Other Languages (ESOL) Endorsement as a tool for improving instruction. Unpublished doctoral dissertation. Kansas State University.

Leithwood, K. (1990). The principal's role in teacher development. 71–90. In *Changing school culture through staff development,* ed. B. Joyce. Alexandria, VA: ASCD.

Lim, H., and Watson, D., (1993). Whole language content classes for second language learners. *The Reading Teacher, 46* (5), 384–93. Newark, DE: International Reading Association.

Menken, K., and Antunez, B. (2001, June). *An overview of the preparation and certification of teachers working with limited English proficient (ELL) students.* Washington, DC: National Clearinghouse for Bilingual Education, The George Washington University.

Milk, R., Mercado, C., and Sapiens, A. (1992). Re-thinking the education of teachers of language-minority children: Developing reflective teachers for the changing schools. *NCBE FOCUS: Occasional papers in Bilingual Education,* 6.

National Clearinghouse for English Language Acquisition and Language Instruction Educational Programs. (2002). *Survey of the states' limited English proficient students and available educational programs and services 2000–2001 summary report.* Washington, DC: U.S. Department of Education, Office of English Language Acquisition, Language Enhancement and Academic Achievement for Limited English Proficient Students.

O'Malley, J. M. and A. Chamot, A. U. (1986). *Learning strategies in second language acquisition.* Cambridge: Cambridge University Press.

O'Malley, J. M., and Chamot, A. U. (1990). *Learning strategies in second language acquisition.* Cambridge, UK: Cambridge University Press.

O'Malley, J. M. and Valdez-Pierce, V. (1996). *Authentic assessment for English language learners.* Reading, MA: Addison-Wesley.

Pelavin Associates, Inc. (1999). *A revised analysis of the supply of bilingual and ESOL teachers: An analysis of schools and staffing survey data.* Washington, DC.

Seguin, C. A. and Ambrosio, A. L. (2002). Multicultural vignettes for teacher preparation. *Multicultural Review: An Official Journal of the National Association for Multicultural Education,* 4 (4), 10–16.

Seguin, C. A., Ambrosio, A. L., and Hogan, E. L. (2000). Committing to critical inquiry: Are new teachers ready to teach in diverse settings? An assessment plan. *Journal of Critical Inquiry into Curriculum and Instruction, 2* (2), 46–49.

Sehlaoui, A. S. (1999). Developing cross-cultural communicative competence in ESL/EFL pre-service teachers: A critical perspective. (Doctoral dissertation, Indiana University of Pennsylvania, 1999). *Dissertation Abstracts International, 60/06,* 2042.

Sehlaoui, A. S. (2001). Developing Cross-Cultural Communicative Competence in Pre-Service ESOL/EFL Teachers: A Critical Perspective. *Language, Culture and Curriculum*, 14 (1), 42–57.

Wood, A. (1988). *The beef packing industry: A study of three communities in southwestern Kansas*. Flagstaff, AZ: Wood and Wood Associates; Topeka, KS: Kansas State Department of Education.

CHAPTER 10

# Linking Ideas to Practice: Effectiveness of Coaching in Teacher Practice

*Xiaoxia Ai and Noelle Rivera*
Los Angeles Unified School District

Dr. Xiaoxia Ai works as a senior analyst in the Program Evaluation and Research Branch (PERB), Los Angeles Unified School District. Her areas of interest include program evaluation, K–12 math education, and school reform.

Noelle Rivera works as an analyst in PERB. Her areas of interest include program evaluation, adult learning, and professional development.

## ABSTRACT

The focus of this study was on the effectiveness of coaching in teacher practice. The study involved 160 elementary and secondary teachers in 40 randomly selected schools and 1,100 teachers randomly selected across the district. Data collection consisted of direct classroom observations of the 160 teachers, interviews of observed teachers and administrators in the 40 schools, and surveys of the 1,100 teachers. Results revealed that despite the potential benefits of math coaches reported by the teachers, the majority of them had not had the opportunity to work one-on-one with their coaches. No significant differences were found between teachers who participated in coaching activities and those who did not, possibly due to the quality and quantity of participation. Several barriers to coaching practice were identified, including: (1) lack of teacher trust; (2) teacher resistance to change; (3) lack of time; and (4) the inconsistency in coach role definition. The results reported by teachers across the district on the overall perceptions of coaching and its effectiveness were consistent with those from the examination of the relationship between coaching and teacher practice in the context of mathematics.

Professional development is the label we attach to activities that are designed to increase the skill and knowledge of educators (Fenstermacher, 1985). In practice, professional development covers a vast array of specific activities, everything from short, "hit-and-run" workshops designed to familiarize teachers and administrators with new ideas or new rules and requirements, to off-site courses and workshops designed to provide content and academic credit for teachers and administrators (Elmore, 2002). Research on the impact of conventional professional development has shown a tenuous connection between these professional development activities and the knowledge and skill of educators (Elmore, 2002). Spending more money on traditional models of professional development, therefore, is unlikely to have any significant effect on either the knowledge or skill of educators or on the performance of students.

Peer coaching has become increasingly appealing to many school districts and evolved as an alternative approach to professional development. The basic premise involves support and training for teachers through collaborative, non-judgmental efforts. Coaches are usually considered exemplary pedagogues, having an abundance of experience and demonstrating excellence in their field. Typical coaching models afford ongoing support provided by on-site peers, follow-up activities, and the opportunities for observation, collaboration, and non-evaluative feedback. Reported effects of coaching include increased ability to facilitate the transfer of training from workshop to classroom, to introduce and assist implementation of innovative techniques, to encourage the development and integration of new instructional skills and strategies, and to foster collegial relationships (Rivera and Sass, 2003).

However, as yet, little work has been done to explore the impact of coaching on teacher practice itself. This chapter reports on early results from a study of how teachers connect new ideas about teaching, learning, and mathematics with their daily classroom practice through participation in coaching. While the primary focus of this study is on the ideas that underlie mathematics education reform, we regard mathematics as a case through which to explore issues that underlie similar reforms in other content areas (e.g., literacy) in our district.

# Research Questions

The study attempted to answer the following research questions:

1. Was there a difference in teacher practice between teachers who had worked one-on-one with their math coaches and teachers without such opportunities?

2. What was teachers' participation in coaching activities and what were the barriers to coaching practice?
3. What were the overall perceptions of coaching and its effectiveness among teachers across the district?

# Method

## SAMPLING PROCEDURE AND SAMPLE

A total of 40 schools consisting of 20 elementary schools, 10 middle schools, and 10 high schools were randomly selected from the district. For each elementary school, two 2nd and two 4th grade teachers were randomly selected. For each middle school, four 8th grade teachers were randomly chosen and for each high school, four 10th grade teachers were randomly selected. A 10th grade math teacher was defined as having more than 50 percent 10th grade students enrolled. This resulted in 160 teachers (or classrooms). A total of 1,100 teachers from across the district were randomly selected to receive a teacher survey on professional development.

## DATA COLLECTION PROCEDURES

*Observations.* Each of the 160 teachers was observed in fall 2001 (three times) and spring 2002 (three times). Observations lasted for about an hour for elementary and for one math lesson (typically about 50 minutes) for middle and high schools.

*Interviews.* Prior to each observation, we briefly interviewed the teacher about the focus of the lesson. In spring 2002, we conducted in-depth interviews with each teacher, focusing on the instructional context for the observations (e.g., how was the lesson planned), teaching preparation, professional development, and teaching background.

Additionally, we interviewed 73 school administrators (principals or assistant principals in elementary and middle schools, math department chairs in middle and high schools) and math coaches. These interviews focused on key issues such as coaching practice and professional development opportunities that had been provided to the teachers at the school.

Trained data collectors used structured interview protocols for the interviews. Interviews were audiotaped and then transcribed by a professional transcription company. All the identification information of interviewees was removed on the transcripts.

*Teacher survey.* Surveys on professional development were mailed to 1,100 teachers. The survey included 17 items focusing specifically on the coaching behaviors, support, and perceived effectiveness of the coaching at their school. Survey data on coaching was drawn from respondents who indicated participation in coaching programs at their schools during the 2001–2002 school year ($n = 293$). These teachers were asked to indicate the type of coach (i.e. peer, expert teacher) and the type of relationship (i.e. one-on-one or group) they participated in regardless of specific content area (i.e. literacy, math) or if they had more than one coach during the school year.

## MEASURES

Experienced data collectors wrote detailed field notes describing: (1) teacher activity; (2) student activity; (3) math content (math problems or tasks that students are working on); (4) social organization; (5) number of students, their gender and ethnicity; (6) materials in use (such as textbooks); (7) interactions between teachers and students, and among students; and (8) where applicable, students' solutions of the problems and/or their thinking processes.

Building on earlier work, this study used four evaluative (scale 1–4) and two descriptive scales to define the quality of teacher practice on the following instructional dimensions.

1. *Clarity of the focus of the lesson.* This dimension consisted of two components: *what* and *why*. *What* captured the extent to which teachers were very clear and specific about the mathematical concepts, skills, and knowledge students were to learn, as well as the degree of emphasis on the mathematical thinking. *Why* examined whether teachers articulated clearly the rationale for students to master the concepts and skills that students were to learn. A 4-point scale was used to describe each component.
2. *Meaningfulness of math tasks in class.* This dimension assessed the meaningfulness of the mathematics tasks teachers presented to students in class. A 4-point evaluative scale was used to describe holistically the degree to which students engaged in meaningful mathematical tasks from the following four perspectives: (1) *types of tasks* (practice routine procedures, invent new solutions, or apply concepts in real-world situations); (2) *alternative methods* (encouraged the development of different methods and examined their relative advantages); (3) *applications increase in complexity* (procedural, conceptual, or both); and (4) *concepts/methods stated or developed* (i.e., derived and/or ex-

plained by the teacher or the teacher and students collaboratively through proof, experiment, or both in order to increase students' understanding of the concept).

3. *Degree of student engagement.* This dimension consisted of two components: (1) *quality of content elicitation*—student participation in instructional conversations or dialogues, and (2) *student opportunities to share* solution methods and learn from mistakes. *Quality of content elicitation* looked at the type of questions teachers asked that requests information directly concerned with mathematics, mathematical operations, or the lesson itself. Such elicitations may request the student to supply a quantity, identify a geometric shape, explain a mathematical procedure, define some mathematical term, or evaluate a mathematical answer. By looking at the types of eliciting questions teachers ask, this component examines the opportunities teachers created for student participation in instructional conversations/dialogues. A 4-point evaluative scale was used to describe student participation in instructional conversations. *Student opportunities to share* solution methods and learn from mistakes assess whether such opportunities exist at all.

4. *Overall instructional pattern of the lesson.* This dimension looked for the overall instructional pattern of the lesson as evidenced in instructional steps of the lesson to examine whether the focus of the lesson is on skill acquisition or on understanding. A 3-point descriptive scale was used to describe or categorize the overall instructional pattern.

## DATA ANALYSES

Descriptive (e.g., means) and inferential statistics (e.g., *t*-tests) were used to explore: (1) differences in the means of teachers in each group on the evaluative scales of the instructional dimensions; (2) differences in the distributions of teachers in each group on the evaluative and descriptive scales of the instructional dimensions; (3) teachers' participation in coaching activities; and (4) the overall perceptions of coaching and its effectiveness among teachers across the district. These analyses helped us to understand teachers' participation in coaching activities, its impact upon teacher practice, and various issues in the implementation of coaching practice.

Using the rubrics we developed to examine the quality of teacher practice, trained raters assessed observation data and assigned scores on each scale. We coded teacher interview transcripts by reviewing responses to each question posed to the respondents and determining the frequency of responses. We also developed categories based on responses to our open-ended questions. The examination of the frequency, categories, and content of responses helped us to understand not only the extent of teachers' participation in coaching activities, but also the experiences of their participation. Additionally, these analyses helped us to comprehend the complexities and challenges imbedded in the implementation of coaching practice.

# Results

## DIFFERENCE IN TEACHER PRACTICE

Teachers did not differ in their practice, regardless of whether they had participated in such coaching activities as coach-modeling lessons and/or coach-observing teacher teaching lessons. There were no significant differences between the two groups of teachers in terms of their mean scores on the four evaluative scales (i.e., *what, why, meaningfulness of math tasks in class,* and *quality of content elicitation*). Additionally, there were no significant differences between the two groups of teachers with respect to the distributions of the scores on the four evaluative and the two descriptive scales (i.e., opportunities for *student opportunities to share* and *overall instructional pattern of the lesson*).

*Teachers' scores on the evaluative scales.* Table 10.1 represents the mean scores of each group of teachers (i.e., teachers who participated in coaching vs. teachers who did not) on the four evaluative scales. Teachers who did not participate in coaching (3.02) scored slightly higher on the *What* scale, than those who participated in coaching (2.80). No significant differences between the two groups of teachers were observed on any other three evaluative scales.

*Distribution of teachers' scores on the evaluative and descriptive scales.* Besides comparing the mean scores, we also examined the distribution of the scores by

**Table 10.1    Means of the Teachers in Each Group on the Four Evaluative Scales (1–4)**

|  | Level of Schooling | |
| --- | --- | --- |
|  | Elementary | Secondary |
| What | 3.02 (2.80)* | 2.26 (2.11) |
| Why | 2.24 (2.07) | 1.42 (1.33) |
| Meaningfulness of Math Tasks | 1.72 (1.83) | 1.15 (1.22) |
| Content Elicitation | 2.02 (2.00) | 2.15 (2.11) |

Numbers in the parentheses represent the mean scores for teachers who had participated in coaching. * Significant at $p < .05$ level.

the two groups of teachers on the four evaluative scales and the two descriptive scales. Table 10.2 summarizes the results.

The majority of the teachers in both elementary and secondary schools, regardless of whether they had participated in coaching activities or not, scored no more than 2 (on a scale of 1–4) on the four evaluative scales (i.e., *what, why, meaningfulness of math tasks in class,* and *quality of content elicitation*). With respect to the two descriptive scales (i.e., *student opportunities to share* and *overall instructional pattern of the lesson*), the majority of the teachers did not provide students opportunities to share their work and/or to learn from their mistakes. The dominant overall instructional pattern among teachers emphasized procedural skills rather than conceptual understanding or problem solving. Chi-square tests showed no significant differences in the distribution of the scores between teachers who participated in coaching and those who did not, regardless of schooling level.

## PARTICIPATION IN COACHING ACTIVITIES AND BARRIERS TO COACHING PRACTICE

Teachers reported limited involvement with math coaches in the two key coaching activities, being observed by math coaches (i.e., classroom observations) and observing math coaches' modeling lessons (i.e., model lessons). There were several issues that might explain why there has not been more involvement of teachers in coaching activities. These included: (1) lack of teacher trust; (2) teacher resistance to change; (3) lack of time; and (4) the inconsistency between the key role that math coaches were supposed to play and the role they were actually playing at schools.

*Teachers' involvement in coaching practice.* This study focused on teachers' participation in either one or two of the following main coaching activities, observing math coaches model a lesson or having math coaches observe actual classroom practices and provide follow-up feedback. We focused on these two types of coaching activities, because they were the most frequently mentioned activities by teachers and math coaches and have been identified by theorists as two of the most effective coaching techniques (e.g., Kohler, et. al., 1997). We examined the coaching involvement from the teachers' perspective. A considerable portion of teachers (62.0 percent elementary and 88.3 percent secondary) had not been involved in any of the two key coaching practices during the first-year implementation of the math program. For those who did, the majority of the teachers (86.7 percent elementary and 66.7 percent secondary) had engaged in only one type of coaching activity. Only a few teachers (4 elementary and 3 secondary) participated in both types of coaching activities.

**Table 10.2  Distribution of the Teachers in Each Group on the Evaluative and Descriptive Scales**

| Scores | Elementary | | | Secondary | | |
|---|---|---|---|---|---|---|
| | 1 | 2 | 3 | 1 | 2 | 3 |
| **Clarity of the Focus** | | | | | | |
| What | 6.1 (3.3) | 4.1 (13.3) | 89.8 (83.3) | 4.5 (0) | 65.2 (88.9) | 30.3 (11.1) |
| Why | 30.6 (23.3) | 22.4 (50) | 47 (26.6) | 75.8 (77.8) | 6.1 (11.1) | 18.2 (11.1) |
| **Nature of Math Tasks** | 44.7 (37.9) | 44.7 (41.4) | 10.3 (20.7) | 84.6 (77.8) | 22.2 (16.2) | 0 (0) |
| **Student Engagement** | | | | | | |
| Content elicitation | 4.1 (10) | 89.8 (80) | 6.1 (10) | 1.7 (0) | 88.1 (88.9) | 10.2 (11.1) |
| Student share | 42.9 (40) | 57.1 (60) | N.A. | 75.8 (77.8) | 24.2 (22.2) | N.A. |
| **Instructional Pattern** | 2.1 (3.3) | 81.3 (83.3) | 16.7 (13.3) | 10.6 (11.1) | 77.3 (66.7) | 3.0 (0) |

*Numbers in the parentheses represent the percentages of teachers who had participated in coaching.*

Except for a few cases, teachers reported positive experiences with their math coaches. For instance, one teacher commented on how wonderful a resource her math coach was:

> I just want to say that, I was thinking for a minute, as far as our math coach is concerned I really love having a person, a go-to person at this school, especially someone like [our coach] who has this depth of understanding and materials for us to go to, because when you're, sometimes you're just hitting your head against the wall with some kids, you don't know what strategies, and I've got five years of teaching but there is so much that I don't know about different ways of teaching, materials, things like that and I have to say whenever I go to my coach with a question or need or something she's there and, you know, gives me a different way of looking at something or a different approach.

According to their self-reports, despite the potential benefits of math coaches, the majority of the teachers had not had the opportunity to work one-on-one with their coaches.

*Barriers to coaching practice.* Coaching practice is intended as an instructional support for teachers. Teachers, however, may think or feel otherwise, which could be a barrier to coaching practice. As one teacher described, "If you ask for help you're criticized. So people don't ask for help anymore." In fact, close to half (45.8 percent) of the math coaches reported "lack of teacher trust" and "teacher resistance to change" as two of the main barriers to coaching practice.

With respect to "lack of teacher trust," math coaches reported that teachers felt "threatened" or "scared," treated math coaches as "an administrator and evaluator," or felt that math coaches were there "to provide more work rather than to be used as a resource." How to build trust with teachers and establish productive rapport with them, therefore, seemed to be of paramount importance in order to "open" teachers up to the idea of coaching practice. Only 50 percent of the math coaches reported "extensive" or "almost complete" confidence in their coaching skills, whereas close to 96 percent and 100 percent of these coaches reported "extensive" or "almost complete" confidence in math content and in using different strategies for math instruction, respectively.

"Teacher resistance to change" was another main barrier to coaching practice, according to math coaches. Some veteran/experienced teachers "think they know it all." Or teachers were reluctant to "try new things." As one math coach put it: "The only thing that I've seen is a little reluctance to change to new ways of doing things." Another coach shared a similar experience with this barrier: "Trying to get some of the veteran teachers convinced that I'm not coming in to tell them how to teach, but to have them feel comfortable in seeing alternatives for teaching strategies." In fact, if teachers were open to the idea of having someone come in to observe and/or demonstrate a lesson, they might learn alternative ways of doing things. Based upon the majority of the math coaches' experiences (54.2 percent), lesson demonstration was the most useful in their role as a math coach during the first-year implementation of the math program. As one coach described:

> Just to show a teacher something new, you can make—you can see a lesson written in writing, you know, on a piece of paper and, but how do you do it, you know? There's a teacher there, she's never used algebra tiles. And she said, you know, I'd like to use this, but I don't know how to do this. Could you come and show me? And I think, you know, we learn by seeing what people do.

Besides teachers' resistance or lack of trust in math coaches, lack of time was the third frequently reported barrier to coaching. According to math coaches, 33.3 percent of them experienced difficulty in providing effective coaching due to lack of time, because they were assigned to work with two schools, which had made them "spread too thin." One consequence of this limited availability of math coaches who had to work with two schools was that teachers who would like to use them as resources for help did not get what they needed in time, which in turn had caused a certain degree of resentment (albeit uncommon) among teachers.

Math coaches were fully aware of problems like this. For instance, one math coach expressed her concern of having to work with two schools:

> I don't think coaches should be at two schools. It's too inconsistent. You know if someone asks for something on fractions and by the time you get it is three days before you come back, so they've either forgotten or found it or improvised themselves.

In some cases, math coaches reported having difficulties scheduling activities with teachers (e.g., post-conference following a classroom observation where one-on-one reflective conversations took place), because teachers did not want to use their break time or stay after school.

Finally, a fourth barrier to effective coaching practice was the inconsistency between the key role that math coaches were supposed to play and the role that they were actually playing at schools. Some math coaches were acting as tutors, sub-teachers, or administrative assistants, rather than being instructional or intellectual resources to teachers. The district had invested a lot in hiring and training math coaches. This has been a good thing, as one math coach described:

It is a wonderful experience; it is giving me more insight into teaching and I am also learning for my personal expertise and knowledge. I have developed professionally a lot just during the year I started coaching.

But if coaches were spending their time doing all this but not working with teachers to support their math instruction, the benefits of training that math coaches received could not reach classrooms, let alone have any impact upon improving teacher practice and student achievement.

## PERCEPTIONS OF COACHING AND ITS EFFECTIVENESS ACROSS THE DISTRICT

Our survey data indicated that the majority of teachers engaged in coaching relationships that involved one specially trained coach working with a group of teachers. As part of these coaching relationships, observing in a classroom or being observed by a coach only happened a few times per year, if at all. Teachers who engaged in any form of observation were more likely to report coaching as effective over those who didn't engage in any form of observation at all.

*Typical types of coaching relationships.* Six types of coaching relationships were delineated on the teacher survey. The "one-on-one" relationships included one teacher partnered with a coach who is a specially trained coach, an experienced or expert teacher, and/or a peer (another teacher). The corresponding list of three "group" relationship types consisted of a group of teachers with a specially trained coach, an experienced teacher, or simply a group of teachers working together (peers). Of the six types presented on the survey, those involving groups, specifically those partnered with a specially trained coach, were the most commonly reported relationships across the district.

*Participation in key coaching activities.* Teachers responded to the frequency of their participation in classroom observations. These included how often they were "observed in their classroom and received feedback from a peer or coach" and how often they "observed in another teacher's classroom" during the 2001–2002 school year. "A few times per year" was the median response for both types of observations. Thirty-two percent responded that "observation in another teacher's classroom" did not occur at all, and 26 percent responded that they did not participate in "observation in their classroom and feedback from peer or coach" at all. Teachers had favorable opinions of the quality of the coaches' model lessons, although they were not conducted often. Overall, teacher responses indicated agreement on the inadequacy of scheduled time. This was particularly evident within the math coach sub-sample where 50 percent of this group strongly agreed that not enough time was scheduled to participate in coaching activities.

*Perceived effectiveness of coaching.* Teachers responded to a series of items in an attempt to determine the level of effectiveness of coaching during the 2001–2002 school year. Exploratory factor analysis revealed the items loading on a single factor with strong internal consistency (alpha = .93) and 75 percent of the total variance explained. Thus, a single factor variable was created to be an indicator of the perceived overall effectiveness of coaching.

A significant positive relationship emerged between the teacher self-reports of the overall impact of coaching on strategies and skills, and coaching as a positive experience ($r$ = .66, $p$ = .00). Comparisons were made to see if the teacher participants in the six different coaching relationships (3 one-on-one coaching relationships, 3 group coaching relationships) had differing perceptions of effectiveness. Among the six different combinations, no significant differences were found. Additionally, no differences were found when the relationships were re-categorized based on the type of coach (special coach, experienced teacher, or peer) or based on number (one-on-one or group). Teachers involved in any type of coaching during the 2001–2002 school year did not vary in their perceptions based on the type of coaching relationship in which they were engaged.

The responses by teachers who had worked only with math coaches regarded coaching as specifically effective in assisting beginning teachers. Fifty-five percent of these teachers responded a "4" or a "strongly agree" to this outcome. This seems to be consistent with our earlier finding that veteran teachers are more resistant to the idea of coaching.

# Discussion

"Coaching," defined as a non-evaluative relationship in which a teacher provides another teacher with opportunities for demonstration, practice, feedback, reflection, and/or collaborative problem solving, provides an alternative way to approach professional development and has been established as a foundational strategy to promote effective instruction and student achievement. As with any new and major initiative, the introduction of coaching led to questions about its implementation and effectiveness.

Our findings revealed that the majority of the teachers had not had the one-on-one opportunity to work with their math coaches. Specifically, teachers reported limited participation in classroom observations or model lessons by math coaches. The limited quantity of coaching practice exists not only in math, but potentially in other subject areas as well (e.g., literacy), because our survey of teachers across the district indicated that these main coaching activities happened a few times per year, if at all.

One of the difficulties math coaches experienced in providing coaching service was due to lack of time, because they were assigned to work with two schools, which had made them "spread too thin." The barrier of math coaches being "spread too thin" (thus limiting their availability as resources to help teachers) could also be true for coaches of other subject areas as well (e.g., literacy), because our survey of teachers across the district suggested that the majority of teachers had coaching relationships that involved one specially trained coach working with a group of teachers. Additionally, teachers reported that not enough time was scheduled to participate in coaching activities.

Besides the problem of math coaches' availability due to lack of time, another barrier to effective coaching practice was the inconsistency between the key role that math coaches were supposed to play and the role that they were actually playing at schools. Some math coaches were acting as tutors, sub-teachers, or assistants rather than being instructional or intellectual resources to teachers.

An additional barrier to coaching practice was "teacher resistance to change." Some veteran/experienced teachers "think they know it all." These teachers regarded coaching as primarily intended to help new or inexperienced teachers. This was consistent with the teacher survey results. When asked whether the practice of coaching had assisted beginning teachers, teachers responded positively regardless of years of teaching experience. It is possible, therefore, that the problem of teacher resistance, particularly among veteran/experienced teachers, could exist in the practice of coaching in other subject areas.

Finally, "lack of teacher trust" was also a main barrier to coaching practice. Math coaches are intended as an instructional support for teachers; teachers, however, felt "threatened/scared," treating math coaches as "an administrator and evaluator" or felt that math coaches were there "to provide more work rather than to be used as a resource."

The barriers potentially have limited the quantity, and possibly the quality, of coaching practice, which in turn might explain the lack of impact of coaching on teacher practice. Our findings revealed that teachers did not differ in their practice, regardless of whether they had participated in such coaching activities as coach-modeling lessons and/or coach-observing-teacher teaching lessons. The discourse norm of mathematics teaching and learning between both groups of teachers put a heavy emphasis on computational and procedural skills instead of conceptual understanding and problem solving.

Interestingly, though, teachers who were engaged in any form of observation reported coaching as effective. Furthermore, teachers regarded the quality of model lessons and the immediacy of feedback by coaches as very positive.

These positive perceptions of coaching practice were observed in both the math evaluation and the survey of teachers across the district. Results from the math evaluation, however, highlighted the inconsistency between teachers' positive perceptions and their actual behaviors (i.e., teacher practice). It remains questionable, therefore, whether positive perceptions could translate into improved behaviors or not.

To summarize, this study has yielded results that help us to comprehend the complexities and challenges that are implicit in the implementation of coaching practice, the understanding of which will provided the bases for our continued effort in ensuring effective implementation of the coaching practice in the years to come.

# Note

The original study upon which the current chapter is based was presented by both authors at the annual meeting of the American Educational Research Association, Chicago, Illinois, April 23, 2003. (Available online at www.lausd.k12.ca.us/lausd/offices/perb.)

# References

Elmore, R. F. (2002). *Bridging the gap between standards and achievement: The imperative for professional development in education*. Washington, DC: The Albert Shanker Institute.

Fenstermacher, G. D. (1985). Determining the value of staff development. *The Elementary School Journal, 85*(3), 281–314.

Kohler, F. W., Crilley, K. M., Shearer, D. D., and Good, G. (1997). Effects of peer coaching on teacher and student outcomes. *Journal of Educational Research, 90*(4), 240–51.

Rivera, N. V., and Sass, J. S. (2003). *Professional development in the reorganized LAUSD: Second year evaluation report*. Los Angeles Unified School District, CA. (Available online at www.lausd.k12.ca.us/lausd/offices/perb.)

# CHAPTER 11

# Moving Professional Development Online: Meeting the Needs and Expectations of All Teachers

*Stein Brunvand*
University of Michigan

*Barry Fishman*
University of Michigan

*Ron Marx*
University of Arizona

Stein Brunvand is a doctoral student at the University of Michigan working on a degree in Learning Technologies. He has been working with a project called Knowledge Networks On the Web (KNOW), which provides online professional development to teachers enacting inquiry-based science. He is particularly interested in the use of video as a professional development tool.

Barry Fishman is an Assistant Professor of Learning Technologies at the University of Michigan. He is also a faculty member at the Center for Highly Interactive Computing in Education (hi-ce) where he works on a variety of projects, including KNOW, focused on learning more about professional development and its impact on teacher learning and student performance.

Ron Marx is currently the Dean of the School of Education at the University of Arizona. At the time this paper was written he was a Professor of Educational Psychology at the University of Michigan and faculty member at hi-ce where he helped with the development and implementation of KNOW.

## ABSTRACT

There is widespread agreement that teacher professional development (PD) is critical for the success of standards-based reform in

U.S. schools (Committee on Science and Mathematics Teacher Preparation, 2001). However, the current infrastructure for professional development is ill-equipped to serve the numbers of teachers who need support in order to employ innovative teaching methods advocated by national standards, such as inquiry-oriented or project-based learning. Online PD is one possible solution for bringing high-quality PD to ever-growing numbers of teachers. This chapter is about a program of empirical research to examine the needs, expectations, and experiences that teachers who are engaged in systemic reform have for online PD. The goal of this research is to understand how to design online PD environments that are useful for and usable by broad populations of teachers, as part of the design of Knowledge Networks On the Web (KNOW) (Fishman, in press), an online PD tool developed for use by the Center for Learning Technologies in Urban Schools (Blumenfeld, Fishman, Krajcik, Marx, and Soloway, 2000).

Chief among the factors motivating this study is the fact that research on professional development (PD) in general does not link directly to outcomes and there is little evidence that PD has an effect on classroom practice, and less evidence linking PD to student learning (Frechtling, Sharp, Carey, and Vaden-Kiernan, 1995; Wilson and Berne, 1999). This is also true of research about online PD where most available studies have focused on issues such as community formation and online discourse patterns (Bautista, 1998; Hammond, 1998), *not* on teacher learning or the impact of online PD on student learning. This link between PD and student learning is an important connection to make if we are to determine the worth of any PD opportunity. This study is the first in a series of studies on the design and use of online PD tools (we plan to explore the connection between PD and student learning in future work). Another important factor motivating this study is that most PD research, both online and traditional, has been conducted with "volunteer" populations of teachers (Bobrowsky, Marx, and Fishman, 2001). Without claiming that there are necessarily differences in terms of professional development needs between volunteer and other populations of teachers, it does seem likely that areas such as motivation are likely to differ, and must be attended to in design. We need to understand the PD needs of *all* teachers if systemic reform is to be effective. Finally, few published studies have focused on needs assessment related to the design of online professional development, so there is little empirical guidance for the design of online PD environments such as KNOW.

In the first part of this chapter we provide a brief description of KNOW, the online professional development environment we studied, and a concise literature review that situates our work within the existing corpus of research surrounding online PD. Next we describe the methods we used to collect our data and the criteria for selecting our sample. In the findings section we discuss the results of our needs assessment and the design implications stemming from our analysis of the logging data and participant interviews. We close the chapter by reviewing the next phase of research we intend to conduct with KNOW.

# Knowledge Networks On the Web (KNOW)

KNOW is an online professional development environment developed by the Center for Highly Interactive Computing In Education (hi-ce). The center is comprised of educators, computer scientists, psychologists, scientists, and learning specialists from the University of Michigan dedicated to educational reform through inquiry-based curricula, learner-centered technologies, comprehensive professional development, and administrative and organizational models. Housed within hi-ce is the Center for Learning Technologies in Urban Schools (LeTUS) whose focus for the past several years has been to create a series of project-based science units to be implemented as part of an urban systemic reform effort. KNOW was specifically designed to support teachers using this set of curricula. KNOW provides an environment that is intended to leverage knowledge held by a community of teachers who enact particular curricula in their classrooms and make that knowledge available to others attempting to use that same curriculum. KNOW is built around standards-based, inquiry-oriented, and technology-rich curriculum materials and uses videos, student work, and other materials and resources designed to help teachers understand how to interpret curriculum so that it becomes more useable in their local context. KNOW provides teachers with access to a level of detail and customization that is impossible to achieve using traditional text-based materials, but is ideally suited to the web. Furthermore, KNOW supports ongoing asynchronous conversations about how to teach specific curricula, linked to an organically growing set of examples and elaborations, generated jointly by the community of teachers using KNOW and by the curriculum developers. In a sense, logging on to KNOW is like walking into a room full of teachers talking about and sharing their personal experiences of curriculum enactment with its multiple challenges. Teachers who use KNOW employ it variously as a substitute for and an enhancement of face-to-face professional development, as a planning tool, and as a community forum and collaboration environment.

# Literature Review

Existing technology affords us the ability to provide a wide range of content via the Internet, but it is important that we maintain a clear objective when designing online learning opportunities. Simply because we possess the technological capability to conduct professional development online is not sufficient rationale to do so (Ely, 1996). Dede (1996) asserts that future advancement in distance education is not dependent on *technological* development but rather on the *professional* development of those who design and participate in these learning environments. In our design of KNOW we are committed to creating an online environment driven by the needs of our users rather than the capabilities of the technology, which is why we decided to conduct a needs assessment for KNOW.

Existing literature related to traditional PD settings suggests that teachers have different expectations and needs based on their experience level (Adams and Krockover, 1997; Hewson, Tabachnick, Zetchner, and Lemberger, 1999). Teachers new to the profession are concerned with gaining more classroom experience so they can hone their lesson planning and classroom management skills. Inservice teachers are often more accomplished in these areas and look to spend time in professional development discussing issues of pedagogy and curriculum at a deeper level (Barab, MaKinster, Moore, and Cunningham, 2001). Research also indicates that teachers differ in their feelings about technology based on their years of experience. In a survey commissioned by the National Center for Education Statistics (NCES) Rowand (2000) found that teachers with fewer years of experience felt more prepared to use computers and the Internet in their teaching than their more experienced colleagues. These findings aren't necessarily surprising but they highlight other differences among users that one might expect to find when designing for a broad population of teachers engaged in systemic reform. Acknowledging that these differences exist, we included questions in our needs assessment that would help us understand the experience level and teaching background of our sample group.

KNOW is designed to serve a population of teachers enacting the LeTUS curricula as a result of their involvement in a systemic reform effort (Fishman, in press). This is unique from other existing online PD environments such as the Inquiry Learning Forum (ILF) (Barab et al., 2001) and TAPPED-IN (Fusco, Gehlbach, and Schlager, 2000, February) that are intended for use by self-selected or volunteer teachers. KNOW must address the needs of all teachers involved in the reform effort, including those individuals whose participation may have been strongly encouraged or even mandated by district policy. This distinction in user population is worth noting because much of the available research on professional development focuses on groups of volunteer teachers who are, more often than not, motivated to change or try something new (Supovitz and Zeif, 2000). It is as yet unclear what the implications of this focus on "motivated volunteers" are for our understanding of the role of online PD, but we argue that the differences are sufficient to warrant investigation (Bobrowsky, Marx, and Fishman, 2001). By drawing our sample from a group of teachers involved in systemic reform we have an opportunity to study the impact of online PD across a broad range of users rather than limiting ourselves to those volunteers who seek out such learning opportunities on their own.

# Methods

This study proceeded in two phases. It involved a focused needs assessment study conducted with 36 middle school science teachers. The sample was drawn from Detroit Public Schools (DPS) teachers based on their anticipated use of a particular middle school science curriculum developed as part of LeTUS. Participation in the needs assessment study was voluntary, and fortunately the majority of eligible teachers agreed to take part. Through their participation in LeTUS the teachers are provided with multiple opportunities for professional development that include monthly workshops, in-class support, participation in focus groups and an educative curriculum (Ball and Cohen, 1996; Schneider and Krajcik, 2002). KNOW is just one of the many PD sites DPS teachers can access in order to help them implement the curriculum.

All subjects were expected to be users of KNOW, though none had used KNOW at the time of this needs assessment. Another unique feature of KNOW was that it was designed to help teachers learn about and enact specific curriculum materials, as opposed to being (for example) oriented around general principles of inquiry-oriented teaching. Our intent in the design of KNOW was to develop a tool that would be immediately relevant to teachers engaged in systemic reform. By conducting this needs assessment we hoped to determine what kinds of features teachers were looking for in an online PD tool and, more specifically, how they expected to use KNOW.

The survey (see Appendix A) was conducted anonymously and included questions about teaching experience, involvement in reform efforts, prior experiences with online PD and computer proficiency. Teachers were asked about how they became involved in the current curriculum effort and about their anticipated PD needs related to implementing the unit. Specific questions pertaining to expected use of various features incorporated into KNOW were also included. Surveys were administered to teachers during two separate workshops held during the summer by Stein Brunvand, a graduate student at the University of Michigan and lead author of this chapter. His primary focus with KNOW over the past two years has been to collect samples of student artifacts and videos of classroom practice to be featured online as sources of professional development. Through these efforts Brunvand has had an opportunity to interact with many of the teachers in the sample both in their respective classrooms and during face-to-face workshops.

The second phase of data collection included observations of how teachers actually used online PD (KNOW). Usage of KNOW was tracked by compiling data from web logs, which allowed us to see what features of KNOW teachers were using and how long they spent accessing each of those features. Logging data for the various features of KNOW was also aggregated across the sample population in order to make comparisons between teachers' *expected* and *actual* uses of online PD. To augment the logging data, informal interviews were conducted with a sub-sample of three users. These teachers were selected on the basis of their login frequency and the different perspectives they each brought to KNOW. Each teacher in the sub-sample was interviewed once, at which time they were asked to explain their decisions in regards to the use of KNOW. For instance, we asked why they spent time using certain features and not others, what they found to be most useful and what they felt was missing in the KNOW environment.

# Findings

In this section we review the results of the needs assessment and analysis of the logging data collected through KNOW. A detailed analysis conducted on the usage patterns of three participating teachers is also included in this section. These mini-cases provide insight into how the system is being used and raise several new design challenges that must be addressed in order for KNOW to be valuable for all teachers.

## NEEDS ASSESSMENT

Teachers in our sample (n = 36) had an average of 9.3 years teaching experience, 4.3 years teaching science, and nearly all of the teachers previously taught the specified LeTUS curriculum. All but three of the teachers were certified to teach science. The majority of the sample considered themselves proficient and comfortable in using computers to create and transfer documents, download files and software and navigate the web.

While all the teachers reported that they had computer and Internet access at home and school, the majority anticipated using KNOW primarily from school in order to take advantage of the faster Internet connection. Everyone in the sample had experience using web search engines to locate content-specific information and lesson plans, but this was extent of the online PD experience for 95 percent of the teachers surveyed. Only four teachers reported having taken a course online and likewise there were only four who had participated in an online discussion group.

To better understand the motivation of our sample we asked teachers how they became involved with the LeTUS curricula and what degree of choice they felt they had when deciding to enact any or all of the units. All of the teachers reported that either a fellow teacher or building administrator introduced them to LeTUS. Twelve of the teachers said they chose to teach the units, eighteen said they were encouraged and five stated that their principals required them.

Results from the needs assessment further indicated that teachers anticipated using the many features available on KNOW with the same degree of frequency. Figure 11.1 shows that the majority of our sample anticipated using

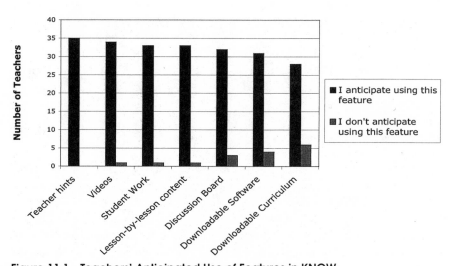

**Figure 11.1 Teachers' Anticipated Use of Features in KNOW**

*every* feature on KNOW with a similar degree of frequency (n = 35, but some teachers did not answer all questions, so values do not always add up to 35). In conducting this survey we expected teachers to show preferences toward those features they felt held more value. As it turned out, the lack of familiarity with KNOW (and all online PD in general) made it difficult for teachers to assign meaningful value to any particular feature and correspondingly to anticipate a greater use of one feature over the next. We also expected that teachers might show a preference toward resources such as videos, student work examples and the discussion board because they represent resources only provided online through KNOW. This wasn't the case because teachers had a difficult time visualizing how these resources would help them implement the curriculum due to their lack of experience with KNOW.

Teachers were given seven different PD formats to select from and were asked first what formats they would *expect* to participate in as they taught the unit and then what formats they would *choose* to participate in to help them implement the curriculum. Online PD was the format teachers expected to use with the highest frequency with 63 percent of respondents indicating that they would use online resources at least once a week or more. The written curriculum, which included all the materials provided to teachers in a curriculum binder at the beginning of the unit, was the only other PD format that teachers expected to use with any frequency. Less than 18 percent of teachers expected to use the remaining PD formats (study groups, focus groups, in-class support, Saturday workshops and for-credit coursework) on a weekly basis. Conversely, when asked what they would *choose* to participate in there was a broader array of responses as illustrated in Figure 11.2. The written curriculum, Saturday workshops and online resources were still the preferred formats but the remaining PD formats all rated fairly high in regards to teacher preference. However, since teachers both prefer to use online resources, and have higher expectations in regard to their use of these resources, it appears that our sample group anticipated a heavy reliance on KNOW and other web-based sources.

## LOGGING DATA

In reviewing the logging data it was clear that teachers expected to use KNOW far more than they actually have. Figure 11.3 indicates that 91 percent of our sample expected to use KNOW at least 1 to 3 times per week. In reality, less than a third of the teachers were using the site with this kind of frequency. During the four-month period in which we reviewed logging data, eight teachers didn't access KNOW at all. The average number of logins for the remaining 27 teachers was 9.3 with a high of 27 and a low of 1. Since KNOW was still in the

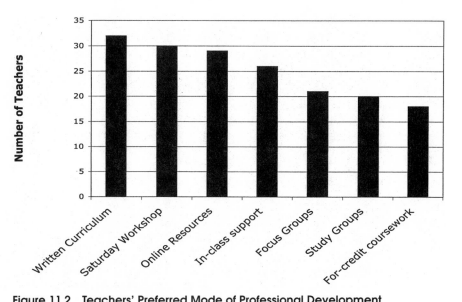

**Figure 11.2   Teachers' Preferred Mode of Professional Development**

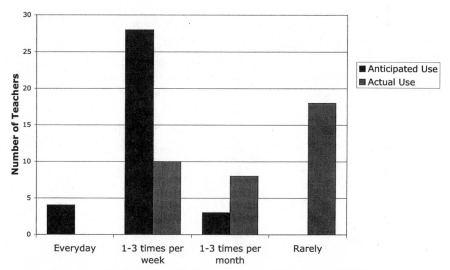

**Figure 11.3   Teachers' Anticipated versus Actual Usage of KNOW**

early stages of developing a community of practice (Lave and Wenger, 1991) this level of usage was not necessarily surprising. The majority of logins occurred during Saturday workshops when teachers were given specific tasks to accomplish on KNOW such as posting in a discussion or viewing a video. We had the opportunity to facilitate this kind of directed use since KNOW is part of a larger reform effort. By embedding the use of an online PD resource within the context of a traditional workshop setting we were able to introduce teachers to the various features available on KNOW in the hopes of increasing their proficiency at using the site as a PD tool.

## MINI-CASES

Considering that KNOW was in the early stages of implementation we weren't surprised by the lack of usage revealed by the logging data. Rather than lamenting the fact that teachers weren't making more frequent use of the site we decided to identify individuals who were using KNOW regularly so we could learn what they found valuable about the site. We wanted to learn from the people who *were* using the site in order to make KNOW a more valuable option for those teachers who *were not* currently logging on. To do this we selected three teachers from our sample and analyzed their use of KNOW. Each of the teachers we selected accessed KNOW 1–3 times a week during our period of data collection and they each came to KNOW with unique characteristics.

Ms. Bradley[1] served in a leadership role within a district. In her role she was asked to lead workshops, review/pilot new curriculums and serve as a content expert for her colleagues. Mr. Jackson represented the population of users who were unable to attend regularly scheduled face-to-face workshops and relied on KNOW to serve as a surrogate in place of the workshops. These teachers may had varying levels of experience and content area knowledge so even within this group there was variation in usage and needs. Ms. Daniels is the third teacher we profiled. She attended workshops regularly, was new to LeTUS, and like many of her colleagues her use of KNOW was largely restricted to directed usage opportunities provided during the face-to-face workshops.

## MS. BRADLEY

Like many schools across the nation, the districts we worked with often utilized their own teaching staff to plan and lead professional development sessions.

---

1 Pseudonyms have been used for each member of our sub-sample.

Teachers were usually selected for these leadership roles as a result of their experience and content area expertise (Fogleman et al., 2003). Ms. Bradley had taught several of the LeTUS units over the past five years and had been a lead teacher for her district since the beginning of the 2002–2003 school year. She planned and facilitated several curriculum specific workshops for her DPS colleagues during the 2002–2003 school year. We analyzed her use of KNOW to determine what unique user characteristics she might have as a lead teacher.

Logging records revealed that Ms. Bradley was one of the most frequent users of the system, accessing KNOW 26 times during our four-month period of data collection. She reported that her primary purpose in logging on to KNOW was two-fold. First of all, she liked to visit the discussion boards to read new messages and reply to questions her colleagues posted. She also used the discussion boards on KNOW to communicate with other lead teachers as they planned upcoming workshops. A discussion conference was created specifically for the lead teachers to facilitate this communication. Ms. Bradley was one of the most frequent users of this conference not only replying to messages but taking the initiative to create discussion threads as well. This initiative stimulated use of KNOW by other lead teachers who replied to the posts. However, Ms. Bradley stated that she wasn't always sure if other teachers were reading her discussion board posts so she often sent duplicate messages via e-mail, which resulted in a higher response rate. The lack of feedback, immediate or delayed, in asynchronous chat environments was often detrimental in the creation of sustained interactions (Barab et al., 2001; Bautista, 1998). Users aren't likely to sustain an online discussion if they perceive themselves as the sole conversant.

Ms. Bradley indicated that she also logged on to KNOW to review lessons in the curriculum and download student worksheets and supplemental reading materials, which were referred to as "student readers" within the unit. While Ms. Bradley appreciated the opportunity to preview the curriculum online she had hoped to be able to customize worksheets and other documents to make them more specialized for her students. Currently, documents download from KNOW as PDF files, making them difficult to edit electronically. This issue of customization will become increasingly significant as the site scales to a larger population of teachers representing a more diverse array of students.

In her needs assessment survey Ms. Bradley indicated that she was particularly interested in using KNOW to view videos of demonstrations and classroom enactments. This hasn't happened as frequently as she originally anticipated for both technical and practical reasons. Initially, Ms. Bradley had trouble downloading and viewing movies because of outdated software on her computer. Technological barriers are often the first hurdles that need to be cleared in order for online PD to be successful. On KNOW, we have taken several steps to break down these barriers so that teachers can access the multimedia content available on the site (Fishman, in press). However, addressing the technological problems for Ms. Bradley did not have a significant impact on her viewing of KNOW videos due to an unexpected consequence of her experience and facility with the unit. Because of her knowledge of the curriculum Ms. Bradley has been the subject of several classroom enactment videos. In addition, she helped narrate and "star" in many of the demonstration videos available on KNOW that showed how to set-up and operate the different apparatus used throughout the unit. Ms. Bradley reported that these videos were not particularly helpful for her since she was familiar with the lessons and activities they were designed to support.

## MR. JACKSON

Mr. Jackson had experience teaching the inquiry-based science units produced by LeTUS, but at the time of our data collection he was teaching at a new grade level and therefore did not have previous experience with the *specific* curriculum he was using. Mr. Jackson reported that he would like to attend the Saturday workshops but personal obligations kept him from participating on a regular basis. Like Ms. Bradley, he visited KNOW 26 times during our period of data collection. Mr. Jackson stated that his usage of KNOW was directly related to his absence at the workshops. He often checked the discussion boards to read any posts that might summarize what took place at the workshops. He also tried to access resources shared at the workshops and made available for download in the discussions area. Mr. Jackson reported trying to post a document that he created on the discussion board, but aside from this attempt he had not initiated any other posts nor replied to any existing posts. Mr. Jackson indicated that he appreciated the opportunity to connect with workshop participants via KNOW but he felt that he often missed important information by not being physically present.

The other reason Mr. Jackson logged on to KNOW was to view the videos, much like his colleagues previously discussed. Unfortunately, Mr. Jackson had yet to experience success in viewing any of the videos due to technical problems associated with outdated software and slow Internet connections both at home and school. He tried to remedy the technical problems he encountered but admitted that he didn't have the time to spend troubleshooting. We acknowledge the difficulty he has experienced, a difficulty that is certainly not unique to his situation judging by the discussion of Ms. Bradley, and realize that we need to take further steps to make the media resources on KNOW more accessible.

## MS. DANIELS

Ms. Daniels participated regularly in the Saturday workshops and roughly half of her 22 KNOW logins occurred during these training sessions. This was her first full year of teaching but she did use the LeTUS units to a limited extent last year as a student teacher. When asked about her use of KNOW Ms. Daniels reported that she logged on almost exclusively to access the discussion boards. She mentioned that her dial-up connection at home made even basic web surfing difficult and that she did not have Internet access in her classroom at school. This lack of access to a high-speed connection was the primary inhibiter to her using other features of KNOW.

Ms. Daniels used the discussion boards both to share information and to ask content-specific questions. For example, Ms. Daniels was teaching a unit on communicable diseases and her students occasionally had questions that they preferred to ask anonymously. To protect their privacy she used a question box in class where her students could submit questions and have them answered without being identified. On more than one occasion students submitted questions that Ms. Daniels was not able to answer. When this happened she posted the questions on the KNOW discussion board. Ms. Daniels reported that she received answers to her questions in a timely fashion and felt confident that the answers she was given by her colleagues were accurate and appropriate for her students.

Her use of KNOW during the face-to-face workshops was also primarily focused on interacting with her colleagues through the discussion board. Ms. Daniels said she preferred using the discussion board during the workshops because she knew other teachers would be posting messages and therefore it was more worthwhile for her to take the time to log in. Another common activity at the workshops involved looking at different parts of the curriculum on the KNOW site. Ms. Daniels reported that this wasn't particularly helpful for her since she had a hardcopy of the curriculum and she preferred using that version to review the unit.

# Discussion

Several design implications can be gleaned from these three teachers. First of all, Ms. Bradley's inability to customize documents means that she is unable to localize the curriculum to meet her needs. This inability to customize learning for her students is in direct contradiction to what KNOW is intended to do. We plan to address this inconsistency by developing an area on KNOW that will house templates for various documents such as student worksheets, lab packets and quizzes. These templates will simultaneously give teachers a framework to follow in creating documents consistent with the tenants of inquiry-based learning and allow them to tailor the materials for their students.

Another issue raised by Ms. Bradley pertains to her inability to access relevant content that was generated by someone other than herself. It seems logical that we would want to disseminate the knowledge and expertise possessed by teachers like Ms. Bradley through KNOW. However, by providing content developed by these expert teachers we inadvertently made the site less useful to teachers like Ms. Bradley. Therefore, we need to make sure we populate KNOW with content from a wide-range of resources. These may include links to relevant websites, ideas for alternative activities and connections to the latest research related to the teaching of science and inquiry-based learning.

The technological problems each teacher had with viewing movies is certainly not unique to KNOW. There simply isn't a foolproof method for providing video online and outdated software coupled with slow or unreliable Internet connection will continue to exacerbate this problem for the foreseeable future. To ameliorate the problems people are having we produced curriculum-specific CDs that house all the movies for that particular unit as well as updated versions of the software we require to play the movies. The CDs work in conjunction with KNOW so that when a user tries to access a movie on KNOW the computer checks first for the presence of the CD. If the CD is inserted the movie is played directly from there, which circumvents the arduous downloading process. This remedy isn't ideal but we believe it significantly reduces the potential problems users may encounter and we are interested to see how it may impact the viewing of videos on KNOW.

Mr. Jackson's concern that he was missing crucial information by not being present at the workshops provides another design challenge. KNOW needs to more adequately capture and reflect what happens at the face-to-face workshops so teachers like Mr. Jackson don't feel like they are missing out. One step we can take toward this goal is to implement a more systematic procedure for collecting the many resources shared at the workshops and ensure that those materials are shared with others via KNOW. This could include scanning documents, taking digital pictures or video and posting a detailed summary of each workshop on the discussion board.

In addition to making modifications to KNOW we are making some changes to our needs assessment survey as a result of this first round of data collection. Users are no longer asked about their anticipated usage of the different features on KNOW. We also are eliminating the questions that asked users to rate their skill and comfort level with computers and technology as we found it difficult to draw any meaningful conclusions from the answers to these questions. In addition, to expedite our data collection we are creating an electronic version of the needs assessment survey. As users log on to KNOW for the first time they will be asked to complete the survey. Results are compiled and aggregated on an ongoing basis so that we can maintain a clear picture of our user population. We also have the capability to administer surveys to a select group of users based on their usage patterns, curriculum affiliation, demographic setting or any other criteria we specify. For instance, logging records may reveal a particular group of users making extensive use of the discussion boards. We could create an electronic survey specifically for this set of users to help us better understand their motivations for using the discussion boards and learn more about the community that might be forming as a result of this communication.

We are not surprised to find a direct correlation between activity on KNOW and the face-to-face workshops. For many of the teachers in our sample, the workshops represent their only experience with KNOW. Interestingly enough, the feature utilized most often at the workshops is the discussion boards, a feature intended to allow teachers to communicate and collaborate from a distance. It appears that this directed usage is beneficial for users in more than one way. Mr. Jackson is able to participate at least partially in the workshops by reading the many posts generated in his absence. Ms. Daniels finds greater satisfaction in accessing the discussion boards because she knows people are populating them with comments, ideas and questions. In her role as lead teacher Ms. Bradley asks teachers to post updates on KNOW detailing where they are in the unit so she can quickly assess how each teacher is progressing through the curriculum. It remains to be seen what kind of impact this directed usage will have on the formation of a more permanent community of learners.

It is important that we take a moment to acknowledge the limitations of this study. First of all, logging records can tell you what pages of a website a user accessed but they have no way of representing the level of engagement of the user at the time the page was viewed. Likewise, we have no way of knowing the intent of a particular user for accessing the various features on KNOW. Much like research on television viewing habits, we can say that a person spent fifteen minutes viewing a specific webpage but we can't say *why* they devoted this length of time or what they gained from looking at a particular part of the site. To capture this type of information we would need to conduct think-aloud sessions with our teachers as they used KNOW in order to find out why they navigated to certain parts of the site.

The other primary limitation in our study is the lack of use of KNOW by our sample population. We were concerned about this from the beginning since we knew that teachers would have access to many other more traditional means of professional development and we weren't sure that KNOW would be able to adequately compete for their attention. We have determined that in future studies we will need to do more to ensure a higher frequency of use among our sample population.

# Conclusion

Our next step in this series of research is to build upon the work of our colleagues (Fishman, Marx, Best, and Tal, in press; Kubitskey, Fishman, and Marx, 2002) and investigate the link between professional development, specifically online PD, and student learning. The real test for KNOW will not only be its ability to sustain a viable community of learners but its ability to positively impact student learning.

We are also interested in exploring the impact of the design changes discussed in the previous section. It is our steadfast belief that teachers will make use of KNOW if it is viewed as a value to them. This means providing them with learning opportunities beyond what is available in the printed curriculum and making it easily accessible so that it is viewed as a worthwhile use of their time. We acknowledge this as an auspicious challenge, but contend that in order for online PD to become a viable alternative for the development of *all* teachers it is a challenge that must be met.

# Acknowledgements

We gratefully acknowledge the collaboration of the teachers and schools involved in this work, and the assistance of Steve Best, Jay Fogleman, Jon Margerum-Leys, Beth Kubitskey, Damon Warren, and Anika Ball-Anthony. The research reported here was funded with support from the W.K. Kellogg Foundation, and the National Science Foundation under the following programs: REPP (REC-9725927); CRLT (REC-9720383); USI (ESR-9453665); and CAREER (REC-9876150). All opinions expressed in this work are the authors' and do not necessarily represent either the funding agencies or the University of Michigan.

# References

Adams, P. E., and Krockover, G. H. (1997). Beginning science teacher cognition and its origins in the preservice secondary science teacher program. *Journal of Research in Science Teaching, 34*(6), 633–53.

Ball, D. L., and Cohen, D. K. (1996). Reform by the book: What is—or might be—the role of curriculum materials in teacher learning and instructional reform? *Educational Researcher, 25*(9), 6–8.

Barab, S. A., MaKinster, J., Moore, J., and Cunningham, D. J. (2001). Designing and building an on-line community: The struggle to support sociability in the Inquiry Learning Forum. *Educational Technology Research and Development, 49*(4), 71–96.

Bautista, A. (1998). A Study of the possibilities of teacher education with computer-based telecommunications systems. *Journal of Information Technology for Teacher Education, 7*(2), 207–30.

Blumenfeld, P., Fishman, B., Krajcik, J. S., Marx, R. W., and Soloway, E. (2000). Creating usable innovations in systemic reform: Scaling-up technology embedded project-based science in urban schools. *Educational Psychologist, 35*(3), 149–64.

Bobrowsky, W., Marx, R. W., and Fishman, B. (2001, April). The empirical base for professional development in science education: Moving beyond volunteers, Annual Meeting of the National Association of Research in Science Teaching. St. Louis, MO.

Committee on Science and Mathematics Teacher Preparation. (2001). *Educating teachers of science, mathematics, and technology: New practices for the new millennium.* Washington, DC: National Academies Press.

Dede, C. (1996). Distance learning—distributed learning: Making the transformation. *Learning and Leading with Technology, 23*(7), 25–30.

Ely, D. P. (1996, June). *Distance Education: By Design or Default?* Paper presented at the Association for Educational Communications and Technology, Tallahassee, FL.

Fishman, B. (in press). Linking on-line video and curriculum to leverage community knowledge. In *Advances in Research on Teaching: Using Video in Teacher Education* (Vol. 10), ed. J. Brophy. New York: Elsevier Science.

Fishman, B., Marx, R. W., Best, S., and Tal, R. (in press). Linking teacher and student learning to improve professional development in systemic reform. *Teaching and Teacher Education.*

Fogleman, J., Fishman, B., Kubitskey, B., Marx, R. W., Margerum-Leys, J., and Peek-Brown, D. (2003, April). *Taking charge of innovations: Shifting ownership of professional development within a district-university partnership to sustain reform.* Paper presented at the National Association of Research on Science Teaching, Philadelphia.

Frechtling, J. A., Sharp, L., Carey, N., and Vaden-Kiernan, N. (1995). *Teacher enhancement programs: A perspective on the last four decades.* Retrieved October 23, 2001, from http://www.ehr.nsf.gov/ehr/rec/pubs/eval/tep/tep.htm

Fusco, J., Gehlbach, H., and Schlager, M. (2000, February). *Assessing the impact of a large-scale online teacher professional development community.* Paper presented at the International Conference for the Society for Information Technology and Teacher Education, San Diego, CA.

Hammond, M. (1998). Learning through on-line discussion: What are the opportunities for professional development and what are the characteristics of on-line writing? *Journal of Information Technology for Teacher Education, 7*(3), 331–46.

Hewson, P. W., Tabachnick, B. R., Zetchner, K. M., and Lemberger, J. (1999). Educating prospective teachers of biology: Findings, limitations, and recommendations. *Science & Education, 83*(3), 373–84.

Kubitskey, B., Fishman, B., and Marx, R. W. (2002, October). *Professional development, teacher learning, and student learning: Is there a connection?* Paper presented at the International Conference of the Learning Sciences (ICLS), Seattle.

Lave, J., and Wenger, E. (1991). *Situated Learning: Legitimate peripheral participation.* Cambridge, UK: Cambridge University Press.

Rowand, C. (2000). *Teacher use of computers and the Internet in public schools.* Retrieved May 12, 2002, from http://nces.ed.gov/pubs2000/quarterly/summer/3elem/q3-2 .html#Table_2

Schneider, R., and Krajcik, J. S. (2002). Supporting science teacher learning: The role of educative curriculum materials. *Journal of Science Teacher Education, 13*(3), 221–45.

Supovitz, J. A., and Zeif, S. G. (2000). Why they stay away. *Journal of Staff Development, 21*(4), 24–28.

Wilson, S. M., and Berne, J. (1999). Teacher learning and the acquisition of professional knowledge: An examination of research on contemporary professional development. 173–209. In *Review of Research in Education*, ed. P. D. Pearson. Washington, DC: American Educational Research Association.

# APPENDIX A

# KNOW Anticipated Needs Survey

**Part One of Four**

The following questions deal with your teaching background and experience as well as your current teaching assignment.

1. What subject(s)/grade(s) are you currently teaching?

   Subject(s): _____

   Grade(s): ($\sqrt{}$ all that apply)

   ☐ 5   ☐ 6   ☐ 7   ☐ 8   ☐ 9   ☐ 10   ☐ 11   ☐ 12

2. How many students will you be teaching the unit(s) to?

   Number of Sections: _____

   Average Class Size: _____

3. How many computers are available for your students in each of these locations and what is the Internet connectivity like in each location? Answer only for locations where students will use computers for the hi-ce units. Write "NA" (not applicable) if a location is not used.

| | Number of Computers Present | Internet Connectivity? | | The Internet connection at this site is reliable. | | |
| --- | --- | --- | --- | --- | --- | --- |
| | | No | Yes | No | Usually | Yes |
| My own classroom | _____ | ☐ | ☐ | ☐ | ☐ | ☐ |
| School library/media center | _____ | ☐ | ☐ | ☐ | ☐ | ☐ |
| Computer lab | _____ | ☐ | ☐ | ☐ | ☐ | ☐ |
| Mobile Computer Cart | _____ | ☐ | ☐ | ☐ | ☐ | ☐ |

4. Typically, how many students operate any one computer at one time during a class? $\sqrt{}$ the most common arrangement, or $\sqrt{}$ two if two are equally common.
   a. One student ☐
   b. In pairs (2) ☐
   c. In groups of 3–4 ☐
   d. Other (Please specify): _____ ☐

**Part Two of Four**

The following questions deal specifically with your access to, and use of, computers.

5.  For how many years, if at all, have you had access to a computer at **school**? Internet connection? If you don't have a computer or Internet connection at **school**, please write "0".

    a.  Computer at **school** ...................... _____ Years

    b.  Internet connection at **school** ....... _____ Years

6.  For how many years, if at all, have you had access to a computer at **home**? Internet connection? If you don't have a computer or Internet connection at **home**, please write "0".

    a.  Computer at **home** ...................... _____ Years

    b.  Internet connection at **home** ........ _____ Years

7.  If you have Internet connection at **home** what speed is your connection?
    a.  Dial-up modem (phone line)        ☐
    b.  Broadband (cable modem/DSL)     ☐

8.  How much experience have you had with each of the following types of computers?

    |  | None | A little | Moderate Amount | Very experienced | Expert level |
    |---|---|---|---|---|---|
    | Windows/DOS PC (IBM style) | ☐ | ☐ | ☐ | ☐ | ☐ |
    | Macintosh | ☐ | ☐ | ☐ | ☐ | ☐ |
    | Apple II series | ☐ | ☐ | ☐ | ☐ | ☐ |

9.  We would like to assess your current **skills** related to using computers and the Internet.

    | I know how to: | No | Somewhat | Yes |
    |---|---|---|---|
    | use a web search engine | ☐ | ☐ | ☐ |
    | participate in a discussion board or online chat | ☐ | ☐ | ☐ |
    | compose, send and receive e-mail | ☐ | ☐ | ☐ |
    | download and install software from the web | ☐ | ☐ | ☐ |
    | download and view documents/files from the web | ☐ | ☐ | ☐ |

install software from a disk ☐ ☐ ☐
copy files from one disk to another ☐ ☐ ☐
create and edit a word-processor document ☐ ☐ ☐
create a slide show presentation (i.e. Power Point) ☐ ☐ ☐
create a new database and enter data into various fields ☐ ☐ ☐
program my own software ☐ ☐ ☐
create a web page ☐ ☐ ☐

10. We would like to assess your current **comfort level** related to using computers and the Internet. √ the statement that best describes your feelings towards each activity.

| Activity | I am not at all comfortable doing this | I am not very comfortable doing this | I am somewhat comfortable doing this | I am very comfortable doing this |
|---|---|---|---|---|
| Use a web search engine | ☐ | ☐ | ☐ | ☐ |
| Participate in a discussion board or online chat | ☐ | ☐ | ☐ | ☐ |
| Compose, send and receive e-mail | ☐ | ☐ | ☐ | ☐ |
| Download and install software from the web | ☐ | ☐ | ☐ | ☐ |
| Download and view documents/files from the web | ☐ | ☐ | ☐ | ☐ |
| Install software from a disk | ☐ | ☐ | ☐ | ☐ |
| Copy files from one disk to another | ☐ | ☐ | ☐ | ☐ |
| Create and edit a word-processor document | ☐ | ☐ | ☐ | ☐ |
| Create a slide show presentation (i.e. Power Point) | ☐ | ☐ | ☐ | ☐ |
| Create a new database and enter data into various fields | ☐ | ☐ | ☐ | ☐ |
| Program my own software | ☐ | ☐ | ☐ | ☐ |
| Create a web page | ☐ | ☐ | ☐ | ☐ |

**Part Three of Four**

The following questions deal specifically with your involvement with the hi-ce unit(s).

11. Which of the following hi-ce units are you planning on teaching next year? (√ all that apply)

    a   Air Quality                           ☐
    b.  Water Quality                         ☐
    c.  Communicable Disease                  ☐
    d.  Big Things (simple machines)          ☐
    e.  Helmets (physics)                     ☐

12. What month do you plan to start teaching each unit?

|  | Sept | Oct | Nov | Dec | Jan | Feb | Mar | Apr | May |
|---|---|---|---|---|---|---|---|---|---|
| Air Quality | | | | | | | | | |
| Water Quality | | | | | | | | | |
| Communicable Disease | | | | | | | | | |
| Big Things (simple machines) | | | | | | | | | |
| Helmets (physics) | | | | | | | | | |

13. Which of the following statements best describes how you became involved with the hi-ce unit(s)?

    a.  I received information about hi-ce while attending a workshop.      ☐
    b.  My building/district administrator gave me information              ☐
        about hi-ce.
    c.  My building/administrator asked me to attend a workshop            ☐
        about hi-ce.
    d.  A colleague gave me information about hi-ce.                        ☐
    e.  The hi-ce unit(s) have been adopted as part of our curriculum.     ☐
    f.  I was contacted by U of M about the hi-ce units.                   ☐
    g.  Other (please explain) _____             ☐

14. Which of the following statements best describes your decision to teach the hi-ce unit(s)?

    a.  Teaching the unit(s) was an option for me.                         ☐
    b.  Teaching the unit(s) was an option for me but I was strongly       ☐
        encouraged to try them.

c. Teaching the unit(s) was required for me. ☐

d. Other (please explain) _____ ☐

15. How often do you expect to participate in the following forms of professional development as you teach the hi-ce unit(s)?

| Professional Development Format | Never | Once a month | 1–3 times a month | Once a week or more | Almost daily |
|---|---|---|---|---|---|
| Saturday Workshop | ☐ | ☐ | ☐ | ☐ | ☐ |
| For-credit coursework | ☐ | ☐ | ☐ | ☐ | ☐ |
| Study groups | ☐ | ☐ | ☐ | ☐ | ☐ |
| In-class support | ☐ | ☐ | ☐ | ☐ | ☐ |
| Online resources | ☐ | ☐ | ☐ | ☐ | ☐ |
| Written Curriculum | ☐ | ☐ | ☐ | ☐ | ☐ |
| Focus Groups | ☐ | ☐ | ☐ | ☐ | ☐ |
| Other: _____ | ☐ | ☐ | ☐ | ☐ | ☐ |

16. If you were given the option to participate in any of the following professional development formats, which would you prefer to participate in most often? If there are two or more formats that you prefer equally, feel free to respond the same for both or all of them. It is **not** necessary that you rank the formats from highest to lowest preference.

| Professional Development Format | I wouldn't participate in this format | I would participate in this format sometimes | I would participate in this format often | I would participate in this format very often | I would participate in this format each chance I had |
|---|---|---|---|---|---|
| Saturday Workshop | ☐ | ☐ | ☐ | ☐ | ☐ |
| For-credit coursework | ☐ | ☐ | ☐ | ☐ | ☐ |
| Study groups | ☐ | ☐ | ☐ | ☐ | ☐ |
| In-class support | ☐ | ☐ | ☐ | ☐ | ☐ |
| Online resources | ☐ | ☐ | ☐ | ☐ | ☐ |
| Written Curriculum | ☐ | ☐ | ☐ | ☐ | ☐ |
| Focus Groups | ☐ | ☐ | ☐ | ☐ | ☐ |
| Other: | ☐ | ☐ | ☐ | ☐ | ☐ |

17. Please indicate the frequency with which you have used the following online professional development resources.

| Online Professional Development Resource | Never | Rarely | Sometimes | Often |
|---|---|---|---|---|
| Websites for subject related information/ideas | ☐ | ☐ | ☐ | ☐ |
| Web search engines to locate subject-related information/ideas | ☐ | ☐ | ☐ | ☐ |
| Frequently Asked Question (FAQ) features of educational or subject related websites | ☐ | ☐ | ☐ | ☐ |
| E-mail listservs to receive newsletters or updates from various organizations | ☐ | ☐ | ☐ | ☐ |
| Discussion groups that allow you to post and view comments and responses | ☐ | ☐ | ☐ | ☐ |
| Online Coursework offered through a university or other organization | ☐ | ☐ | ☐ | ☐ |
| Other _____ | ☐ | ☐ | ☐ | ☐ |

18. If you have used online professional development, how would you charac-
terize your overall experience with these resources? If you have not used
online professional development resources, skip questions 18–19.

| Online Professional Development Resource | Never Satisfied | Rarely Satisfied | Often Satisfied | Always Satisfied |
|---|---|---|---|---|
| Websites for subject related information/ideas | ☐ | ☐ | ☐ | ☐ |
| Web search engines to locate subject related information/ideas | ☐ | ☐ | ☐ | ☐ |
| Frequently Asked Question (FAQ) features of educational or subject related websites | ☐ | ☐ | ☐ | ☐ |
| E-mail listservs to receive newsletters or updates from various organizations | ☐ | ☐ | ☐ | ☐ |
| Discussion groups that allow you to post and view comments and responses | ☐ | ☐ | ☐ | ☐ |
| Online Coursework offered through a university or other organization | ☐ | ☐ | ☐ | ☐ |
| Other _____ | ☐ | ☐ | ☐ | ☐ |

19. Please use the space below to further describe your experience with online professional development. Explain why you have been satisfied/dissatisfied and whether or not you find it an effective way to learn. For instance, do you usually find the information you need in a timely fashion?

20. What do you hope to gain from online professional development? (√ all that apply)

   a. Strategies for implementing the curriculum ☐
   b. Increased understanding of content specific material ☐
   c. Assessment techniques and alternate ideas ☐
   d. Strategies for teaching with inquiry-based learning ☐
   e. Strategies for teaching with technology ☐
   f. Monetary compensation ☐
   g. To earn CEU's/fulfill certification requirements ☐
   h. Opportunities for peer collaboration/interaction ☐
   i. Other _____ ☐

**Part Four of Four**

The following questions deal specifically with the KNOW website that has been developed at the University of Michigan. KNOW has been designed as an on-line professional development resource to support teachers using the hi-ce units.

21. Place a √ in the box that best matches your anticipated use of each feature. Please make sure to √ a box for each feature.

| KNOW Feature | I wouldn't choose to use this feature | I don't anticipate using this feature much | I anticipate using this feature occasionally | I anticipate using this feature often |
|---|---|---|---|---|
| **Downloadable curriculum:** | | | | |
| • Download and print the entire unit including student readers & worksheets | ☐ | ☐ | ☐ | ☐ |
| **Student work samples:** | | | | |
| • View samples of student work | ☐ | ☐ | ☐ | ☐ |
| • Read teacher comments about each piece of work | | | | |

**Videos:**
- View teacher demonstrations,
  software tutorials &
  classroom enactments       ☐       ☐       ☐       ☐

**Downloadable software:**
- Download software associated
  with each unit       ☐       ☐       ☐       ☐
- Download software updates
  associated with each unit

**Lesson-by-lesson content:**
- View each lesson with
  individual lesson objectives,
  materials, assessments and
  instructional sequence       ☐       ☐       ☐       ☐
- Links to relevant videos,
  student work and teacher
  helpful hints are organized
  within the lesson

**Teacher testimonials & hints:**
- Comments, tips and
  alternative ideas from teachers
  who have taught the units
  before       ☐       ☐       ☐       ☐

**Discussion board:**
- A forum to communicate
  with other teachers using the
  units.       ☐       ☐       ☐       ☐

22. What other feature(s) not already mentioned would you look to find on a website like KNOW in order to help you teach the hi-ce unit(s)?

23. Please select one of the KNOW features from item 21 that you consider to be valuable. Use the space below to explain why that feature is important to you. Include in your response any specific uses you anticipate for this feature.

24. Where do you anticipate using KNOW?

    a. At school primarily       ☐
    b. At home primarily       ☐

c. Both home and school equally ☐
d. Other _____ ☐

25. **When** do you anticipate using KNOW? (√ all that apply)

| Time of Day | Minimal use | Less than 25% of use | 25–50% of use | At least 50% of use | Primary use |
|---|---|---|---|---|---|
| Early morning (before school) | ☐ | ☐ | ☐ | ☐ | ☐ |
| During school hours (prep period) | ☐ | ☐ | ☐ | ☐ | ☐ |
| After school hours (afternoon) | ☐ | ☐ | ☐ | ☐ | ☐ |
| Evening | ☐ | ☐ | ☐ | ☐ | ☐ |
| **Time of Week** | | | | | |
| During the week (Monday–Friday) | ☐ | ☐ | ☐ | ☐ | ☐ |
| On the weekend | ☐ | ☐ | ☐ | ☐ | ☐ |

26. How often do you anticipate using KNOW while you are teaching the hi-ce unit(s)?

a. Almost everyday ☐
b. 1–3 times per week ☐
c. 1–3 times per month ☐
d. Very rarely ☐

Thank you for taking the time to complete this survey. Your answers are very important to us and we appreciate your participation.

# Summary and Conclusions
## NON-TRADITIONAL MODELS OF PROFESSIONAL DEVELOPMENT

*Christy L. Faison*
Rowan University

## Summary

Today's professional development must go far beyond adding a few more days or even weeks of "drive-by" in-service training to teachers' calendars. Strong professional development opportunities must be embedded in the very fabric of public education. . . . Furthermore, professional development for teachers cannot be "one size fits all." (National Commission on Teaching and America's Future, 2003, p. 28)

The studies in the three chapters in this division present alternative methods of providing professional development for classroom teachers. Each shows promise as a delivery model as we struggle to provide meaningful learning experiences for a cadre of teachers with varying needs, expectations, and experiences. These studies provide the necessary research-based evidence to assist us in efforts to meet No Child Left Behind's goal of providing highly qualified teachers for all students.

The Sehlaoui, Seguin, and Kreicker study (chapter 9) investigated an online collaborative teacher education program developed at Emporia State University to provide ESOL training (English for Speakers of Other Languages) to districts across the state of Kansas. This grant-funded program was designed for inservice classroom teachers and led to ESOL certification. The goals of the program included improvement in teaching efficacy and development of appropriate instructional and assessment strategies. The 15-credit-hour graduate program was delivered online via WebCT with supporting resource materials and online learning communities. Participants were selected based on strong pedagogical skills and principals' recommendations. The project's evaluation included multiple assessment measures such as observations, tests, teacher logs, Teacher Work Samples (TWS), Praxis results, and external review. Project assessments indicated that as a result of participating in the online training, teachers were well-prepared and possessed appropriate content knowledge for the delivery of ESOL instruction. The study concludes that the use of online teacher training is proving to be an effective delivery model.

Using Levin, Kim, and Riel's Framework for Evaluating a Network Community (as cited in Stephens and Hartmann, 2004), this project meets several of the criteria necessary for online programs to succeed. The framework consists of five network qualities: organization of network, network task, response opportunities, response obligations, evaluation and coordination.

1. Participants had the shared interest of meeting the needs of ESOL students in their classes and because the teachers were located in rural and suburban districts throughout Kansas, participants were unable to meet in the same place or at the same time. (Organization of Network)
2. Online participation was tied to course requirements and teachers were motivated to participate as indicated by their applications and recommendations for the program. This created a sense of response obligation and commitment to the process. (Response Obligation)
3. Grant faculty were available in person. Ongoing assessment, evaluation and coordination were built into the program design. (Evaluation and Coordination)

The Emporia State University online teacher training program has the potential to provide a successful alternative method for the delivery of professional development. Based on the project's use of multiple evaluation and assessment strategies, and attention to successful online methods and techniques, this project provides a valuable professional development model.

The Ai and Rivera study in the second chapter, chapter 10, focused on the effects of coaching on teacher practice and involved more than 1,200 teachers in a large urban district. The study provided an in-depth look at 160 of those teachers and the use of two coaching strategies: modeling lessons, and observing lessons and providing feedback. Coaches were hired as part of the district-wide professional development plan and were assigned to multiple schools. The project was assessed using observations, interviews, and teacher surveys. The study concluded that there were no significant differences in the practices of teachers who used coaches and those who did not. Several barriers to the successful implementation of peer coaches were cited including confusion about the role of the coaches, lack of trust and time, and teacher resistance to change.

Reviewing current literature on the use of peer coaching, several elements required for success were missing from the project studied by Ai and Rivera. In McLymont and da Costa (1998), trust and the concept of a critical friend are foundational elements of coaching. Trust must be established for growth to take place and viewing the coach as a critical friend provides valuable feedback about one's practice. In Ai and Rivera's study, participating teachers lacked trust in the coaches and were confused about the role the coaches played.

According to Feger, Woleck and Hickman (2004), peer coaches must have interpersonal skills and a repertoire of coaching strategies. Although coaches in this study had opportunities for professional development, it was apparent from comments from teachers and principals that not all coaches were successful in their interactions with teachers and in their abilities to provide useful feedback.

The biggest barrier, however, appeared to be time. Coaches did not have sufficient time to provide one-on-one assistance for teachers, and teachers did not have sufficient time to avail themselves of these opportunities. Nonetheless, teachers in the district still perceived coaching as positive and the limited number of teachers who engaged in coaching reported their experiences as effective. Given appropriate skills and training for coaches, support from administration at all levels, and sufficient time for teachers and coaches, this alternative method of professional development holds great promise.

In the final study, Brunvand, Fishman and Marx examined teacher needs, expectations, and experiences with online professional development. Unlike the study in the first chapter in this section, which looked specifically at the use of online courses, this study looked at using an online professional development environment (KNOW—Knowledge Networks On the Web), to support the use of specific curriculum materials. Teachers in the study used the online network in conjunction with workshops and in-class support. The study showed that although teachers anticipated frequent use of the online environment, they actually made limited use of the tool as part of their professional development experience. Barriers to use included lack of access to high-speed connections, delay or absence of feedback in the asynchronous environment, and teacher preference for face-to-face interaction and hard copy materials.

When reviewing this online experience against the criteria of Levin, Kim, and Riel (in Stephens and Hartmann, 2004), teachers in this study were not volunteers, but were involved based on their use of the district's curriculum materials. Further, use of the professional development environment was not required, but made available as one of multiple formats of professional learning experiences. These elements may have limited participants' commitment to use the online environment and their response obligation. Additionally, since specific tasks were limited to the workshop experience, participants' use of the online environment outside of the workshop was infrequent. Technological barriers also played a role in the limited use of KNOW. The researchers intend to use this study and future studies to understand how to design effective online professional development tools that meet the needs and expectations of teachers and to investigate the link of online professional development to student learning. As such, this study shows promise as a model for alternative professional development.

# Implications

All of the above studies investigated alternative ways to provide meaningful learning experiences for teachers. Implementing effective professional development initiatives will require the educational community to look beyond the traditional in-service delivery models and be receptive to research-based, nontraditional methods of professional development. The ultimate goal of professional development, however, is the improvement of student learning. While designers of professional development need to take into account the factors that enhance the success of professional development experiences regardless of delivery method, researchers must continue to investigate the impact of professional development on student learning, and offer models that can be used to enhance classroom teaching and learning for all teachers and students.

# References

Feger, S., Woleck, K., and Hickman, P. (2004). How to develop a coaching eye. *Journal of Staff Development, 25*, 14–18.

McLymont, E. F. and da Costa, J. L. (1998, April). *Cognitive coaching: The vehicle for professional development and teacher collaboration.* Paper presented at the annual meeting of the American Educational Research Association, San Diego, CA.

National Commission on Teaching and America's Future. (2003). *No dream denied: A pledge to America's children. Summary report.* Retrieved June 3, 2004, from http://documents.nctaf.achieve3000.com/summary_report.pdf

Stephens, A. C. and Hartmann, C. E. (2004). A successful professional development project's failure to promote online discussion about teaching mathematics with technology. *Journal of Technology and Teacher Education, 12*, 57–73.